DON JOHN OF AUSTRIA

ARMS OF DON JOHN OF AUSTRIA
Drawn by Major T. Shepard, F.S.A.

The shield party per pale, the dexter side per fess Castile and Leon, the sinister side per pale Arragon and Arragon-Sicily, over all an escutcheon of pretence Austria impaling Burgundy (Ancient).

Crest, out of a coronet a bush of peacocks' feathers.

Round the shield the collar of the Order of the Golden Fleece.

DON JOHN OF AUSTRIA

By MARGARET YEO

" There was a man sent from God whose name was John "
(*Inscription on Don John's tomb in the Escorial*)

NEW YORK

SHEED & WARD INC.

MCMXXXIV

LINES FROM "LEPANTO"

By G. K. Chesterton

. . . Dim drums throbbing, in the hills half-heard,
Where only on a nameless throne a crownless prince has stirred,
Where, risen from a doubtful seat and half-attainted stall,
The last knight of Europe takes weapons from the wall,
The last and lingering troubadour to whom the bird has sung,
That once went singing southward when all the world was young.
In that enormous silence, tiny and unafraid,
Comes up along a winding road the noise of the Crusade.
Strong gongs groaning as the guns boom far,
Don John of Austria is going to the war,
Stiff flags straining in the night-blasts cold,
In the gloom black-purple, in the glint old-gold,
Torchlight crimson on the copper kettle-drums,
Then the tuckets, then the trumpets, then the cannon, and he comes.
Don John laughing in the brave beard curled,
Spurning of his stirrups like the thrones of all the world,
Holding up his head for a flag of all the free.
Love-light of Spain—hurrah !
Death-light of Africa !
Don John of Austria is riding to the sea. . . .

*　　　*　　　*　　　*　　　*

(*Don John of Austria is going to the war.*)
Sudden and still—hurrah !
Bolt from Iberia !
Don John of Austria
Is gone by Alcalar. . . .
Don John calling through the blast and the eclipse,
Crying with the trumpet, with the trumpet of his lips,
Trumpet that sayeth ha !
Domino Gloria !
Don John of Austria is shouting to the ships. . . .

Don John's hunting and his hounds have bayed,
Booms away past Italy the rumour of his raid.
    Gun upon gun, ha ! ha !
    Gun upon gun, hurrah !
    Don John of Austria has loosed the cannonade.

     *   *   *   *   *

Don John pounding from the slaughter-painted poop,
Purpling all the ocean like a bloody pirate's sloop,
Scarlet running over on the silvers and the golds,
Breaking of the hatches up and bursting of the holds,
Thronging of the thousand up that labour under sea
White for bliss and blind for sun and stunned for liberty.
    Vivat Hispania !
    Domino Gloria !
    Don John of Austria has set his people free !

     *   *   *   *   *

Cervantes on his galley sets the sword back in the sheath
   (*Don John of Austria rides homewards with a wreath*)
And he sees across a weary land a straggling road in Spain
Up which a lean and foolish knight forever rides in vain,
And he smiles, but not as Sultans smile, and settles back the blade
   (*But Don John of Austria rides home from the Crusade.*)

     *   *   *   *   *

These verses from the poem are reprinted by kind permission of the author and Messrs. Methuen & Co. Ltd.

CONTENTS

PART I

CONTENTS

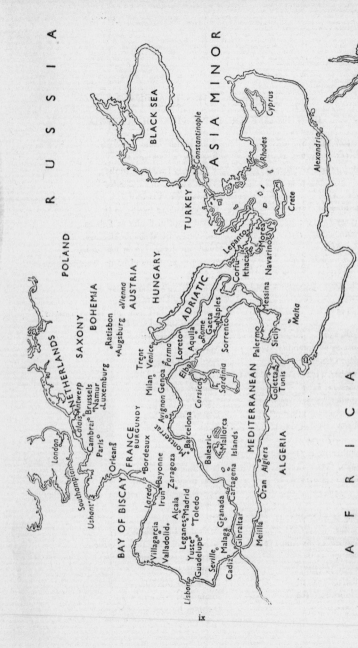

Map showing places, marked in roman letters, which Don John visited.

TABLE OF DATES

IN THE LIFE OF DON JOHN OF AUSTRIA

February 24, 1547 . . .	Born at Ratisbon.
July, 1551—Spring, 1554 . .	Leganes (near Madrid).
Spring, 1554—October, 1559 .	Villagarcia (near Valladolid).
July—September, 1558 . .	Yuste (till death of Charles V).
May 21, 1559	Auto-de-Fe, Valladolid.
September 28, 1559 . . .	Acknowledged by Philip II.
February 22, 1560 . . .	Takes Oath of Fealty at Toledo.
Autumn, 1561—1564 . . .	University of Alcalá de Henares.
May, 1565	Flight to Zaragoza and Barcelona.
May—October, 1568 . . .	First trip as Admiral of the Mediterranean Fleet.
April, 1569—November 30, 1570 .	Granada. (Morisco Rebellion.)
February 10, 1570 . . .	Capture of Galera.
May, 1571	Commander-in-Chief of Holy League's Forces on Sea and Land.
July 26, 1571	Sails from Barcelona.
August 23—September 16, 1571 .	Messina.
Sunday, October 7, 1571 . .	Battle of Lepanto.
November, 1572—August, 1573 .	Naples.
October 11, 1573 . . .	Capture of Tunis.
November, 1573—April, 1574 .	Naples.
April—August, 1574 . .	Genoa, Milan, &c.
August—October, 1574 . .	Sicily.
November, 1574 . . .	Genoa.
December 30, 1574—March, 1575 .	Spain.
Summer, 1575	Naples.
Winter, 1575—1576 . . .	Pilgrimage to Loreto.
May 3, 1576	Appointment as Governor of the Netherlands.
August 22—October 23, 1576 .	Spain.
November 3, 1576 . . .	Arrival at Luxemburg.
November, 1576—end 1577 .	Namur, Louvain, Brussels, &c.
January 31, 1578 . . .	Battle of Gemblours.
June—July, 1578 . . .	Ill at Namur.
August 1, 1578	Battle near Mechlin.
September 16, 1578 . . .	Again ill at Namur.
October 1, 1578	Death at Bouges (near Namur).

PART I

I

COMING AND GOING

(August, 1556—July 1, 1558)

The castle of Villagarcia de Campos had buzzed like a hive of bees about to swarm ever since the arrival of the courier with news that its lord, Don Luis de Quijada, was coming home from Flanders. Jerome was in such a state of breathless excitement that he lay wide awake as the narrow patch of moonlight pouring in through the arched window in the thick wall shifted right across his bed. He had not yet seen his hero who had been at Brussels with the Emperor Charles V ever since he himself had arrived here with the stout Fleming over two years ago.

It was five years since Don Luis had married Doña Magdalena de Ulloa and his visits home had been few and hurried, for the Emperor was always loth to part with his faithful friend and Chamberlain. His wife managed the castle and estate twenty miles from Valladolid, with the help of the steward, de Valverde, and the old squire, de Galarza, who had taught Jerome to ride and was now showing him how to handle a small sword and throw a miniature lance.

Jerome sat up in bed. It was still hot and he could smell the fragrance of the myrtle, bay and lavender bushes round the well in the middle of the patio. He unhooked the Crucifix which hung on a string above his head and held it tenderly in his small brown hands. In the brilliant August moonlight he could see plainly the black charring all down one side of the rudely carved Figure and the wooden cross. Of all the stories that Doña Magdalena had told of her husband—his fights and travels and wounds in Tunis, Italy and Flanders—the one Jerome loved most and was never tired of hearing was how Don Luis, single-handed, had fought a band of Moors in southern Spain and had snatched the Sacred Image from the bonfire onto which they had thrown it. It had been the proudest moment of Jerome's life when he had been given the Crucifix for his own and had vowed to himself never to part with it and to spend his life fighting for Christ against the infidels.

He lay down again with his hands folded over the Crucifix on his breast and began to think about the time he had spent here and how he loved his Tia (as he had been told to call her) better than anyone in the world. When he had been at Leganes there had been no one to love. Ana de Medina had kept him fed and clothed, but she was always busy with the house and farm and he could hardly remember her husband, Francisco Massuin, who had been the Emperor's musician. Then one day the fat Flemish gentleman, Charles de Provost, had arrived. Jerome laughed to himself as he remembered the excitement in the village over the coach, for such a thing had never been seen before. " The house on wheels," the boys had called it and Jerome had been very proud and excited when he had been carried off in it, north to Madrid and all those

miles on to Valladolid. He could still remember very vividly how he had first seen Doña Magdalena, standing in the patio with her two duennas, Isabel and Petroñila de Alderete,—old widowed sisters,—and the chaplain, Don Garcia de Morales. She had been in black velvet, with the long sweeping sleeves which she affected, pearls round her neck under the ruff of Flemish lace, a lace veil shading her black hair and oval face, and the lonely boy of seven had thought her the most beautiful person he had ever seen,— more beautiful even than the famous Virgin of the Hill of the Angels, who was carried down in state to Getafe every year at Whitsuntide.

Doña Magdalena, too, in the great bed hung with brocade, was awake. She too was remembering Jerome's arrival in the spring of 1554, and the puzzling letter from her husband. "I beg you by the love you have and have always had for me to receive this boy as if he were indeed your own and so to care for and train him. He is the son of a great friend of mine, whose name I cannot reveal but for whose honour and high position I will go surety." When she had read and re-read this a sudden fierce rage of jealousy,—of which she had not known herself capable,— had surged up in her. Whose child could the boy be, except Luis's own? The one way in which she had failed him, and which was an unceasing ache in her heart, was the fact that she had not given him a child, and would never give him one. Then Jerome had come—small and thin for his age, pale from the fatigue of the long journey and from nervousness at being flung into a strange place among strangers whom he had never seen before. His yellow curls had been dusty, his blue eyes under their thick lashes dark with suppressed emotion. He had kissed her hand. She had caught him in her arms and taken him to her heart. From that moment the old castle had been a different place, life had been a different thing and that ache of emptiness in her had ceased.

She wondered what Luis would think of the boy ; if he would be satisfied with his riding, fencing, and exercises. He certainly would not be with the result of lessons, although, not content with Don Garcia, she had installed at the hermitage near the castle Dr. Prieto, a learned professor of Salamanca. Well, it was no good worrying. She would not make Jerome nervous by too many instructions. Anyhow she would be too busy, after the daily morning almsgiving to the local poor, for the castle would be full of friends, relations and neighbours come to welcome home the lord of Villagarcia.

The great day dawned at last. Everyone was up before the sun was over the long range of hills towards Valladolid. De Galarza was posted on the north-west tower, looking up the wide valley of the Rio Seco towards Medina Seco, to give warning when the cavalcade appeared. The corn was already cut and carried and the stubble fields showed a pale ochre, though the vines were still green. Fields, orchards and vineyards were deserted. The primitive wooden ploughs stood idle. Only a few shepherds were to be seen, still as statues, leaning on their tall crooks, wrapped in the striped brown and grey blankets which enveloped them from head to foot like an Arab burnous.

Brown and grey too were the hills, the shades of rust and ash, with, here and there, a darker patch the colour of dried blood. There was a jingle of bells as a small ass pattered down the village street, two girls sitting sideways on his bare back.

Peasants and farmers were collecting in the outer court of the castle and at the entrance to the village just below. Their sunburnt faces looked almost as dark as their wide black hats, waistcoats and breeches, their folded belts of scarlet or yellow the only bright patch of their sombre attire. The women, however, in their feastday dress, supplied plenty of colour, in their wide, heavily embroidered skirts, and brilliant shawls and handkerchiefs. They, with the excited, chattering children and cocoons of tightly swaddled babies, huddled in the deep patch of shade under the castle walls in the dry moat. De Valverde and the gentlemen mounted in the yard and rode off towards Medina. The clergy, in cassocks and cottas, gathered in the patio—Don Garcia, Dr. Prieto, the parish priests from San Pedro and neighbouring villages—and started out in procession, preceded by a cross-bearer. Galarza was perched on the highest tower, watching north where stubblefields, vineyards and dried river-bed quivered in the heat.

Jerome, white and nervous, stood in a corner of the patio holding the huge old iron keys of the castle on a brocade cushion.

Galarza signalled the approach of the cortège and a clash of bells began, the deep clang from the round arches of San Pedro's tower, a shrill tinkle from San Lorenzo.

Little white puffs of smoke from arquebuses were followed by the crackle of shots, almost drowned by the gay harsh voices of boys and girls shouting the old Quijada hymn to the traditional tune, a roar of welcome and the clatter of hoofs. Altogether a thrilling, deafening din that made Jerome's heart beat so fast that he could hardly breathe. Hoofs sounded hollow on the drawbridge. There was a jingle of spurs as men dismounted. The cannon thundered from the battlements till the old walls seemed likely to collapse.

Doña Magdalena stood in the patio with duennas and maids. Through the archway Jerome saw Don Luis get down from his big mule, a burly figure, his wide hat, linen tunic, riding boots and gloves, his neat beard and strong cheekbones all grey with dust. He strode into the patio, pulling off hat and gloves. As his wife came forward he kissed her hand ceremoniously, then caught her with both arms in a tight hug.

He took the keys from the kneeling boy, then, still holding his wife's hand, led her into the dining-hall, followed by priests and friends.

Once more the cannon roared. Rockets soared noisily and burst invisible in the sunshine. The roll of drums, the blast of trumpets, the last verse of the lengthy hymn drowned the cries of excited women and the screams of frightened children.

Jerome still stood in the corner of the patio by himself, his hands clutching the cushion, his lips parted as if he were literally drinking in the noise and excitement. Cannon, musketry, drums, trumpets, a roar of welcome,—it was his first taste of life's thrilling draught.

Jerome was doomed to disappointment if he had hoped that Don Luis's return would mean freedom from lessons. The very next morning the chamberlain came into the room where Don Garcia was putting together Latin grammars and exercises to make room for Dr. Prieto with his French and history books. Jerome fidgeted uneasily while *el Señor*, one thumb slipped into his twisted leather belt, enquired about progress. That the result of the catechism was anything but satisfactory appeared in a report penned by Quijada a little later.

" The person in my charge . . . is in good health, is growing and is of a good disposition considering his age. He is getting on with his studies, but they are hard work and a lot of trouble. He is learning French and has a good accent in the few words he knows, but time and more concentration are needed. He enjoys riding far more . . . and can throw a lance in good style though not yet very strong."

Nearly every day the two rode out together, Don Luis on his big weight carrier, Jerome on his small mule. He listened enthralled to tales of the Emperor's expedition to Barbary in 1535 and the capture of the port of Tunis where Luis had been wounded,—of the taking of Terouanne, where Juan, Luis's younger brother, had been killed at his side,—of the Emperor's great victory over the Germans at Mühlberg. Luis would tell again and again the story of how he had rescued the little charred Crucifix from the

Moors and how, just before Mühlberg, they saw on the river bank a Crucifix which had been broken by the heretics. Charles had reined in his horse before it. "God grant that I may avenge Thy wrongs," he had said and had then ridden on to victory.

Don Luis would look down at the small face flushed with anger and enthusiasm, the brown fingers clenched tight on the reins, and sighed, thinking that here was little sign of a vocation to the religious life for which he had been bidden to prepare his ward. Then he would tell of the scene in Brussels ten months ago when Charles V, leaning on the shoulder of his dark, handsome young favourite, William, Prince of Orange, had laid down the burden of empire with the noble words which brought tears to all eyes. "I have done what I could and am sorry that I could not do better. I know well that I have in my day committed many faults. But I can testify truly that I have never done violence, wrong nor injustice knowingly to any of my subjects. If I have done any it has been unconsciously and I ask pardon for it."

Meanwhile the days grew shorter and cooler. Stubble fields bleached to cream. Chaff fluttered down the wind in a haze of golden dust. Women were grinding the new wheat and barley in round stone hand-mills. Vineyards were bare and ravaged, the last leaves like patches of spilt blood on the rusty earth. Jerome had a fine time with the noisy, merry half-naked men in the wine-presses and came home late, bare legs and linen smock covered with ruby stains. In the evening he sat on his cushion between Don Luis and Doña Magdalena before the fire of applewood logs in the wide Flemish grate which Don Luis had installed in the castle, much to the wonder and admiration of the neighbours who had never seen anything like it.

Doña Magdalena had her embroidery or her plain needlework. She herself spun the flax, superintended the weaving of the linen, and, with her own hands made all Jerome's things. All his life he would never wear a shirt made by anyone but her. There was a low hum from the spinning wheels of the maids in the next room as an accompaniment to Don Luis's big, booming voice. As Jerome listened the dry names and dates of lessons took on flesh and blood. He learnt—from one who had been the inseparable companion of the great Emperor—the history of the last half century, its play and interplay of European politics, treaties made and broken, cities and countries conquered, lost and reconquered, as the tide of war ebbed and flowed from Germany and the Netherlands, through France and Italy to Northern Africa, from Vienna to Constantinople. He followed the tangled skein of old enmities between Spain and France and Germany, the shifting Papal policy as Paul III succeeded Clement VII, and the present Pope, Paul IV, followed Julius III. He heard how Philip, Prince of the Asturias, had come to Brussels to be present at the Emperor's abdication, and how glad the Prince had been to escape from the foggy white cliffs of England and from his unhappy, lovesick wife, Queen Mary, whose hopes of motherhood had proved to be only the onset of a mortal disease.

Most eagerly of all Jerome listened to the incidents of that ceaseless struggle between Cross and Crescent. He pondered over it when he should have been working at Latin and mathematics, when Doña Magdalena had kissed him goodnight and he lay under the old Crucifix. It was only twenty-seven years ago when Suleyman the Magnificent and his vast armies had besieged Vienna. If the Janissaries had captured it and the Crescent had floated from its sharp high towers, the tide of Islam would most likely have submerged the Christianity and civilisation of Europe. Suleyman was still Sultan at Constantinople, still dreaming of fresh conquests. Hungary, once Europe's strongest bulwark against the East, was a Turkish province. There was a Turkish empire of more than forty thousand square miles and a Turkish fleet which swept the Mediterranean from the Straits of Gibraltar to the shores of the Holy Land.

Early in October a courier arrived with a summons to Don Luis from the Infanta Juana, Regent during her brother Philip's absence, to say that the Emperor had landed at Santander. Don Luis had everything to arrange for the journey of Charles V and his suite to the cloister-home planned at Yuste, so that he had to leave home at once.

Jerome's eyes were full of tears as he waited to say goodbye in the court, but little sympathy was shown by the old man, cross and fussed at this sudden departure.

"Keep your tears till you confess your sins," the harsh voice barked at Jerome: "A man should only weep when on his knees at the feet of his confessor."

Then, at sight of the quick flush of shame, the crusty, faithful heart softened. Luis leant from his saddle, gave

Jerome his hand to kiss and made the sign of the Cross over the bent yellow head before he set out north for the Biscayan coast.

The winter months slipped by, their passing only marked by letters from Don Luis, who was finding his job at Yuste anything but a bed of roses. It was something to have got the gout-racked Emperor and his unwieldy train of followers down the long road from Santander to the Estremadura, but the cloister home in the Hieronymite friary was far from ready and, not till February, 1557, could the imperial household move into the annexe built onto the side of the Yuste chapel.

Luis expressed a fervent hope in every letter that, once this installation was completed, he would be able to resign his post as Chamberlain and come home for good. Charles, however, had no intention of losing the indispensable services of his old and honest friend. It was with the greatest difficulty that Luis got home and then only temporarily. His cordial detestation of the wooded Estremadura valley was freely and frequently expressed. He saw no resemblance to the Homeric Elysium with which learned local tradition identified it, " the green land without snow or winter or showers," gentle and fertile as " the island valley of Avilion."

During the four months that he was at home (April–August, 1557) his wife had the full benefit of his grumbles and worries. Crippled by gout, the Emperor was incapable of controlling his immense Flemish appetite. A menu of rich fish, game, oysters, Guadelupe veal, lamb specially fattened on beer, all washed down by sweet, heavy *vino bastardo* from Seville, inevitably resulted in a violent attack of gout and fever. Shivering in bed under a pile of quilts and eiderdowns, the invalid worried himself over the troubles of the world he had left—the broken hopes of Mary Tudor's pregnancy, the raids of Turkish and Algerian corsairs under Dragut Reis, the varying fortune of war in Flanders. Well might Quijada declare irritably : " Kings seem to think their stomachs different from other peoples'." Indeed he was to find his dream of peace at home as completely upset as the imperial digestion.

An urgent summons recalled him to prepare for a visit of Charles's two sisters—the fragile, dovelike Queen Eleanor of Portugal and the burly, bronzed, Amazonian Queen Mary of Hungary, who had ruled the unruly Netherlands with masculine efficiency for years. By the end of August Luis was back at Yuste. " Cursed be the man who built it here," he wrote crossly. Of course everything had gone wrong during his holiday and, with more than his usual bluntness, he made plain to the Emperor his desire to spend his remaining days at Villagarcia. He was finally pacified by the suggestion that his wife and household should join him at Quacos, the little village a mile from Yuste. He arranged for three small houses to be knocked into one for their accommodation and made a flying visit home in the spring of 1558 to arrange the move to Yuste, " though I should be better pleased never to return there to eat asparagus and truffles ! "

The midsummer sun beat down mercilessly on the bare, scorching plains of Old Castile and, by the time Quacos was reached, on July 1, poor Doña Magdalena had collapsed with the heat. She was fit only for bed and quite incapable of appreciating the Emperor's messages of welcome or the delicacies supplied from his larder.

Even his Tia's illness could scarcely cool Jerome's simmering excitement on the evening of arrival. He leant from his little window under the roof and looked out over a view very different from the wide, treeless valley of the Rio Seco. The undulating hills were covered with beeches, oaks and chestnuts, pierced here and there by the tall spearheads of cypresses. The valleys were filled with orchards of mulberry, olive, fig, almond, peach and apple, and the lower slopes were clothed by vineyards. Above the huge old walnut tree which shaded the arched entry in the monastery wall he could see the high, narrow chapel of yellow stone and, on its right, looking down the garden slope, the cruder yellow of the new two-storied E-shaped building. A light was shining in one of the upper windows. Was it the Emperor's ? Jerome wondered. And was it really possible that tomorrow he might see and hear the victor of Mühlberg, great soldier, ruler, statesman and Christian ?

II

THE SANDS RUN OUT

(JULY 2—SEPTEMBER 21, 1558)

Jerome was not to see the Emperor the next day nor for some time. When Doña Magdalena had recovered the old man was down with a sharp attack of gout. Luis took the boy to Yuste one morning, under the big walnut tree, through the arch in the high friary wall. The new wing looked raw and uncomfortable. The Emperor's bedroom, facing north, therefore dark and chilly, had a window into the chapel so that, from his bed, he could see the High Altar, participate in Mass and Divine Office. Always passionately fond of music he had insisted on new voices being added to the choir and when his sensitive ear detected a false note or a harsh tone his loud and unprintable criticisms echoed the camp rather than the cloister.

Jerome was taken into the long living-room on the ground floor, with its large Flemish fireplace and a wide view from the window over the sloping garden to the wooded hills. In one corner stood the little organ which had accompanied Charles in all his campaigns and travels. The walls were hung with priceless Brussels tapestries, sacred pictures and portraits. The boy stood spellbound before the superb Titian of Charles at Mühlberg, the calm, strong face, handsome in spite of the protruding Hapsburg jaw, partly masked by the fair beard, the gorgeous gilding

16

and embossing of the plumed helmet and armour, the prancing Flemish charger, plumed and armed too, proud of carrying the world's mightiest ruler. It was all the splendour and romance of war, and the hero-worshipper forgot Don Luis's tales of the greedy, sick old man and remembered only the glamour of the young soldier of Christ.

He saw Fray Juan de Regia, the Emperor's confessor, in his full-sleeved white habit and brown scapular, then was given leave to run into the garden. He explored the new paths and fountains, the summer house shaded by mulberry trees and ventured as far as the hermitage of our Lady of Solitude, a mile away. Perched on the rock at the top of the hill it was easy to pretend that he was on the high prow of a ship and that the green and russet treetops below were rolling waves. Ever since he could remember he had had this love of the sea, though he had never seen it,—unless a vivid picture of a long semicircular row of white buildings, with a tall campanile protecting a harbour as thick with masts as a pond with reeds, and a far background of snowclad hills, were a memory, not a dream.

The midday Angelus rang. Jerome looked back at the crude yellow of the new building, thinking of the fifty-eight years which had been so stormy, so glorious, so adventurous, so sorrowful, but all so intensely vital, crammed with trouble and disappointment, with defeat, victory, treachery, statesmanship and triumph. Now it was all over. With his own hands Cæsar had laid aside both crown and sword. It was a great way to live, thought Jerome. To fight for the Cross against the Crescent, for the Faith against infidelity and heresy, then, when the world was in one's hands, and one's enemies—the enemies of God—under one's feet, to leave it all and find reward in the peace of the cloister.

This pious and thoughtful mood was naturally followed by reaction. His Tia was still resting, Don Luis busy at Yuste. There were no lessons, always a trial and burden to pupil and teachers. A troop was soon organised among the small boys of Quacos, who were awed and thrilled by the Quijada page's commanding manner, his white skin, yellow hair and bright blue eyes. Orchards were raided, goats and hens chased, passers-by pelted. The great excitement of the day was the return in the evening of the herds of gaunt, half-wild pigs from their feast of acorns and beech-mast in the forest. They came thundering back at sundown and, in the village, each one turned unhesitatingly into his own home. One evening Jerome was caught in the cataract, swept off his feet and only just able to avoid being trampled under the galloping hoofs.

Then, one day, he found Don Luis with a face like a thundercloud. Complaints had been made by farmers of stolen fruit, stone-throwing and frightened beasts. He had the worst scolding of his life and, worse still, was threatened that the long awaited visit to the Emperor, fixed for the next day, would be cancelled. He cast a look of agonized appeal at his Tia and no doubt it was she who softened the sentence, for Jerome rode beside her litter the next afternoon, mounted on the little mule, unnaturally clean and tidy in his best linen smock.

They went into the chapel to wait their summons.

Over the high altar, where the Emperor could see it from his room, hung Titian's "Gloria," a crowded blaze of light and colour, the irresistible swift upward rush of figures towards the divine centre, the young Charles V transfigured and eager, his fair lovely young wife beside him.

Don Luis stood in the doorway and beckoned. Jerome followed the two, carrying a silver tray on which lay Doña Magdalena's present to the Emperor, discreetly veiled by a square of brocade. They went upstairs. After the blazing July sunshine outside it was hardly possible to distinguish anything in this dark north room. Jerome was shaking with excitement at the thought of seeing his hero and with terror lest he should stumble in the gloom and drop the tray with a resounding crash.

He knelt, holding the tray and not daring to lift his eyes, while a low tired voice greeted Doña Magdalena. He saw knees and feet outlined under a coverlet of silk edged with feathers, and two small grey Siamese cats asleep on the knees. A gnarled hand, with veins like blue cords was cold under his lips. It slipped under his chin and tilted it. At last he lifted his eyes and met the piercing gaze of an old eagle. Then, at a sign from Don Luis, he drew back and stood in a corner.

Oddly enough he could never remember a word that was said, yet every visual detail was stamped on his mind for always. The beard, grey-white like the face with its jutting jaw, hair hidden under a silk cap, bowed, frail body wrapped in a silk eiderdown and sunk in a big chair padded with cushions—this broken ghost was the Emperor. The only patch of colour in the gloomy room was a scarlet and emerald parrot chained to a perch near the window.

After that Jerome saw the Emperor several times. One day the old man was leaning on Quijada's arm and a stick as he inspected the garden, looking to see if the Indian pinks from Tunis and the newly planted orange trees had been well watered. Another time he was with a tall, thin priest whose black gown was green with age. Jerome noticed the high, bald forehead, hollow cheeks and temples, long beaked nose and jutting chin. He had an uncomfortable feeling that the keen eyes, under their queer, square eyebrows, had pierced to his soul and seen all his small, half forgotten sins. He learned from his Tia that this was Francisco de Borja, once Duke of Gandia, Viceroy of Catalonia, friend of the Emperor and Empress, now Father Francis of the Society of Jesus. Don Luis was chuckling over the results of the visit to Charles V of this old friend, who had succeeded in persuading the Emperor that after all there might be some good in the new Order founded a few years before by Ignatius of Loyola—even though Fray Juan had declared that, if the Jesuits were not emissaries of the devil himself, they were certainly secret agents of the Grand Turk.

The weather this August of 1558 certainly gave the lie to the tradition identifying Yuste with Avilion. It was bitterly cold, with terrifying storms of wind and hail and thunder. Trees and cows were struck by lightning. Most of the royal household were down with fever or some illness. The Emperor had an attack of dysentery accompanied by

violent headaches. Don Luis was at the friary from dawn
till dark, and only his wife's serene patience and unfailing
sympathy kept his frayed nerves and ruffled temper from
getting quite out of control.

Instead of Doña Magdalena the old man woke Jerome
very early on the morning of August 30. Still half asleep
the boy tumbled out of bed into his clothes and jogged
along on the little mule. When he got into the monastery
chapel, however, he gave a cry of fright. The walls were
draped in black. A huge black catafalque, surrounded by
tall yellow candles, stood before the high altar. The three
friars were vested in black chasubles and dalmatics. The
household filed in, all in deep mourning. The Requiem
Mass, the *Dies Irae* were solemnly chanted. Utter misery
filled Jerome. The Emperor was dead and nobody had
told him. Then he saw the Emperor in his stall, black
too from head to foot, saw him advance, kneel at the altar
steps and hand a lighted taper to the celebrant, in token
that he gave back his life and all he had and was to God
from Whom he had received all.

Three weeks later, at midnight on September 20, the
Emperor was in his last agony. The room was crowded,
the prior, the confessor, the doctors, the Chamberlain,
who had not left his master day nor night, Bartolomé
Carranza, Archbishop of Toledo, whose harsh voice,
earlier in the day, had irritated the dying man's musical
ear. Within the curtains of the great bed was ebbing the
mightiest life of the century. As its sands ran out there
passed with them the last of the Middle Ages, of a Europe
united in Faith, in culture, in chivalry, when men had

lived hardly and been glad to die hard deaths in the service of Christ.

Jerome stood by the open window, almost hidden by the brocade curtains, dazed with grief and loss of sleep, forgotten by all. It was the first time he had watched the approach of death and few men grow impervious to the sight of death. The face under the silk nightcap was terrible, a yellow grey above the white beard. The blue lips were open, the jaw protruded more than ever in the fight for breath. A taper from Montserrat guttered as the twisted fingers relaxed their hold. The Crucifix which the Empress had clasped in her death-agony at Toledo slipped too. Suddenly the sunken eyes opened wide and a strong clear voice rang out from the shadow.

" *Ya voy, Señor !* " (I come now, Lord). " *Ay Jesus !* "

III

AUTO-DE-FE

(Winter, 1558—May 21, 1559)

The winter days slipped by as uneventfully as they had always done. Luis Quijada remained behind at Yuste to wind up the Emperor's business after his wife and Jerome had returned to Villagarcia, then was summoned to Valladolid by the Infanta Juana, Regent till her brother Philip could return from the Low Countries.

The three months at Yuste seemed to Jerome like a vivid dream, only the three days between the Emperor's death and funeral were a blurred haze of misery and exhaustion. All day he had stood behind Don Luis by the black bier in the black-hung chapel, while friars had come and gone, had chanted Masses for the dead, Office for the dead, replaced the thick yellow candles as they burned down and brought in neighbouring prelates and nobles who came to pay their last respects to their sovereign. Even the visit to the famous shrine at Guadelupe with his Tia had left little impression on a mind dazed with fatigue and emotion.

Now, though life and lessons went on as before, Jerome had changed. He was no longer the child who had dreamed before the fire to the hum of spinning wheels and the murmur of women's voices. He had seen and heard the man who for nearly half a century had held the fate of

Europe and the New World in his hands. It had given a
more definite shape to his vision of future wars and glory,
had opened up new and wider horizons.

Jerome was now twelve, not tall for his age, will and
spirit stronger than the slender, graceful body which often
burned and shivered with fever. Lessons were still, as
they would always be, a burden but, sitting on his stool
beside his Señora Tia's chair, he listened with new interest
to news from the great world. Mary of England and Cardinal Pole, last Papal Legate to England and last Catholic
Archbishop of Canterbury, had died in November, 1558,
and Philip, victor in the battle of St. Quentin, had sent a
tentative offer of his hand to her successor.

" You owe your crown, Madam, to my master's support,"
the Duke of Feria had said tactlessly to the new Queen.

" No, I owe it only to my people," had been her quick,
proud answer.

In spite of the crushing defeat of the French at St.
Quentin, August, 1558, the war was not ended till the peace
of Cateau Cambrésis was at last signed in April, 1559.
Philip now saw some hope of escaping from the Netherlands, where climate and people were equally odious to
him. Though he had not been elected Emperor, still his
father's death had left him with crushing responsibilities
and complications. The war with France was ended for
the time being, but there were still difficulties with the
turbulent Netherlanders and doubts whether to lay claim
to the English throne, as Elizabeth, born out of wedlock,
had now declared herself definitely in favour of the new
religion. The most Catholic King also found himself at

loggerheads with the terrifying old anti-Spanish Neapolitan, Paul IV. Decisions of the Council of Trent on the reforms of ecclesiastical chapters had not been put into effect in Spain. The Pope retaliated by questioning the royal right of appointment to church preferments. The Council of Castile riposted by refusing to allow Papal Bulls to be promulgated in Spain and the Regent ordered the arrest at any port or frontier of messengers carrying a Bull of excommunication against her brother. A paradoxical situation for the most Catholic king and country in the world. No doubt Philip murmured a most fervent *De Profundis* for the soul of Paul IV when news reached him in Brussels of the fiery Pope's death in August, 1559.

The King's arrangements for his homecoming were at last complete. On June 22 he married by proxy Isabel of Valois, the thirteen year old daughter of Henry II, who was accidentally killed in a tourney a few days later. He appointed as Governor of the Low Countries his half-sister, Margaret of Parma, an illegitimate daughter of Charles V, with de Granvelle as her chief adviser, an able, subtle, diplomatic young prelate, son of an old minister of the late Emperor. Young William of Orange was made Governo of Holland, though de Granvelle's shrewd summary of his character foretold friction between them. " A dangerous man, subtle, rusé and a pretended democrat." These settlements made Philip's thoughts turn eagerly to his beloved Spain, which he had left so unwillingly at his father's command five years ago, and which he was never to leave again.

Before the King sailed, however, the even tenor of life at Villagarcia had been interrupted twice. One night when Don Luis was at home he woke to find the room full of smoke. The servants, hurriedly wakened by him, were amazed to see him rush through blazing tapestries and furniture to Jerome's room, snatch the sleeping boy and carry him to safety before he returned to rescue his wife. There were murmurs and head shakings. One duenna ventured to express surprise and disapproval in her mistress's hearing, only to be silenced with unwonted sharpness. Doña Magdalena's doubts and jealousy were stilled finally. The fact that her husband had left her, whom he loved more than anyone in the world, to save the boy, had shown her that Jerome was a sacred trust and responsibility which came before all personal affections.

Suddenly there was a bitter cry from Jerome, who had remembered the precious Crucifix. It was impossible to force a way back to save it. Later, when Don Luis managed to pick his steps through the smouldering *débris*, he found the string burnt but the Crucifix intact in the heap of ashes.

One May day in 1559 Jerome came in from a ride on the Emperor's mule, which had been kept for him "because she is very gentle and the rider rather reckless." Don Luis, dusty from the ride out from Valladolid, stood in the patio beside Doña Magdalena, who sat as if turned to stone, pale as death, staring fixedly before her. Jerome, terrified, stole away, afraid to ask what was amiss,— though Luis flung over his shoulder the curt announcement that they were to go to Valladolid.

The chaplain told Jerome later what had happened.

Her younger brother, Juan de Ulloa, had been accused of heresy. A Knight of St. John, he had fought for Spain and the Cross in Tunis and Algiers. Now, stripped of military honours and knightly rank, he was in the Inquisition prison at Valladolid. Don Garcia explained how, a year ago, the Emperor had been roused to his old vigour by news of the discovery in Spain itself of those new beliefs which he condemned both as a Catholic and as a sovereign. Ruler and statesman, as well as soldier, he felt certain that the new religious doctrines would lead inevitably, sooner or later, to rebellion and anarchy. He had written strongly to his son at Brussels and his daughter at Valladolid that heresy must be instantly and ruthlessly suppressed and threatened himself to return to the capital : " If I had not entire confidence that you would do your duty and arrest the evil at once by chastising the guilty in good earnest."

The heresy hunt was now up " in good earnest." The dungeons of the Holy Office were crowded. Fernando Valdes, Archbishop of Seville and Inquisitor General, had a remarkably keen nose for anything that he fancied savoured of Lutheranism. Intellectual argument or research grew so dangerous that an acid proverb became current. " He is so clever he must be a Lutheran."

Carranza, whose harsh voice had irritated the Emperor, had held a Crucifix before the dying man with the words : " Behold Him Who answers for all. There is no more sin. All is forgiven." A spying friar had reported the saying to the Inquisition as tainted with the Lutheran doctrine of salvation by faith alone. Valdes looked with no special favour on the man, younger than himself, who had been appointed to the Primacy and the richest see in Spain which he too would have liked. Carranza awoke one night to find the dreaded familiars at his bedside and was hurried off to the damp and gloomy prison in Valladolid.

The Spanish Inquisition, which has proved such a godsend to English writers of historical fiction, had been instituted in 1480 by Ferdinand and Isabella, to deal with the special and complicated problems presented by heresy in Spain forty years before Luther nailed up his famous Theses : the problems, in particular, of those Jews whose conversion to Christianity was purely fictitious and later of the Illuminists with their tinge of diabolism. They had wrung a reluctant consent from Pope Sixtus IV under plea of an urgent and temporary measure. It had now acquired political as well as religious power and was securely defended against Papal and foreign interference. Even the Vicar of Christ himself (as Carranza's case was to prove) could only with the greatest difficulty obtain the release of a prisoner of the Holy Office in Spain.

The best known of those now under sentence in Valladolid was Dr. Agustin Cazalla, a popular preacher, a doctor of Salamanca University and a chaplain to the late Emperor. This Agustin Cazalla, his brother Francisco a *cura* of Palencia, a younger brother Juan and his wife, and a sister Beatriz, were all members of a distinguished family of Jewish converts in the capital. There were other priests and laymen, members of the same secret society, whose meetings had been betrayed to the Inquisition. Altogether fourteen were condemned to death—of whom

Juan de Ulloa was not one. His sentence was that of
imprisonment.

On May 15, 1559, came a courier from Vallodolid with
an invitation, which was in fact a command, to Doña
Magdalena from the Regent " that she would do her the
favour of coming to witness the auto and would bring with
her the boy in her charge." Doña Magdalena was puzzled
by this. She had not heard, for she did not listen to gossip,
the talk and rumours about Jerome which had been current
at Yuste, had reached Vallodolid and even the ears of the
Infanta Juana; so she wondered why his appearance
should be insisted on and was thankful that she would not
have to hear sentence of death passed on her brother.

Jerome was blissfully ignorant of these cross-currents
and convinced that the visit to the capital was to be the
greatest event of his life after his meeting with the Emperor.
So far his experience of town life was limited to a few
visits to Medina del Rio Seco, ten miles away on its hill
above the shallow river. There had been one unforgettable
moment there when, at one of the bull-fights, he had been
blooded. He had been allowed to go down and give the
coup-de-grace and, as he had plunged his small Ferrarese
sword into the bull's great neck, a gush of hot blood had
drenched his linen smock. He had come home enormously
pleased with himself and his gory appearance but somehow
his Tia's reception of him had been disappointing. But an
auto-de-fé was vastly more exciting than a bull-fight and he
wondered if the five days till their departure would ever
pass.

The long straight road was gilt by the May sunshine. As Jerome's mule trotted beside the litter he felt very grown up and very different from the small boy who had bumped along this sandy track five years ago, feeling shy and sick. The grey-dun fields were veiled now by the young corn. The vines stuck queerly from their pyramids of sand, their two bent branches like the horns of goats half hidden by the vivid yellow green of the new leaves. Then, as the last hill was reached, there was a bird's eye view of Valladolid below, its wide, dishlike plain bounded to the north by the spurs of the Penas de Cervera. The river Pisuerga was running sluggish and yellow under the arches of the old bridge, and inside the walls progress was as slow, for the narrow, twisting streets were packed with excited crowds. Hardly had they reached the house of the Count of Miranda, a cousin of Doña Magdalena, than Jerome obtained leave to go out with Juan Galarza.

Even the familiars of the Inquisition on horseback found it almost impossible to force a way for the officials and cryers who had to proclaim the decree forbidding anyone to carry arms, under pain of death, during the next twenty-four hours. It seemed hardly necessary to add that none but pedestrian traffic was allowed along all streets leading to the Plaza Mayor. A double row of guards already prevented entrance to the square, but Jerome, mounted on Galarza's shoulder, could see the stage prepared for to-morrow's tragedy. Workmen were putting the final touches to the huge, two-storied scaffold where the prisoners would hear sentence. From the Palace of the Inquisition in the Calle del Obispo, through the Plaza del Fuente

Dorada to the Plaza Mayor, black-draped stands had been
erected at every street opening. All the seats in them and
at all the windows and balconies along the route of the
procession were already sold at high prices. Pulpits, also
in funeral garb, stood at other corners, and friars, black,
grey and white, were preaching impassioned sermons to
the curious, excited, half-frightened crowds.

The greatest spectacle of this evening was still to come.
As four o'clock sounded from the cathedral tower sermons
ended abruptly, while stands, windows and balconies filled
for the Procession of the Green Cross.

Galarza found a place for himself and his charge which
commanded a view down the street to the front of the
Inquisition Palace, its big stone blazon carved with the
Dominican arms. From the big arched entrance emerged
an apparently endless stream of all the religious com-
munities in the city, each man carrying a lighted candle.
They were followed by the officers of the Inquisition in
their white habits and black cloaks, the mayor and municipal
dignities with still larger candles. Last of all, under a
canopy of velvet, came a Dominican friar carrying the
huge Cross of green wood, veiled in crape, while the choir
behind him intoned the " *Vexilla Regis.*"

It was dark by the time the long procession had finished
the slow circuit of the principal streets. The Green
Cross was solemnly enthroned on the altar on the lower
stage of the scaffold in the Plaza Mayor, to remain there all
night, lit by a dozen monster candles and guarded by friars
and a picket of troops.

Nothing had been forgotten which could contri-

bute to the horror and importance of the morrow's
ceremonies.

There was little sleep for Jerome that night after his
exciting day, for the stars were still shining when he started
again for the Plaza with Doña Magdalena and her niece
Maria, daughter of the Marques de Mota. By half past
four in the morning the streets were packed to suffocation
and every seat on stand and balcony filled. Places had been
reserved near the royal seats for the Quijada party, on the
balcony of the Casa Consistorial. This faced the scaffold,
where the candles round the Green Cross were flickering
palely in the growing daylight. As five struck there was a
roll of drums, a blare of trumpets and the royal guards
appeared, followed by the Council of Castile, grandees,
dukes, marquises, counts, archbishops and bishops. Next
came the maids of honour and the household of the Regent
and, last of all, Juana herself, veiled in crape from head to foot
and walking beside her Don Carlos, Prince of the Asturias.

Jerome, wedged between his Tia and her niece, was all
eyes, specially for his first sight of Don Carlos, only two
years older than himself. Like everyone else the Prince
was in mourning for this solemn occasion. The crooked-
ness of his shoulders showed even under the black serge
cloak and his spindly legs looked thinner than ever in
black stockings.

The royal party swept down the narrow gangway kept
for them on the balcony. Doña Magdalena flung her
cloak right over Jerome just before the Infanta stopped
and held out her hand as she whispered :

" Well, and the muffled mystery ? "

Doña Magdalena was forced to draw back her cloak.
Jerome emerged, cheeks scarlet and eyes blazing with rage
at the ignominy, his cap off and his hair ruffled. To his
amazement and indignation the Princess stooped, took him
in her arms and kissed him several times before she moved
on to her place. Don Carlos, delayed by this extraordinary
behaviour on his aunt's part, scowled sullenly and fingered
his dagger while his yellow face went a dull red. He was
not the only one who had noticed this odd incident.
There was a buzz of whispers. Attention was only diverted
by the tolling of all the church bells which announced the
arrival of the prisoners. The only splashes of colour in
the long procession were the great crimson standard of the
Inquisition, with the Dominican black and white and the
royal arms of Castile and Aragon, and the *sanbenitos*.
These yellow woollen tunics, worn by those condemned
to death, had a replica of the Green Cross on the breast.
Tall pointed caps were hideously painted with devils and
flames of hell and in their right hands the wretched creatures
carried green tapers. Among the prisoners were Beatriz,
sister of Dr. Cazalla, a young and exquisitely lovely girl,
and four other women.

There was a low growling murmur, a movement in the
dense crowds like the swaying of corn-ears in a wind. Some
women sobbed aloud. The Regent put a handkerchief to
her eyes under her veil. Pity, terror, horror had been
skilfully aroused and the atmosphere was electric. Fray
Melchior Cano, one of the most famous preachers in Spain,
mounted the pulpit opposite the scaffold where the prisoners

were massed, and in deep, blood-curdling tones, gave out the text : " False prophets, in sheep's clothing but inwardly they are ravening wolves."

His sermon lasted for over an hour and was succeeded by a solemn promise by Juana and Don Carlos of fidelity to the Catholic Faith. Then came interminable sermons, sentences on the guilty, and lectures, which altogether lasted till four in the afternoon. The May sun blazed down impartially on princes, nobles and people. Women fainted. Children cried. Jerome, worn out with excitement and lack of sleep, rested his head against his Tia's knee and slept peaceably in the shadow of her cloak.

At last the long ceremonies were over and the fourteen condemned prisoners were taken away to the Campo Grande, outside the city walls, where they were strangled before being burnt, only officials being allowed to be present.

Once more public curiosity veered to the Quijada page, with his brilliantly fair colouring. The mob surged round the party as they left the Casa Consistorial. Jerome got separated, crushed, nearly suffocated and would have been trampled to death under the crowded feet had the Count of Osorno not come to the rescue and carried him shoulder-high while he battled his way to Doña Magdalena and her niece.

" What has happened ? " cried the puzzled, frightened Jerome. " What is it ? Have the heretics escaped ? "

He got no answer. His Tia could bear no more. She ordered her litter and, late as it was, started home.

Dawn was breaking when Jerome at last fell asleep in his own bed under the charred Crucifix.

IV

THE KING !

(May—September 28, 1559)

That May day left its mark on Jerome. He did not talk to Doña Magdalena about it for he saw that even her serenity had been broken. Nor did he ask any explanation of the strange behaviour of the Infanta Juana and the crowd. He listened silently to the talk of Don Garcia and Dr. Prieto, to the argument of the latter that heresy was a cancer which, if not cut away, would spread and bring the whole body to death, that rebellion against authority ends in anarchy and destruction.

As usual, summer at Villagarcia passed in hot, drowsy peace, but there was a queer feeling in the air, like that moment before the storm when all is brilliant, sharp-cut and still as enamelled metal. Jerome was treated more ceremoniously, dressed better, but lessons were as rigorous as ever. Don Luis came and went, more brusque and irritable than before till he could hand over his responsibilities to the King, now ready to sail.

Harvest was over, vintage begun. The sound of stone mills grinding, the songs and shouts of men and boys bringing home the grapes in slow, ox-drawn waggons, deadened the shrill twitterings of swallows on their way back to Africa and the bleating of the first Mesta flocks of sheep on their way down from the Galician mountains to

winter quarters. Jerome lived feverishly, in harvest fields
and wine-presses, off on the Emperor's mule with gun or
bow. Galarza rode with him sometimes, further afield, to
the woods below the Espina monastery, where he got
glimpses through oaks and ilexes of wild boars rootling
for truffles, or heard the clash of the antlers of fighting
stags. He became expert at tilting, lance-throwing and
sword-play, learned to swim and play tennis, to train and
fly a hawk, brought home partridges, hares and quails.
The days passed quickly, Mass said by Don Garcia in the
castle chapel, or heard on Sundays and holy days in the
parish church of San Pedro, breakfast followed by the
almsgiving of Doña Magdalena, whom the poor had named
" God's Lady Bountiful."

It was her strong, sweet selflessness which was the
inspiration and keynote of life at Villagarcia. It seemed to
have distilled the essence of golden peace from the vast
stretches of ripe corn, the fruitfulness of the vintage, of
apple, pear and olive orchards, the austerity of the castle
within its square yellow walls, the stability of the low,
grey-red hills,—all mellowed and touched to unearthly
beauty like one of the sunsets when the western sky was
topaz and the crescent moon was poised on the far horizon.

The five and a half years that Jerome spent at Villagarcia
set an indelible seal on his character, put before him an
ideal which, though sometimes dulled or obscured, yet
was always to be the pole-star of his short and stormy life.
Looking back he recognised them as his happiest years
and when, as youth and man, he would still sit at his Tia's
feet he would live again with her the joys and sorrows of

his childhood which they had shared. Her love for him and his for her were, as he was to write to her, " the greatest love that has ever been or ever will be in this life."

Meanwhile King Philip was sailing down the Channel with a following wind. Muffled in his cloak he stood silent on the prow of the galley and watched the white Kentish cliffs give way to the flat Sussex shore. He looked at the opening to Southampton Water, where he had landed to marry the elderly, amorous Queen. He had nothing but unpleasant memories of his time in England. These tall, fair northerners were a blunt, arrogant, undisciplined race. Ruy Gomez, Prince of Eboli, had summed them up well. " The English steal unblushingly under one's very nose. We Spaniards are more refined about it." Philip remembered the acute discomfort of his own position as Prince Consort among an inimical people, the worse discomfort of his delicate stomach condemned to menus of endless roast joints and copious drafts of heavy, bitter ale. He saw a battered little English ship beating up-channel against the wind. It reminded him of a note he had made on the minutes of a Council meeting which had declared ships unready for sea. " England's chief safety depends on her navy being always in good order to serve for the defence of the kingdom against all invasion," he had scribbled in that cramped, illegible hand of his. " Ships should not only be ready for sea, but instantly available." Strange words for the future master of the " Invincible Armada." Ushant rose on the starboard horizon and the King looked eagerly south across the tumbling waves of the Bay of

Biscay, already in fancy sighting the Basque hills and the first view of the beloved Spain which he had resolved never to leave again.

He landed at Laredo (Santander) on the Feast of the Nativity of our Lady, 1559, and three weeks later (Michaelmas Eve) Don Luis told Jerome to put on his best smock to come riding. As he changed, the boy thought of a conversation between his Tia and Don Garcia about the famous shrines of the Mother of God : Guadelupe, whose statue had lain hidden during the Moorish domination ; Montserrat, the Benedictine monastery perched on the queer mountains which the Moors had called the Stone Watchmen ; Zaragoza, where tradition said that Our Lady had appeared " in mortal flesh " to Sant'Iago ; Loreto, where the humble house of the Holy Family was enshrined in golden domes and marble cloisters. Jerome had seen Guadelupe. He resolved that some day he would visit the other shrines too,—perhaps stop at Montserrat, as the Emperor had done in 1535, on his way to fight the infidels.

To Jerome's surprise a black horse was waiting for him in the yard instead of the mule, but he knew the old man's moods too well to ask any more questions. They rode off in silence, followed by Galarza and the hounds. Only when they reached the edge of the Espina wood did Jerome make bold to regret that he had not brought his hawk.

" We are flying at higher game today," was all the answer he got.

Oaks and chestnuts were touched with rust and flame that toned with the umber and sepia of the bare stubble-fields and vineyards. There was an exhilarating tang in the air under the great trees. Presently hounds got onto the scent of a stag and ran deeper and deeper into the wood till, at the top of the hill, they checked and, to Jerome's deep disappointment, lost the trail. Just as Galarza called them in, over the shoulder of the hill came the sound of a horn and the baying of a pack in full cry. Across the end of a long glade flashed a splendid stag, followed by hounds and a group of well-mounted huntsmen.

Jerome had difficulty in holding the black, who was as keen to follow as his rider. He cast an appealing look at Don Luis, who shook his head and gave a curt order to Galarza to take home the hounds.

" The King's huntsmen," he explained as he and the boy continued towards the Bernardine monastery. " We must leave the way clear for them."

He pulled up as two horsemen emerged from a group of ilexes and trotted towards them. One was tall and lean, with shaggy hair and beard turning grey, a long hooked nose and light piercing eyes deepset under a lined forehead. The other was small and slight, all in black, with the collar of the Golden Fleece on his breast. Jerome recognized him from the fair hair and beard and the protruding jaw like the Emperor's even before Don Luis whispered: " The King ! "

The two dismounted and knelt to kiss the hand which the King held out in silence. Jerome found he could not reach it,—a terrible moment of humiliation. The King dismounted too and held out his hand again, then, as the Emperor had done, put it under the boy's chin, tilted it and studied the young face. Jerome felt his cheeks turn scarlet under the searching gaze of the heavy-lidded hazel eyes, but his blue ones met them without faltering.

" What is your name ? " asked the King in his slow, quiet voice, motioning Jerome to stand up.

" Jerome, your majesty."

" A great saint but unfortunately he is dead. Do you know who was your father ? "

Jerome's face went white. If anyone else had dared to ask such a question. . . . But they would not have dared. He remained silent, head up and his gaze still fixed on the King, in a mixture of shame and defiance. The King laid a hand on his shoulder and spoke gently.

" Be of good heart, *niño mio*, for I have good news for you. The Emperor, my lord and father, was your father too. I now recognize and love you as my brother."

He bent and kissed the boy on both cheeks then, as horns and baying announced the return of the hunt, he spoke a few words to Don Luis, mounted and rode off with the Duke of Alba.

The ride home was as silent as the one to Espina had been. Jerome sat very straight on the big black, made no comments and asked no questions.

Still composed, though pale, he slipped down from the saddle as soon as they entered the court, ran across the inner patio and up the stairs. Doña Magdalena was in her room alone. She knelt to kiss his hand, whispering " Your Highness." He pulled her to her feet, to her chair, then, after bearing this amazing turn of fortune with dignity and calm, he broke down, flung himself on his knees, his arms round her and, burying his head in her lap, burst into tears.

V

THE QUEEN

(October, 1559—February 29, 1560)

Philip II of Spain was not called the Prudent without reason. He realized, as clearly as did Don Luis and his wife, the danger of such an amazing change of fortune to an ardent and ambitious character. In gratitude to Don Luis he made him a Knight of Calatrava and a member of the Council of Castile and appointed him Tutor and Head of the semi-royal household assigned to Don John of Austria as Jerome was called from henceforth. Under the " *Ayo* " were two Major-domos, a Master of the Horse, a Chamberlain, three gentlemen of the Bedchamber, a Captain of the Guard, a Secretary, bodyservants, and the rest— altogether a formidable establishment for a boy not yet fourteen. The royal court at Valladolid, however, continued the Burgundian splendour and ceremonial with which Charles V had superseded the old democratic simplicity of the Castilian court. Philip, whose recognition of his half-brother was full and generous, ordered that the boy was to be treated in every way as an Infante of Castile, except that he was to be addressed as Excellency instead of Highness,—a rule which was honoured more in the breach than in the observance.

Don Garcia and Dr. Prieto were left behind, but unfortunately lessons were not. It was a point on which the

King was inexorable. However, Don John found them less boring when in the company of boys of his own age. The three who now studied together in the palace were all in their teens, Don John's two nephews, Don Carlos and Prince Alessandro Farnese, both being two years older than himself. All three were to leave names known to the whole of the civilised world, though for very different reasons.

Don Carlos, silent and sulky when his young uncle was first presented to him, was soon captivated by his charm and in saner moments remained faithfully and generously devoted to the young prince whom he inscribed first on his secret " List of Friends." This was to the credit of the Infante, who had every reason to be jealous of the physical beauty and personal charm of his uncle. Don Carlos was a perfect example of the terrible results of interbreeding and marriages between cousins, uncles and aunts. His mother, Maria, had died young and he had always been sickly, undersized, ailing and slightly deformed. One shoulder was higher than the other and he had an impediment in his speech. His pear-shaped head, prominent eyes and ears, sullen sensual mouth and long Hapsburg chin made a handsome portrait impossible even for the flattering brush of the court painter. He was a trial to masters and governors, for he had already shown the queer, moody temper, alternating fits of laziness and flaring rage which were later to develop into dangerous insanity.

Alessandro, like Don John, was in every way a contrast to the heir to the throne. In him Don John found at once a twin soul, and from now on the fortunes of these two beautiful and brilliant young princes were to be intertwined, as boys, youths and men. Alessandro was the eldest son of Ottavio, Duke of Parma, and of Margaret of Austria, illegitimate daughter of Charles V by his first youthful amour with Margaret Vangest, now Governor of the Netherlands. Philip, with his usual caution, had considered it prudent to hold a hostage for his sister's behaviour, so had brought her son back to be educated at the Spanish court. Probably too he already saw in the boy of fourteen the intellectual capacity, cool calculation, courage and ruthless subtlety which were to make Alessandro one of the greatest military captains of the age.

Scarcely had Don John and the Quijadas settled into the house assigned to them at Valladolid than the court moved to Toledo, where the Cortes was to meet and the young Queen to be solemnly received on her arrival from France. The ride of a hundred and fifty miles to Madrid and fifty more on to Toledo was the first of many such journeys for Don John. Mounted on the new black horse he jogged beside Luis on the big mule and Doña Magdalena in her litter. He saw the great yellow Castillo de la Mota at Medina del Campo, dominating the country for miles round, one of the favourite homes of Isabel the Catholic, his great-grandmother. Then came the long climb up the mountains to Arevalo and over the Guadarramas to Avila. Hardly a house or village broke the desolation. Only here and there groups of pines pushed through the piles of grey granite boulders covered with a green bloom like patina on bronze. The mighty walls and towers of Avila,

its nine gates, the east apse of the cathedral, jutting, like
the stern of a ship, beyond the wall, were a symbol in stone
of the long war against Islam which had ended less than a
century ago. Outside the city, on the slope from the Puerta
del Sol rose the fortresslike convent of the Encarnacion.
Among the Carmelite nuns there was one, Teresa, daughter
of an hidalgo of the city, Alfonso de Cepeda. Already
people were talking of Sister Teresa de Jesus, for Francis
Borja, on his way back from visiting the Emperor at
Yuste, had stopped in the new Jesuit house of San Gil in
Avila and, after an interview with the young nun, had
reassured her that her mystic experiences were truly of
God.

The grey-brown country, bare and arid, its dun sandhills
covered here and there by a purple bloom of moss, was
left behind. The deep valleys between the granite mountains were full of pines and the sound of streams running
full from the snows not far above. From the highest
point of the pass was a glimpse, behind the blue line of the
nearer peaks, of the distant Toledo mountains. There
was still far to go, though, before Toledo was reached,
long miles across the wide upland of the Escorial, with its
grey rocks, grey olives, dark pines and little streams
gleaming like quicksilver. There, in four years' time the
first stone was to be laid of the monastery vowed to San
Lorenzo by Philip at the battle of St. Quentin. Thirty
miles on to Madrid, and then the two days' journey to
Toledo.

Jerome recognised, as one recaptures a half-forgotten
dream, the shrine on the steep hill of the Angels, Getafe,

with its two churches and the school where he had managed to learn nothing. Everything was the same, the peasants' houses of dried mud or wood, thatched with rushes or sods of withered turf, scattered among the olive orchards where the gnarled trees were the same dun-grey as the earth. It was all as it had been the first three years he could remember. Only he himself was no longer the same.

The massed trees of the royal gardens at Aranjuez, bare though elms and poplars were, came as a revelation of beauty after the bare, wide, burnt plains of Castile that he knew so well. The final stage of the long journey came as the short December day was drawing to a close— the winding Tagus, fringed with grey rushes and blood-red osiers, queer flat-topped mountains which looked as if some hungry Titan had taken a bite out of them, and one of those sunsets which El Greco has expressed in four dimensions, where a world out of time and place takes on a tangible as well as a visible reality. In a gulf edged by low hills a fleet lay at anchor on a sea that was red as blood and fire. Piled clouds of molten steel, lined with tenderest lavender, were a stage set and waiting for angelic actors or the conference of immortal gods.

It was dark as Toledo was entered over the Puenta de Alcantara, and the Alcazar towered black into the starry sky.

During the next two months Don John grew to know Toledo better than he had known Valladolid—the wide view from the terrace of the Alcazar, over the yellow Tagus encircling the city ; the splendour of the cathedral, with the chapel where Mass was celebrated according to the Mozarabic rite, and the marble tomb of Alvaro de Luna, who had been executed at Valladolid; the Franciscan church of San Juan de los Reyes, built by Ferdinand and Isabel for their burial place and ornamented with their initials; the churches which had been synagogues; the Moorish gate of the Sun, with its double arch, its battlements and arcading of fire-red brick. But most of all he loved El Cristo de la Luz, its straight white columns, horseshoe arches of brick and marble and intricate, interlacing arcades.

This he loved not because of its beauty, nor because it was the oldest mosque which had been converted into a church, but because of the legend which gave it its name. Always as he passed it he would stop to picture the entrance of the victorious Christians in 1085 under Alfonso VI (who had also taken Avila from the Moors) and see the Cid's horse kneel down before the mosque and refuse to rise till the wall was opened and the Crucifix found with the lamp before it which had burned miraculously during the three and a quarter centuries of the Moorish occupation.

Here every narrow crooked street, every tower, the name of the market, the " Zocodover," of the palace where he lived, the Alcazar, spoke of those centuries of Islamic domination, were a live expression of the force against which he had promised to devote his life.

Christmas and Epiphany were gone. Lessons continued. At the end of January the King left for Guadalajara to complete in person the marriage which had been celebrated by proxy seven months ago. The Queen was to make her state entry into Toledo on February 12, 1560 and this was to be Don John's first public appearance, no longer a page nor a pupil, but acknowledged by the King as prince and brother.

The King, who had come on ahead, waited for his bride outside the new Puerta Visagra, with Don Carlos on his right and Don John on his left. Between the two great round towers, over the arch, was a huge double-headed Austrian eagle supporting the arms of Charles V who had built the gate in 1550 and above that a tall angel towered into the sky. Even here, though, the Moorish spirit intruded in the brilliant *azulejo* tiles roofing the smaller square towers. As usual in Toledo a gusty wind whipped round the corners, filling eyes and nose and hair with dust and setting rubbish and dead leaves going in a devil's dance. Cloaks fluttered, feathers tossed and horses fidgeted, but at last along the Aranjuez road came the thicker cloud of dust which heralded the arrival of the Queen. John was not the only one who was excited. All Spain, without a Queen since the death of Don Carlos's mother ten years before, was ready to welcome the young French Princess not only for herself but as a visible sign of the peace which had at last ended the long drawn out war with France.

To Don John of Austria the Queen must indeed have seemed an incarnation of all the romances he had read at Villagarcia, a fairy princess of dew and light. Mounted on a white palfrey, with sweeping trappings, she was shaded by a canopy of fringed brocade embroidered with F's and I's, Philip's initial and her own. Her pale clear skin, thick dark hair, fine black eyebrows and liquid dark

eyes were set off by the richness of her brocade gown ;
the glitter of diamonds and soft gleam of pearls. Her
straight nose, softly rounded chin and generous mouth—
the lips curled as if about to break into laughter—made an
irresistible ensemble that justified the praises of that gossip
Brantôme. " Gentlemen dared not look at her for fear
of falling in love with her . . . Even churchmen avoided
looking at her for fear of temptation."

No wonder that she won the hearts of the young princes
on either side of the King, that Don Carlos (for whose
bride she had originally been intended) should look with a
jaundiced eye on a father who had robbed him of such a
prize, that Don John laid at her feet his first romance,
selfless and devoted.

Isabel *de la Paz*, as the people lovingly called her, had
loveliness of soul as well as of body. She possessed in a
supreme degree the courage which was the hall-mark of
noble and royal blood. She had already had need of it.
Crossing the Pyrenees in mid-winter, in snow and hail,
the child of fourteen was reproved by the Archbishop of
Burgos at Roncesvalles for her tears when she parted from
her French escort. Received at Guadalajara by the Princess
Juana, as always robed in funereal garb and her face hidden
by a black veil, Isabel stared in silence at her quiet, middle-
aged husband till, half in fun, half angry, he asked if she
was trying to count his grey hairs. Fresh from the Valois
court, with its gay, easy freedom, from the splendid royal
chateaux, with their Renaissance architecture and high,
ornate windows letting in all the sun and air, Isabel must
have thought Toledo, with its crooked streets darkened

by tall leaning houses, as gloomy as the grim square bulk
of the Alcazar and the hidalgos with their sombre clothes
and their warlike air.

She had found the heavy-jawed, reserved, grave King a
kind and affectionate husband, if over amorous. She had
hardly time to enjoy the long programme of festivities
prepared for her reception when she sickened with small-
pox. Couriers rushed to and fro between Toledo and
Catherine de Medici, whose fear for her daughter's possible
loss of beauty was diplomatic rather than motherly. It
was essential to the Queen-Mother's intricate schemes that
Philip's somewhat fickle heart should remain tangled in his
wife's dark hair.

The absence of the Queen, not yet completely recovered,
took some of the brilliance off the ceremony of February 22,
when the Cortes were to swear fealty to the Prince of the
Asturias. This, however, was not regretted by the ladies-
in-waiting of the Infanta Juana, whose dowdy sombreness
of attire would have been thrown into greater relief by the
chic of the Frenchwomen.

Juana, though she and her ladies were black as crows,
knew her young half-brother's un-Spanish passion for
colour and, the evening before the cathedral ceremony,
sent him a complete and gorgeous outfit, doublet and coat
of crimson velvet, trimmed with gold and silver embroidery,
the buttons and ornaments of diamonds. Doña Magdalena's
heart must have thrilled with pride to see her " Jeromín "
on the great day, splendid in silk and velvet and plumes,
eyes shining and hair as bright as his gold embroideries.

Bartolomé Carranza, Archbishop of Toledo, being a

prisoner of the Inquisition in Valladolid, his part was
taken by the Cardinal Archbishop of Burgos, who had
rebuked the poor little Queen at the frontier. Before the
cold spring day had dawned the streets were so crowded
that it was only with difficulty that way could be made for
the Cardinal in his scarlet robes, who was the first to arrive
in the gorgeously decorated cathedral for the Pontifical
High Mass.

Toledo does not lend itself to pageantry. Its crooked
streets are so narrow that, even when a donkey with laden
panniers appears, it is often necessary to take refuge in a
neighbouring door to allow it to pass. Any imposing
procession from the high-perched Alcazar to the great
triple west door of the cathedral, opened only on state
occasions, was out of the question. The scene on the wide
terrace of the Alcazar, though, was splendid, with the
sombre splendour of the Spanish spirit. There was the
King, the fairness of hair and beard accentuated by the
black plumed cap and black velvet doublet, the only
relief the heavy gold collar of the Golden Fleece and the
fine Flemish lace of ruff and cuffs. El Greco's wonderful
painting of the burial of the Count of Orgaz might portray
the crowded grandees and hidalgos on their fidgeting
horses—the long, lean faces, dark above the stiff ruffs,
the pointed beards, fine brows and dark eyes smouldering
with a fire that was of the spirit rather than of the flesh,
hands pale and slender, but strong and supple as the Toledo
blades that hung at their thin thighs. Here and there the
red-crossed surcoat of a Knight of Santiago or the gleam
of an order broke the mass of black. Above it fluttered in

the wind a gay foam of pennons and banners and, as the long files began to move off, there was one brilliant splash of colour as Don John of Austria moved by, on his prancing black horse, his gold hair shining, his crimson doublet and flying cloak glowing in the sun. Behind the three young princes came the litter of the Princess Juana and her ladies, a flock of funereal crows doubtless watched with catty amusement from the windows by the quarantined French ladies.

After the Pontifical High Mass the Cardinal ascended his throne, with the Duke of Alba, staff in hand as chief royal major-domo, and the Count of Oropesa with the drawn sword of justice, on his right. The oath of allegiance to " Don Carlos, eldest son of His Majesty, as Prince of this realm," was first read from the altar and then solemnly taken by grandees and Cortes. After the Infanta Juana had sworn, an announcement was made that, though not yet fourteen, Don John was considered by the King " of sufficient discretion, courage and understanding " to be able " to swear and perform full homage." He then left his seat, knelt before the Cardinal and laying his hands on the Gospels and the Cross answered in a clear, unfaltering voice : " I swear." He knelt also before the King and the Prince and, placing his two hands feudalwise between those of the King swore " once, twice and thrice, on faith and word " to do him full and complete loyalty and homage.

This oath, taken when he was not yet thirteen, at his first public ceremony, Don John of Austria was to keep faithfully and fully all his life. Never in word or deed did he fail in loyalty to his King and brother, and his obedience was to be as absolute as his loyalty. In an age when diplomacy was a thin mask for treachery, when truth was unknown in international politics, when honour meant only the etiquette of the tilting yard or the battlefield, loyalty was so rare that it may be counted as one of Don John's most remarkable characteristics. Loyalty to him was all the more difficult as he was the opposite of Philip in every way. Even when it seemed to him, as in those dark days in Flanders, that fealty to the King clashed with his own private code of honour, obedience stood the strain. He realised that the King, whatever his faults of government, his incorrigible and fatal procrastinations, his wrong decisions, never set up as his ultimate aim anything but what he believed to be for the service of God and the Faith.

As the procession wound its slow way back to the Alcazar the bitter wind carried the martial music of drums and trumpets far to the south. Don John of Austria, in his crimson cloak, on his big black horse, had started on the road that led south to Granada, east to Lepanto, north to Namur.

VI

STUDENT PRINCES

(March, 1560—Summer, 1564)

Even before the Emperor's death Don Luis Quijada had mapped out a peaceful old age for himself with his wife at Villagarcia, after half a century of continual fighting and travelling. Hardly had he got home after the King's return in September, 1559, that he had to move, wife, bag and baggage to her house in Valladolid. A month later the Court moved to Toledo. A few weeks after the oath of fealty to Don Carlos came another move, this time to Madrid, which had finally been decided on as the new capital.

Shifting a semi-royal household was a slow and complicated business, as was all travelling when coaches were an almost unknown luxury and roads a delusion. Luckily in this world everything comes to an end and no doubt the old man heaved a vast sigh of relief when at last Don John's establishment was settled at Madrid, in a large house belonging to Pedro de Parras, opposite the cathedral and close to the Alcazar (now the *Capitania General*).

Doña Magdalena, accustomed to the brusque manners and gusts of temper of the " rusty old Christian," treated him as most sensible women treat their husbands in such moods, like a petulant small boy. She was happy to have him with her, prizing his sterling worth, his rare honesty, his Christian virtue and the deep love for her hidden under his blunt exterior. She was happy too because her boy, in spite of the upheaval in his life, remained unchanged to her. Every morning he saw her before he went off with his escort to the Alcazar, for lessons and games with Don Carlos and Alessandro Farnese. Every evening when he came home he ran in, as at Villagarcia, to tell her the day's doings and to regale her with his boy's romantic devotion to the Queen. She was only too pleased that his first love should be for the lovely girl so little older than himself, whom the unlucky fate of royal birth had forced into the web of international politics at an age when the normal child's mind is absorbed by toys and dolls. Isabel *de la Paz* was indeed an inspiration to her young brother-in-law, not only by her charm and beauty but in her unselfishness, courage and loyalty.

But there was another influence which Doña Magdalena feared and distrusted—that of the Princess of Eboli. Ruy Gomez de Silva, a slightly older contemporary and friend of the King, was the confidential secretary to whom the reserved and cautious ruler revealed more of his secret thoughts and schemes than to anyone else but his confessor. Gomez, descendant of an old Portuguese house, had been rewarded for his services to Spain and his master by being made Duke of Pastraña, with an income from the dukedom of 25,000 crowns, and Prince of Eboli. He was one of the most powerful men in Spain, both from his influence with the King and as leader of the Peace Party in the Council of State which opposed the War Party led by the Duke of Alba. His charm of manner and speech, his tact and conciliation enabled him to steer a difficult course with success, while making the minimum of enemies. His knowledge of the world and of courts, his keen judgment of men, his mastery of court, council and diplomatic relations made him an invaluable adviser to Don John, whose friend he remained till his own death in 1573.

In 1553 he had married Ana de Mendoza, daughter of Diego Hurtado de Mendoza, Viceroy of Peru. Though only twenty now (1560) the Princess had already shocked old-fashioned people by her modern and advanced ideas and behaviour. Beautiful, witty, intelligent and original, she broke loose from the traditional and almost Oriental seclusion of Spanish women of the noble class. She kept open house and, as usual in such cases, her salon was as popular with men as it was disapproved of by women.

Doña Magdalena disapproved no less than others, though she was too charitable to bandy gossip. Instead she added a few extra petitions to her daily prayers for her beloved boy. It was only natural that he should be fascinated by the Princess, the dead pallor of her face accentuated by the blue-black of the curly hair which was piled high on the narrow head, and the scarlet of her mouth, its upper lip a perfect Cupid's bow, the lower full and petulant. Admirers said that her beauty was enhanced by the triangular black patch over the right eye, which had been damaged in a childish accident, that this gave added lustre and expression to the remaining eye. If Don John was fascinated by her it was equally natural that he should be her favourite of the three young princes. His brilliant fairness, his ardour, frank ambition and northern romanticism appealed to her by force of contrast. Alessandro's youthful and clear-sighted cynicism, his Italian sophistication and ruthlessness were too akin to her own nature. As for poor Don Carlos, with his crooked shoulder, uneven legs, fever-wasted body, stammering speech and fits of temper, the most he could hope for was pity and patience, and these he received in full measure only from his young stepmother.

So the summer of 1560 passed. The sun blazed down on the narrow, smelly streets of Madrid, on the scorched, barren tableland of Castile. At midday the big houses were shuttered and silent. Everyone gasped and sweated, longing even for a breath of that breeze which, according to the proverb, " *mata a un hombre y no apaga a un candil* " (is strong enough to kill a man but not to blow out a candle). With autumn the wind came sweeping down from the snow peaks of the Guadarramas sharp as a knife. Games and riding became a pleasure again, lessons a little less of a misery. Sleep was possible in the long, cold nights.

Early on the morning of November 24, 1560, a peasant coming up from the Manzanares with an ass-load of vegetables for market was turning into the Calle Mayor when he saw smoke and flames coming from a window of the house opposite the cathedral. He battered on the heavy door, with shouts of " Fire, fire ! " Don Luis, with the light sleep of the old soldier, was again the first to wake and, in his nightcap and woollen gown, to rouse the household. Don John, much to the destruction of his thirteen year dignity, was caught in the old man's arms, carried out and dumped on the cathedral steps. *El Cristo de sus Batallas* was saved, but the great chest containing all the family papers of the Quijadas was burnt, a loss which Don Luis never ceased to regret. The house blazed like a gigantic bonfire and in a few hours nothing was left but a pile of smouldering débris.

Kind neighbours were providing the shivering refugees with clothing, blankets and offers of hospitality when the crowd parted to make way for Ruy Gomez, suave, handsome and neat in spite of the early hour. To Doña Magdalena's dismay he was accompanied by the Princess, who insisted on their all coming home with her. There was no alternative but to accept and for the next few months Don John and his guardians were lodged in the Eboli palace till another house was ready for their reception.

There was one quiet and unnoticed inmate of the house who regretted the eventual departure of Don John—Maria de Mendoza, a small relation of the Princess's. It was inevitable that this inconsiderable little girl should worship from afar the gold-and-ivory young god, equally inevitable that with the magnificent arrogance of the healthy young male, he should ignore her very existence and grieve only for leaving his " *Tuarte* " (one-eye).

Another year went by. Alessandro left his uncle far behind in lessons, but in horsemanship, feats of arms and games there was nothing to choose between the two. Don Carlos shone in nothing—awkward and unattractive as the third brother of fairy tales but, unlike him, destined neither to health, wealth nor happiness. His odd moods and sulky fits alternated with storms of almost maniacal rage, even against those of whom he was fondest. His devotion to his stepmother increased his bitterness against his father, whom he grew to hate for having deprived him of so lovely a bride. Rumours that he was unfit for marriage reached his ears, as unpleasant talk always reaches those whom it hurts most, and, though only fifteen, he grew eager to prove his manhood.

Philip, who watched his son with anxious care, saw that the time had come to make a change and resolved to send the three boys to the University of Alcalá de Henares, which, though only founded by Cardinal Ximenes in 1499, was now at the zenith of its fame. By the end of October, 1561, Don Carlos, Don John and the Prince of Parma were settled at the University in charge of Honorato Juan, a stout, pompous old gentleman who had studied at Louvain, fought with Charles V at Algiers and had been the King's tutor. Carlos and John were lodged in the Archbishop's palace, for its unfortunate owner, Carranza, was still imprisoned at Valladolid, while a continuous stream of couriers went to and fro between the offices of the Spanish Inquisition and Rome. It was a gorgeous Mudejar building, a mixture of Renaissance, in the decorations and balustrades of the great arched patio and noble stairs, with pure Moorish in the huge Council Chamber, whose horse-shoe arches and *artesonado* ceiling was a riot of intricate geometric moulding and a blaze of red, blue, green and yellow. Round the walls ran Cufic inscriptions, whose messages were lost in the darkness of an unknown tongue, though their square stiff lettering accentuated the lavish beauty of honeycomb carving and rainbow colours.

This was Don John's first experience of a world of men. The dusty, windswept streets of the old Roman-Moorish town were filled by a noisy crowd of over ten thousand students. The wide, arched patios, the marble stairs, the shell-topped Renaissance doorways of the University, rang with the gay laugh and talk of youth, the jingle of spurs, the smack of pelota balls, or, in the *Paraninfo*, the heated arguments of those who took study seriously.

The University, by its Bull of Creation granted by Alexander VI to Cardinal Ximenes, was modelled on that of Salamanca, one of the most famous in Europe. It had the power to confer degrees, and its graduates enjoyed the same privileges as those of Valladolid, Salamanca and Bologna. In the Spanish universities, probably alone among those of the Middle Ages, degrees were conferred in the name of the King as well as in that of the Pope, and their connection was a close one with the Crown, which generally provided a third of their endowment—thus following the course of keeping as much power as possible in royal hands rather than in those of ecclesiastics.

The famous press which had printed Cardinal Ximenes' Polyglot Bible—said still to be the most beautiful printed Bible in the world—was keeping up its reputation of scholarship and scientific research, and lecturers were chosen from the best brains of Spain.

The King, with his usual conscientious care, drew up a detailed time-table for the studies of Don Carlos and Don John. Alessandro, who lodged in the town, not with the other two in the archiepiscopal palace, had naturally more freedom. The Spanish princes were to get up at seven in winter, six in summer, to attend household prayers, after breakfast to hear Mass in the private chapel. Two hours of study, begun by the " *Veni Creator*," ended by " *Dios gracias*," were followed by dinner in public at eleven and an hour's music lesson from twelve to one. The afternoon was devoted to riding and fencing and, from four to five, games and amusement. After six o'clock supper came recreation, and at nine o'clock Rosary and bed.

Alessandro easily outstripped the others in Latin, philosophy and the humanities. Learning came as naturally to him as riding, swimming, sword play and all outdoor sports to Don John. Short winter afternoons and long summer evenings were a joy to both. Races, horse and foot, tilting at the ring, javelin-throwing were all staged in the flat meadows on the banks of the Henares. Tennis, pelota and quoits were played in the university precincts. Don Carlos, clumsy at such exercises at the best of times, did not often take part in them, for he had come to Alcalá a wreck from two years of quartan fever. When he did play he could not bear to lose. On one occasion there was a discussion about a doubtful service at tennis. Carlos, his yellow face dark with one of his sudden, ungovernable rages, turned on Don John, his opponent.

" I cannot argue with you because you are my inferior. Your Mother was a harlot and you are a bastard."

John answered quietly enough, though he was white with anger at such an insult.

" At any rate my Father was a much greater man than yours is."

Don Carlos repeated the story to his Father, whose answer was :

" Don John was right and you wrong. His Father and mine was a far greater man than I have been or ever shall be."

The incident was forgotten and Carlos's affection for John ranked only second to his devotion to his stepmother. But in the following spring came catastrophe. Carlos, to prove his disputed manhood, started an affair with the porter's daughter. Proud of this clandestine romance, he confided it to Don John, who greeted it with laughter, then, disgusted, walked off. The tutor and Don Luis got wind of the business. Doors were shut at nine o'clock so that ingress and egress were impossible. The boy, however, managed to get hold of the key of a small door out of the court. As he was creeping out on the night of April 19, 1562, he slipped on the dark stairs, fell and fractured his skull.

He lay at the point of death for nearly a month. The King rushed to Alcalá. Quijada and Honorato Juan remained day and night by the sick-bed. The best doctors, Spanish and Italian, came, consulted, disagreed, consulted again and finally trepanned the patient. The streets of Madrid were crowded with processions. Blood streamed from flagellated shoulders. The Queen spent hours on her knees. The Infanta Juana walked barefooted on an icy morning to the shrine of our Lady of Consolation. A Moorish doctor was fetched from Valencia to apply his famous ointment. The body of one Fray Diego, who had died in the odour of sanctity, was disinterred to be laid on the invalid's bed. Mercifully Don Carlos was unconscious. To find as a bed-fellow a century-old corpse in a mouldering Franciscan habit would hardly have steadied an already unbalanced mind.

Whatever the reason—Moorish unguent or holy corpse —the Prince at last took a turn for the better and on July 5 was able to attend Mass.

During illness and convalescence he had shown exemplary patience and unselfishness. In one of his lucid moments, between fits of delirium, he had whispered to his father that his chief regret in dying was that the Queen had not yet borne a child. That there had as yet been no hopes of one was a deep grief to herself and the King. He, when he saw the contrast between his own sickly boy and the health and brilliance of Don John and the Prince of Parma, must indeed have found resignation difficult.

The years passed, full of study, games and cheery young society at Alcalá, holidays in Madrid or at the royal country seats of Segovia or Guadalajara. Don John was now seventeen, of medium height, beautifully made, graceful, slender, agile, with perfectly trained body and muscles like whipcord. He looks out from Antonio More's picture of him at sixteen with a steady, enquiring look in the deepset blue eyes, while the full red lips curl a little scornfully under the straight nose with its sensitive nostrils. A high ruff frames the soft, smooth young face, and the curve of the jaw from the small flat ear to the rounded chin is fuller than it will be a few years later. He is fully armed, in a richly engraved and gilded Italian cuirass and arm-pieces, with the collar of the Golden Fleece below the gorget. One sinewy long-fingered hand holds a baton, the other grips his sword-hilt. That grip is typical of the unwavering determination and hardening resolve of these years of adolescence. All the physical training, the perfection in sport and arms, the self-control and asceticism were directed to the one end. War was the means to an end with Don John and Alessandro Farnese. To the Italian it was the way to become the greatest military leader of his age. With the Spaniard his own glory and ambition were secondary. His first aim was the extermination of infidels and the triumph of God and His Church.

If Luis Quijada, in his rough, soldier's heart, sympathised with this warlike ambition of his charge, Honorato Juan had the King's wishes to consider. He would stand with his pupil before the splendid monument of Cardinal Ximenes behind its fine gilded *reja* in the chapel of the University. The Florentine artist had carved the strong features, the sharp nose and grim mouth, the long, nervous hands, the spare frame in the Franciscan habit, with so lifelike a touch that it seemed that at any moment the sunken lids might lift, the thin lips open. Honorato, in his booming voice, extolled the great statesman and churchman, his learning, his wisdom, his power, his foundation of the University, his patronage of the world-famed printing press. But Don John saw the Cardinal not in the purple in his metropolitan cathedral, nor in the printing room, but saw him fronting the rebel nobles, answering their query as to his authority with a proud gesture which pointed to his troops in the Plaza below—saw him, his Franciscan habit girt with a sword-belt, as he led the Spanish troops into battle against the Moors and uttered the warrior words : " The smell of gunpowder used against the infidel is sweeter than the perfume of incense."

Don John, aware of plans for his ecclesiastical future, forgot such remote and unpleasant contingencies, till suddenly the small cloud on the far horizon advanced and darkened all the future. When the Aragonese Cortes met early in 1564 the King had already written to the Pope asking for a Cardinal's hat for his brother. His relations with Pius IV were a pleasing contrast to his endless quarrels with Paul IV. Giovan Angelo Medici, unlike his predecessor, was strongly pro-Austrian in sympathy and made up for his lack of blue blood by a cheery good nature and an appreciation of the good things of life. He wrote accordingly that he was delighted to grant the King's request and, at this one fatal blow, all Don John's dreams and ambitions were shattered.

Those fair curls, though, were destined to a laurel crown, not a tonsure. In the nick of time, as if in answer to his anguished prayers, the perpetually smouldering quarrel about precedence between the French and Spanish ambassadors flamed up suddenly. The Pope pronounced in favour of France. Diplomatic relations between Spain and the Holy See were broken off. Negotiations about the red hat were at an end and the future victor of Lepanto, his student days over, rejoined the court at Segovia, in the autumn of 1564, in time to welcome his cousins, the Archdukes Ernest and Rudolf, whose father, the Emperor Maximilian II, had sent them to be educated in Spain.

VII

"RIDING TO THE SEA"

(Autumn, 1564—November 15, 1565)

Months passed. The days, in their quiet regularity, were much the same whether the court was at Guadalajara, Segovia or Madrid. The King and Queen heard Mass, went for a short, gentle walk or ride, took a siesta after dinner. Every spare moment was spent by the King at his writing desk, making those interminable marginal notes, minutes and letters, which he insisted on penning in his own difficult hand. Hunting, specially in the woods of Valsain, near Segovia, was a favourite but genteel pastime. Deer and boars were driven from the forest into big, railed enclosures where they were shot from butts and stands. The Queen, with her ladies, watched the " sport " from a coach and even, on one memorable occasion, herself shot a stag.

The gay, brave, little French princess of whom Brantôme said that no man could look at her without falling in love, had little chance of turning men's heads or stealing their hearts, even if she had wished to. The etiquette of the Spanish court reeked of the harem. No man was allowed to dance with the Queen except the King. No men were allowed the entrée to her apartments except the three young princes. In the evenings she would sit with the King, while her ladies danced those stately *branles* and *pavanes* at which Don John and Prince Alessandro were such expert performers. Or at Valsain the King, feeling rustic, summoned the country boys and girls to dance the Castilian *Habas Verdes* or the wild old war-dances, to the accompaniment of pipes, drums, castanets and hand-clapping. Sometimes a band of wandering gipsies would perform their age-old *Zarabanda*, " the pantomime of love," which by its wild abandon shocked the ecclesiastics but thawed the King's habitual staid reserve.

On May 15, 1565, the Queen bade a tearful farewell to the grave elderly husband whom she had learnt to love and rode north to meet her mother at Bayonne. With her going sunshine went too. Don Carlos, who, with Don John, had been continually with her all the spring, relapsed into a mood of black melancholy shot, like a thundercloud by lightning, with outbreaks of furtive and terrible sadism.

The court moved to Valsain. Philip buried himself in papers and reports. There was trouble everywhere. The Council of Trent had at last ended its quarrelsome and often interrupted sessions on December 4, 1563. Its decrees on the reform of ecclesiastical chapters and their immunities had not yet been enforced in Spain where the King appointed the bishops and therefore wished to keep Church patronage in his own power. The Netherlands, once known as " the Black Indies " from the money their coal and manufactures had poured into the Spanish treasury, were now a continual thorn in the flesh and drain on the exchequer. A stream of letters flowed in from Alessandro's mother (the unfortunate Governor), from the Protestant nobles, whose leaders, the Prince of Orange, the Counts of Egmont and Horne, had resigned as a protest against the policy of de Granvelle, now a Cardinal. The religious houses objected, naturally enough, to the appropriation of part of their revenues for the endowment of the three new archbishoprics and fourteen bishoprics for whose foundation Philip had obtained a Bull from Paul IV. There was too the spread of that new teaching which Philip had in vain tried to suppress. " Better not reign at all than reign over heretics," he had written and had refused to withdraw his edicts against Lutheranism.

At the Prince of Eboli's palace politics were naturally in the forefront of the conversation and the young princes were often in the salon of the fascinating one-eyed beauty. Alessandro's interest in the Low Lands problem was accentuated by the fact that, since Cardinal de Granvelle had left for Rome, his mother was in the unenviable position of buffer between the inflexible Catholicism of the King and the turbulent independence of Protestant nobles and burghers. Don John's thoughts were directed elsewhere. The Turkish Fleet was gathering in strength in the Golden Horn (spring 1565). The sea-wolves of the Mediterranean had found, under the able leadership of the brothers Barbarossa, that their interest was furthered by submission to the Ottoman ruler. Now the armada commanded by Sinan Pasha contained the galleys of the renegade Dragut, bravest, cruellest and cleverest of the corsairs.

Jean de Valette, Grand Master of the Knights of Malta, had no doubt of the objective of this great fleet. He sent out an appeal from Malta to all the Christian princes. It fell on deaf ears. Jealousies and selfish struggles for

personal advantages drowned the call to sacrifice for a
noble end.

The Pope himself, now that the Council of Trent had
done its work, felt that his own was done too and that he
was entitled to some relaxation from effort. " He began to
act more freely according to his inclinations," wrote
Tiepolo with the usual caustic cynicism of Venetian
ambassadors. " One saw in him more a prince busied
about his own affairs than a pontiff caring for the welfare
of others."

In France the young King Charles IX was a puppet in
the hands of his able and unscrupulous mother, Catherine
de Medici. She was now with him at Bayonne to meet her
daughter and to discuss with the Duke of Alba the best way
of checking the Huguenots, whose tenets she only condemned when they threatened her own power and designs.

Elizabeth of England, as was inevitable on account of
her illegitimate birth, was showing herself as determined
to stamp out Catholicism as Philip was to crush
Lutheranism.

The Emperor Maximilian, married to Philip's sister
Maria, was a garrulous and ineffectual gentleman, sure of
his own judgment only as a collector of artistic works.
He had lately concluded peace with the Turks whom he
preferred as powerful neighbours and allies rather than as
ruthless enemies.

There remained only Philip II, whose interest as well as
his conscience marked him out as the most likely helper
of the Knights of St. John. De Valette's letter came, was
read, annotated and placed among the piles of other corre-

spondence. Philip remained true to his favourite saying :
"*Yo y tiempo contra otros dos*" (I and time against any
other two).

To Don John the delay was insupportable. He was
eighteen. He had done nothing. He was doing nothing
except ride and fence and hunt and swim to keep his body
fit for an emergency which refused to materialize. Evenings in the rich, brocade-hung, scented rooms of the
Princess of Eboli, music, dancing, soft or witty words
from her curling red lips, a caressing touch of her white
fingers, rides and talks with Alessandro, these sedatives
had no longer power to still the effervescent ambition of
passionate youth. Alessandro, so much older than his
nineteen years, with the sophistication and worldly knowledge of his Italian blood, would laugh at his uncle's
simplicity. He himself, though only nineteen, was this
year to be married to Princess Maria, niece of King Manoel
of Portugal.

As the two rode onto the heights of the Siete Picos,
Alessandro would tease Don John about his romanticism,
the relics of Amadis de Gaul and the tales of chivalry he
had read at Villagarcia and Alcalá. North, beyond the
sweep of oak and pine and chestnut, lay the plain of Castile,
russet-red, burnt sienna and yellow ochre, blazing yet
barren. South, over the Sierra de Guadarrama, the grey
walls of the Escorial were rising under the direction of
Juan Batista de Toledo. East, through Guadalajara and
Zaragoza, ran the road to Barcelona and the sea.

Don John's thoughts and desires flashed over mountains
and rivers, by Cataluyd and Lerida and Montserrat to the

Catalan harbour and the silver-sapphire Mediterranean.
The wind in the pines was like the distant murmur of the
sea. The movement of the black horse under him was the
stirring of a ship as she comes alive on the waves. Dreamer
of dreams, Alessandro sometimes called him. Perhaps,
after all, dreamers were the doers of the greatest deeds.

Don John had gone. He had ridden out with Don
Carlos and vanished. There was a hue and cry. The
King sent for Luis Quijada. *He* had thought Don John was
with the Prince of the Asturias and the Archdukes. Nobody
knew where he had gone nor what had become of him.

And Don John, with two attendants, was away to
Barcelona to sail with the galleys bound for the relief
of Malta (April 9, 1565). The news leaked out. The King
sent couriers post-haste to all ports and officials with
orders : " That Don John return at once, since his journey
is against my wishes and since he is too young for so long
a voyage and so dangerous an undertaking." But Don
John galloped east, along the banks of the Henares, through
Sigüenza, crowned by the pinnacled ruins of the old
Moorish Alcazar, through Medina Celi, perched high on its
hill, with its triple Roman arch, along the Roman-Moorish
road to Cataluyd, its houses of crumbling sun-dried brick
round the Templars' church of Santo Sepulcro. Up and
up into the mountains, grey like scarred iron, with streaks
of tawny sand, furred here and there by grey scrub of
rosemary and thyme, a weird country like some strange
fierce dream, red copper, burnt brown gorse, ochre sand,
black cows like splashes of ink on pewter, high spurs of

hills thrusting square towers and broken battlements of
Moorish castles into the steel sky. On and on, while
heart and pulse beat loud and hard as the hoofs of the black
horse on the stony track.

On to the galleys and out to sea, dreamed Don John,
away from that half forgotten menace of the tonsure and
the shadow of the red hat, on to the crash of iron-beaked
prows, the thunder of cannon, the clash of sword and shield,
the shrill music of bugles, the fierce shout of " Santiago "
and white decks red with blood. There lay his destiny.
For this fate had he been born of the warrior-emperor's
passion for the German singer. He knew it as every man
in his soul knows the work for which God has created him.

Before them lay the green valley of the Jalon, with its
cornfields and vineyards and olive orchards, almond and
peach blossom flushing into rose here and there, water-
wheels and ox-drawn ploughs. Don John had dreamed.
Now things fused into a muddled nightmare. The flash
of magpies' wings, black goats with devils' horns, steel
stained with blood—was it a sword-blade or a tumbled
rock ?—whirling wheels, creaking carts, weird music of
Aragonese *Jotas*. . . . Heart and pulse beat faster and
louder till he was shaken and scorched, then icy and
shivering.

Blindly and reeling in the saddle he rode into Frasno,
five leagues short of Zaragoza and there the two terrified
men put him to bed in a miserable inn, too racked with fever
to be conscious how his flight had been abruptly ended.

Tidings flew swiftly as by wireless. Young nobles
began to pour out of Madrid to join the young hero in his

enterprise. Information of his plight reached the local grandee, the Duke of Villahermosa, widower of Doña Luisa Borja, Father Francisco's sister, and at once he sent to the dirty tumble-down *fonda* his own two doctors, beds, hangings, furniture, and a litter to bring the invalid to his castle as soon as the doctors considered him fit to be moved. But the news had reached Zaragoza too.

Never had the little village known such excitement nor seen so much life. Hardly were beds and furniture crowded into the grimy little inn-rooms than down the street rode the Governor of Zaragoza with a cavalcade of gentlemen sent by Don Hernando de Aragon, grandson of King Ferdinand and Archbishop of Zaragoza. The ducal litter was commandeered, and in it Don John was carried the fifteen miles into the city, surrounded by the escort of noble cavaliers—all little calculated to bring down the temperature of a fever patient.

Lying in a great room in the Archbishop's palace the invalid looked down on the old seven-arched Puente de Piedra, the bases of whose piers, sharp as ships' prows upstream, and rounded like a ship's stern downstream, made the flooded, muddy river foam angrily. Beyond the green vega on the far side of the river, where cypresses cut darkly upwards above the drooping willows and grey olives, row behind row of mountains rose in the distance, the snowpeaks of the Pyrenees dominating the rest and, in this clear, hard, dry air, seeming almost within reach of an outstretched hand. It was pleasant to lie in the canopied, curtained bed and to feel strength return, but with convalescence came a fusillade of argument and persuasion.

A curt and decisive message came from the King:
" That Don John is to go no further . . . the more so as
the galleys have already sailed." The Archbishop, grown
old in command and with the added authority of his royal
blood and cousinship, the Governor, the local nobility
all with one voice urged obedience. Don John, still pale
and weak, replied courteously but inflexibly :

" My expedition is for the service of God and my lord
the King, and for the sake of my reputation I cannot give
it up."

So, in his first recorded speech, sounds the keynote of
his life, the service of God and the King and the winning
of glory.

Frontal attack had failed. Subtler tactics were tried.
Let his Excellency wait till fifteen hundred men had been
raised as an escort fitting to his rank, till a loan had been
negotiated for the expenses of his voyage. His Excellency
politely but firmly declined all offers, sent one of his gentlemen on to get lodgings at Barcelona and prepared to ride
as soon as possible.

At Guadelupe he had knelt beside Doña Magdalena.
Now he was out of favour with Luis as well as with the
King—the more reason for fervent prayers at the shrine
of the famous Virgen del Pilar. The little chapel, a copy
of the Holy House at Loreto, was dark but the columns of
gilt bronze and purplish, brown-red marble glowed warm
in the yellow candlelight. Behind the silver *reja* and the
forest of candles the chased silver of the Pillar was pale
against the star-studded sky-blue brocade. The stiff,
fringed mantle of white satin was heavy with gold and

jewels. Under the high, jewelled crown the carved face
was dark with the passing of centuries and the flames of
millions of candles. Broken fragments of song drifted
in as a procession came across the Plaza. " *Virgen Santa,
Madre mia . . . Pilar Bendito, Trono de Gloria, Tú a la
Victoria nos llevarás* ! " (Blessed Virgin, my Mother,
Holy Pillar, Throne of Glory, Thou wilt lead us on to
victory.)

Don Carlos and Don John rode north from Segovia to
meet the King and the Queen on her return (July 30,
1565). The Infante dismounted and limped forward
eagerly to kiss his stepmother's hand. Don John had a
more difficult task. It was his first meeting with the King
since his flight and his homecoming from Barcelona. He
had lingered in the port though the galleys had sailed for
Malta, had even thought of riding overland through France
to try and catch them at Genoa. Scarlet with embarrass-
ment, though still quietly dignified, he too dismounted,
kissed the hand of the reserved, alarming sovereign and
begged forgiveness for the trouble and anxiety he had
caused. The King, instead of showing the displeasure
which self-control made more effective, leaned from his
saddle and warmly embraced his brother. Then with a
hand on his shoulder he told him to be patient, that it
would not be long before the whole Mediterranean fleet of
Spain would be ready to sail against the infidel and that he
should be in command, since this last escapade was proof
positive that he had no vocation to an ecclesiastical career.
It is likely that Philip admired most in his brother the

qualities of reckless courage, ardour and romance which had been omitted in his own mental make-up.

As Don John kissed the Queen's hand she asked with a laugh :

"Did you find the Turks very brave when you got to Malta ? "

Still scarlet-faced he lifted his head and met her look proudly.

"I have not *yet* had the chance of testing their mettle, not *yet*."

She was lovelier than ever, glowing with pleasure at being home again, and the King smiled lovingly at her as she rode to Valsain with that ill-assorted pair—Caliban and Ariel—on her right and left.

To Don John the stars danced for joy. The King's forgiveness, that whispered promise, the Queen's loveliness, her gay jests and laughter—he could not but know, for all her diplomacy, that he was nearer her heart than her uncouth stepson—and if Don Luis was still crusty because he had been kept in ignorance, well the old bear's growl was worse than his bite and Señora Tia would soon smooth his ruffled fur.

Dragut, the old seawolf, was killed. At last the Spanish galleys under Don Garcia de Toledo were sighted (Sept. 8, 1565). The Turkish fleet weighed anchor. The siege of Malta was over. La Valette and his few surviving Knights, gaunt, haggard and bloodstained, welcomed the tardy Don Garcia to the shattered walls of Il Borgo, the shreds of the white, eight-pointed Cross on its black ground still

crowning the ruins. In those four terrible months of
siege thirty thousand Turks and eight thousand Christians
fell—a blood sacrifice on the altar of Philip's dilatoriness—
but the name of Jean Parisot de la Valette was blazoned
for ever in the roll of great Christian heroes and immortalized in the name of Valetta.

Winter was here again. The Court moved to Madrid.
Don John stayed with the King to superintend building
operations at the Escorial, a spot more bleak and windswept
even than Madrid. The visit was more honourable than
comfortable, for the accommodation in the village was of
the worst and scantiest and the " Royal Tribunal " in the
temporary chapel of the friars, equally draughty and leaky,
consisted of a tattered curtain.

All was peaceful at the court, but it was no secret that
both King and Queen were anxious and unhappy that, after
five years of marriage, no children had been born to them
—a misfortune the greater because Don Carlos's health
did not improve, in mind or body.

After the battle of St. Quentin Philip had captured the
saint's head, but, now that relations were again friendly
between Paris and Madrid, an exchange had been arranged
by which the skull was to be restored to France in return
for the relics of St. Eugenius. At Bordeaux a French
embassy had handed over the bones to a Spanish one and
the royal progress of the sacred remains to Toledo was now
in its final stages. Strangely enough it was at Getafe,
their nearest approach to Madrid, that the Queen chose to
visit them, with the Infanta Juana and Don John. So the
small frightened boy in peasants' clothes, who had left

Getafe eleven years ago, now returned as a royal prince in attendance on the Queen.

He left the two ladies still at their prayers and stood at the church door, looking out at the half-forgotten land-scape, the hill of the Angels, the wide plain in its dreary winter garb of dun-grey, the snow peaks of the Guadar-ramas in the north, sinister under a sky of dull steel. It had for him no sentiments and no regrets. He had never taken root here, rather had been a boat waiting in harbour the signal to put out onto an unknown sea. Perhaps, though he did not know it, this grim, hard country had strengthened in him the endurance, the capacity for hardness which contrasted so oddly with his love of richness and splendour.

The Queen came out alone, smiling at him through her tears. He knew for what she had been praying. He too had asked that her desire might be fulfilled. He would gladly have sacrificed himself to gain it for her. He held her hand a moment after he had kissed it and all his youthful, romantic devotion was shining in his blue eyes.

VIII

CHIAROSCURO

(November, 1565—January 18, 1568)

It is always hard to wait, hardest of all when one is young, ardent and ambitious. But there was the King's promise, and the only thing was to fill every day and hour to make weeks and months pass more quickly. Good-natured Pius IV died in December, 1565, and the Spanish ambassador in Rome, Luis de Requesens, urged Philip to support the election of the Dominican, Michele Ghislieri. The austere and saintly friar became Pope Pius V in January, 1566, and in this election Don John saw the further-ance of his hopes of action. Not only were rigid and ruth-less reforms carried out in church matters, but the new Pope showed, in his relations with Venice, that he had no sympathy with that republic's Laodicean attitude towards the Turks.

One activity of the Pope, however, met with no approval from Don John nor any of his fellow countrymen. In 1567 was issued a Bull forbidding attendance at bull-fights or the baiting of any wild animal. Philip, though he himself did not share the national passion for such sports, realized that the promulgation of the Bull in Spain would rouse a storm of fury as well as being disobeyed, so, prudent as usual, he played for time by setting the Spanish theologians to start an interminable discussion on the rights of the case.

Meantime Don John, since his flight to Barcelona, had become the idol of society, " the glass of fashion and the mould of form," to such an extent that his characteristic gestures and style of dress were slavishly copied by the young bloods. His thick, wavy hair, brushed straight back from his wide forehead, fell naturally to the left and he had a trick of tossing his head to that side. All hair, then, black, brown, straight or curly, had to be trained carefully " à l'Autrichienne." All heads, ugly or handsome, empty or brainy, had to be turned in the same direction. " Beautiful as Apollo, splendid as an archangel," an Italian wrote of Don John later, and the Madrileños were of the same opinion.

First in the tilting field, at hunting, riding, swimming, dancing, with sword and lance, little wonder that the young Prince Charming was a social success. Doña Magdalena was often asleep long before her boy came in, but her prayers for him were all the longer and more fervent. She knew that his activities were mostly physical ones, that he was more at home in the fencing school than in the society of women—with that one fatal exception, the Princess of Eboli.

On May 19, 1566, the Court moved to Valsain, as being more healthy for the Queen, who at last, after five fruitless years of marriage, was hoping for a son. It was a daughter, though, who was born on August 11. Don John had the task of holding his little niece at the font and carrying her back to the Queen's apartments, as her godfather, Don Carlos, was hardly able to stand after one of his frequent bouts of fever. The Infanta's third name, Eugenia, was given in gratitude for the answer to the prayer made before the saint's relics at Getafe.

That autumn at Valsain Don John spent a lot of time swimming with the Prince of the Asturias. The streams in the woods of Segovia were icy cold from the high valleys of the Guadarramas and Don John, from their chill, was seriously ill for several weeks.

Back to Madrid went the court, for Christmas and the New Year. There was a new habitué of the Eboli palace, Antonio Perez, a suave, handsome young dandy, illegitimate son of a priest who had been secretary to Charles V and the present king. He threaded his way skilfully through the intrigues of court and Council and was gaining more and more influence with the members of the Prince of Eboli's party. Oddly enough, Don John inclined to their policy, though they stood for peace and diplomacy as opposed to force and war advocated by the old Duke of Alba.

Thanks to Eboli interest Perez, on his father's death, was appointed confidential secretary to the King and still further assured his future by his marriage early in 1567. To celebrate the wedding of her protégé the Princess gave a series of balls and banquets which lasted till Twelfth Night. She danced often with Don John, the guest of honour, sometimes those wild, amorous country dances which the Queen would only have watched done by peasants to amuse the King.

Outside, the bitter wind from the mountains cut like a sword. In the Eboli palace all was warm and bright, fires, candlelight, laughter and wine. One night the Princess

asked Don John if he remembered his little admirer, Maria.
He shook his head. She laughed and called the girl.

By June the brief, fierce passion was forgotten, for Don
John was preparing, with Don Carlos and the two young
Archdukes, to accompany the King to Flanders. Things
there had been going from bad to worse. In August,
1566, the Protestant mob had sacked the cathedral of
Antwerp. The revolution spread. Margaret of Parms
was forced to suspend the Inquisition in the Low Countries
and to allow the new doctrines to be preached. Philip,
however, refused to ratify his half-sister's concessiona,
though the lack of troops on the spot made strong measures
impossible for the moment. He wrote to the Duke of
Alba in Italy orders to concentrate all available Spanish
troops in Milan and to march at their head through Switzer-
land, Savoy and Lorraine in order to succeed the Duchess
of Parma as Governor of the Netherlands. It was necessary to gain time for concentration and march, so Philip
announced his intention of proceeding to the Low Countries
himself.

In June, 1567, Don Carlos, Don John and the Archdukes were told to be ready to start with the King who was
going by sea to Antwerp. The Queen, who was expecting
another baby, was to follow later, leaving the Infanta as
Regent. Everything and everyone was in a hum and
bustle of preparation. A squadron assembled at Coruña to
escort the royal travellers. Don Carlos arranged for the
fifty horses of his stables to go through France. Don
John was happiest of anyone. At last the long time of

waiting and inaction was over. Over too was the affair
with Maria de Mendoza. It was confessed, forgiven and
almost forgotten. He had no intention of repeating such
folly.

The King's bluff probably deceived few experienced
diplomatists. At any rate it fulfilled the purpose with
which he had put it up—that of enabling Alba and his
tercios to reach Brussels in August and to begin the conquest
of the revolted provinces with the ruthlessness which has
made his name satanic in the pages of Protestant historians.
Philip II, like Charles II of England a hundred years later,
had no desire to set out on his travels again. " The List
of The King's Voyages," which his son compiled in a
flash of savage sarcasm, was to extend no further north
than Valladolid, no further south than Seville.

For Don John once again hope was deferred. The
mirage of glory vanished beyond the horizon of the future.

On October 10, 1567, a second daughter was born to
the Queen and, nine days later, was baptized with great
pomp in the royal chapel adjoining the Alcazar of Madrid.
Don John was the central figure in this gorgeous pageant.
Splendid in cloth of silver, edged with green silk and gold,
belted with huge pearls and rubies, over it a cloak of his
favourite crimson velvet, he carried the baby, inappro-
priately attired in a gold dress and a crimson cloak like his
own. Preceded by guards, kings-of-arms and officers of
the household, Don John had the Papal Nuncio on his
right, the Imperial ambassador on his left, behind him the
French and Portuguese ambassadors, followed by the
Archdukes Rudolf and Ernest and the Queen's household.

At the church door the procession was received by Cardinal Espinosa, President of the Council of Castile, tall, handsome and haughty, with four other bishops, members of the various Councils, including Luis Quijada, now President of the Council of the Indies. The five premier dukes of Spain carried the white christening hood, taper, salt, napkin and ewer. The silver font in which St. Dominic had been baptized stood under a brocade canopy and there the little Princess received the name of her grandmother, Catherine.

It was an extraordinary honour for Don John to have been made the central and principal figure of this splendour. Loving colour and magnificence as he did he was always to play his part on such occasions with the perfection of one born to them. This day, however, there was something which filled him with even greater pleasure than the outfit with which the Princess Juana had presented him. He had received his appointment as Admiral of the Fleet, which assured him that the King had finally relinquished all idea of an ecclesiastical career for him.

Life smiled then even more than usual that day and, at the ball given that night by the Princess Juana in honour of her niece's baptism, Don John was one of the gayest and happiest. All the ladies of the Queen's house were there. The Princess of Eboli was not, nor—Don John noticed with relief—was Maria de Mendoza. The ball over, none of the young men felt like anything so dull as going to bed, so Don John suggested an " encamisada," a wild ride through the streets in disguise.

The cavalcade, then, assembled outside his house in the

Plaza Santiago. Each cavalier was dressed up in a hood or turban, a false beard, a white domino, carried a lighted torch in his left hand, wore his lady's colours on his right shoulder. It was a weird sight, the flaring torches in the pitch-dark streets giving an uncanny look to the white figures, the horses, frightened by glare and shouts, dancing and rearing.

All the young bloods were there with Don John, Ernest and Rudolf. Only Don Carlos was missing, lost on one of those mad, furtive night wanderings, when he would seize and insult women, force kisses and caresses on them or brutally ill-treat them.

Off went the rout—clatter of hoofs on cobble-stones, shouts, laughter and songs. Every now and then they would stop to serenade some favourite. When shutters were flung open and sleepy spectators applauded, the riders would twist in and out in the figures of a dance. The feelings of the good citizens and their wives whose virtuous sleep was so rudely shattered are not recorded. Anyhow the children must have loved the shouts and lights and prancing horses, all the wild spirits of youth so little older than themselves.

Don John was feeling at the top of the wave. The honour that had been shown him by casting him for the most showy part in today's pageant, the ball, this wild, happy riot, best of all the knowledge that he would soon be at sea and in command, all these united to make him drunk with pleasure and enjoyment.

A halt was called and a serenade begun in front of the Eboli palace. Like all other houses at this hour between night and dawn, it was dark and shuttered. Unlike the others not a light was shown, not a shutter was flung open to greet the revellers.

Don John felt a queer foreboding. A shiver ran through him. He drew a little away from the singers and, as he did so, a man slipped out of the wicket gate of the palace nearest the cathedral, muffled to the nose in a black cloak. He laid a hand on the bridle, whispered a few words and vanished. Don John was missed, called back to take the lead in the musical ride in the Plaza de la Armería. He played his part to the end, then, still in his disguise, galloped back to the corner where the cloaked messenger was still waiting.

Jorge de Lima, his favourite gentleman-in-waiting, sat up all night waiting anxiously for his master. As dawn began to show grey through the uncurtained window, there were quick steps on the stairs and his master came in and tore off cloak and turban. Jorge dared ask no questions. The ravaged young face, deathly white, eyes like pits of darkness, told him without words that something terrible had happened. Up and down, to and fro like a caged beast, paced the young prince. In vain Jorge begged him to rest, to eat, to drink. The only answer was a gesture of refusal.

As the day crept on Jorge, in despair, fetched Doña Magdalena. She, wise and understanding as always, asked no question, made no fuss. With her own hands she beat up some eggs, as she had done when, a child, he had had fever, made him sit down by her, eat and drink a little. Then, a child again, he broke down as he had done that day nine years ago, flung himself at her feet and, his head in her lap, sobbed himself to sleep, with her gentle hand on the yellow head.

That night she went out in her litter, nobody knew where—except Galarza, the old squire, who went with her. A few days later she obtained leave from the King to return to Villagarcia.

Her boy rode the first day's journey beside her, up into the piercing air of the Guadarramas, a desolate country of grey-green granite rocks, dark pines and grey twisted ilexes that accorded well with his mood of melancholy and remorse. The moment came when he had to leave her. He knelt to ask her blessing as if he were a child again and kissed her hand again and again as if he sought to express his gratitude which could never be spoken.

He never saw Maria de Mendoza again. She vanished from court, to the Princess's country house, then to a convent. Doña Magdalena, who had fetched the newly born baby, took it home to Villagarcia, educated the girl there for sixteen years and then sent her to the Augustinian convent at Madrigal. So closely was the secret kept that no one in the convent knew the girl's parentage and even the King did not know of her existence till Alessandro wrote to tell him after Don John's death.

This sequence to the short and almost forgotten madness of last winter was a greater shock than any Don John had yet known. It branded indelibly on his mind the fact that no man can sin lightly and escape without punishment. It taught him that " the occasions of sin " are only less dangerous than the sin to which they lead. He faced the fact that he would not marry anyone less than royal, that, to win queen or princess, he must have honour and glory to offer her which would efface the bar sinister of his birth. He resolved then, that there was no place for women in the career of action and danger he had mapped out for himself —any more than Alexander the Great had found time to dally with women till half the world was at his feet.

But for his Tia, with her selfless devotion and absolute discretion, there would have been public scandal and disgrace. Now she was gone to Villagarcia and he had to do without her care and sympathy. Remained the Queen—sympathetic too, lovely, charming, with a splendid courage which hid physical and mental weariness under a delightful gaiety. It was her part now to cheer and distract the King, buried under mountains of letters and minutes, harassed with bad news from Flanders, more distressed about his son. With his stepmother Don Carlos was a rational human being, affectionate, gentle, generous. In the pathetic, childish list of his friends, found among his papers, hers is the first name, Don John's the second. Carlos was devoted to his uncle, generously pleased at his appointment to command the fleet, but even Don John was powerless to keep him from those secret, sinister night wanderings through the streets and into the brothels of Madrid. There were darker things too—his orders to burn a house with its inhabitants because some water had splashed on him when passing it, to mutilate a man who had visited him uninvited. One day he shut himself into the royal stables. Twenty horses had to be destroyed. When the Duke of Alba came to take leave of him before starting to the

Netherlands the Infante drew his dagger and attacked him.

On December 20, 1567, the King went to the Escorial and Don Carlos determined, during his father's absence, to carry out a plan for which he had been raising money— that of a flight from Spain to the Low Countries, where he considered he should have been appointed Governor instead of Alba. On Christmas Eve he confided this mad scheme to Don John, commanded his help as Admiral of the Fleet and offered him the choice of the kingdom of Naples or the duchy of Milan as reward. Don John, finding the young lunatic deaf to arguments and advice, realized the seriousness of the matter, mounted and rode straight to the Escorial.

Philip, with his usual iron self-control, listened, said nothing and continued his religious exercises. There was worse to come. Carlos went to make his confession on the eve of the Jubilee, December 28, but was refused absolution because of his deadly hate and desire for a certain person's death. Finally, he was persuaded to divulge the name of the enemy whose death he was plotting. It was his father.

On January 17, 1568, Philip returned to Madrid and, accompanied by Don John, visited the Queen in her apartments, where they were joined by Don Carlos. The Prince took Don John away to his own rooms where they were alone together for two hours, he trying to obtain a promise of help and galleys, Don John pleading for delay. The next day prayers were offered in all the churches of Madrid, by the King's orders, for guidance in a matter of importance. No one knew what was afoot, but there was a feeling of tension that grew stronger as the day went on. Just before midnight the Prince of Eboli, the Duke of Feria, the Prior of the Atocha were summoned by the King, who, in armour under his silk gown, led the way to his son's room. The bolts which the Infante had had fixed on the door had been removed, as well as the sword, dagger and pistol under his pillow. He woke to find his weapons gone, the five men round his bed.

He jumped to his feet with a cry: " Who is there ? " Then, when he saw his Father :

" Has Your Majesty come to kill me ? "

" That would be the act of a madman."

" I am not mad, not mad ! " screamed the wretched young man, then tried to dash his brains out, tore out his hair and was only with difficulty restrained and put back to bed.

The King's marble imperturbability remained unbroken during this dreadful scene. When news of the Infante's arrest became known next day both the Queen and the Princess Juana tried in vain to shake his inexorable decision. Leave to visit the prisoner was refused. Even the Queen's tears and prayers were of no avail. Don John appeared in her apartments dressed not in his usual gay colours but in deepest black from head to foot. The King quietly told him to go and change into his ordinary clothes.

The living tomb had closed upon the heir of all the Spains.

IX

DRESS REHEARSAL
(May—October, 1568)

There was a feeling of dread and doom in the air. Don Carlos had vanished from court and the world. His establishment was broken up. His horses, of which he had been so proud, were sold or distributed to Don John and the Archdukes. To all practical purposes the Prince of the Asturias was already dead. The Queen's pale face and red eyes, the Princess Juana's outspoken reproaches, the gossip of ambassadors and common folk left the King as unmoved as Don John's mourning had done. He knew that he had taken the only course open to him. Life went on as usual.

In the spring of 1568 Don Garcia de Toledo, who had been so long in coming to the relief of Malta, resigned the Viceroyalty of Sicily and his office of " General of the Sea." Don John was appointed to succeed him in command of the Mediterranean fleet of Spain. Don Luis de Requesens was recalled from the embassy at Rome to act as Vice-Admiral and adviser. Luis Quijada, whose experience had been all on land, was to remain at home. Fond as he was of the old man, Don John, now twenty-one, had probably few regrets at being freed from the supervision of his " Ayo." His dream was at last to materialise. He was to leave Madrid for Cartagena at the end of May, 1568, with his secretary, de Quiroga.

Philip, with his usual meticulous carefulness, wrote a long letter of directions and advice to the young Admiral in his own hand, " on account of the great love I bear you " (Aranjuez, May 23, 1568).

" Be very devout and God-fearing and a good Christian, not only in reality and essence, but also outwardly, giving a good example to all. By this means and on this foundation God will give you grace and your fame and glory will continue to increase." He is bidden to go frequently to Confession and Communion, to hear Mass daily, " and to perform your private devotions and prayers with great recollection and regularity, at the time set aside for that purpose." This last direction was faithfully observed. When Don John was dying he asked for the book in which he had written out his private prayers and told his confessor that he had never devoted less than an hour a day to them, whether afloat or ashore, in war or peace.

" Truth in speech and the fulfilment of promises are the foundations of confidence and esteem among men." The words are startlingly unexpected in an age unrivalled for lies, deceit and treachery. The King goes on with warnings against flattery, backbiting, gambling and bad language. " Live and move with great care for your own purity, for an offence against chastity is not only a sin against God but it entails many troubles and does damage to business and duty." " Be modest and controlled, avoiding hot temper and angry words. . . . Preserve a pleasant, gentle and courteous manner, as well as the dignity entailed by your rank. . . . In winter and when ashore keep yourself busy with active exercises, specially military ones. . . . I trust you will carry out my advice better than I have written it. This letter is for your eye alone."

The long, affectionate letter, with its mixture of Christian morality and sound commonsense, was worthy to be read, studied and memorized.

The young Admiral had said goodbye to Doña Magdalena, who was half sad that her fledgling was at last to try his wings, yet glad because he was happy—to old Luis, full of gruff, soldierly last words—to the Queen, hardest farewell of all.

For a moment, instead of leaping seaward, his heart returned to have ineradically engraved on it the last memory of its first and best love. For a moment, when Don John lifted his head from her long white hands and looked into her haggard face and black-ringed eyes, the future was shadowed by a dark presentiment that he should not see her again.

During those last few days of May, 1568, Don John rode south into a country unknown to him, across the plains of la Mancha, over the watershed, from which, on the right, the Guadiana and Guadalquiver started to the Atlantic, and on the left the Jucar and the Segura began their course to the Mediterranean. Past Albacete, down the Segura to Murcia, over stretches of hill and marsh, barren of all but esparto grass and saltwort, between bare, treeless hills, into the fertile irrigated country, rich with corn, wine and oil, through orchards of orange and lemon, waxy blossom and yellow fruit on the boughs together, under tall, feathery palms and into Murcia. Then the last day's long trail of forty miles, over the Sierra de Carrascoy, past the long salt lagoon of the Mar Menor, to Cartagena at last.

The May evening was still light enough to see the town crowded within its brick walls, with its castle looking over the finest harbour of Spain. In the deep bay, guarded by the narrow entrance and the four fort-crowned hills, lay the fleet, thirty-three galleys and, towering above them, glowing with paint and gold, the new flagship, the *Real*, a sight to fill any naval heart with joy.

Carthaginian galleys, Roman triremes, the lighter craft of Moors and corsairs had all in turn sheltered here. Philip of Spain meant no enemies to lie again by the town piled up to the high hill crowned by the *Castillo de la Concepción*. Within another two years the work of new fortification, already in hand, would render the port impregnable. So Philip thought, till Drake and Carleill, under orders from that " daughter of the devil," Elizabeth, took it in 1585.

The next morning (June 2) the Admiral of the Fleet presided over his first Council, in the *Commandancia de Marina*, which looked south across the bar to the entrance of the harbour. Round the long table sat old Luis de Requesens, whose life was to be interwoven with that of Don John for the next few years, the famous old sea-captain, Alvaro Bazan, Marques de Santa Cruz and the veterans Juan de Cordona and Gil de Andrade.

Don John took his seat at the head of the table among the old men. His profile was cut against the gilded leather on the walls with the sharpness of a cameo : the wide forehead, slightly aquiline nose, small fair moustache which did not hide the lines of the well-cut mouth. He was grave and a little pale. His manner had the modesty, courtesy and dignity recommended by the King and he soon showed that, though a novice in naval matters, he would prove himself an apt pupil. Orders were discussed and then signed by him for reinforcements to be sent to Giovanni Andrea Doria (nephew of the great Andrea Doria), who was watching for the Turkish fleet off the Sicilian coast—for two hundred men to be supplied by each governor of Murcia, Granada and Seville—for the Barcelona fleet to be ready to sail in two days' time to meet the fleet returning from the Indies and escort it to Cadiz.

De Quiroga sanded the wet ink of the signatures and gathered up the papers. The Council was over.

Before sunrise on June 4, 1568, Don John had made his Confession and Communion and by nine in the morning he was ready to go on board his flagship. The thirty-three galleons of his fleet were dressed from bow to stern, pennons at mast heads and yard-arms, standards at the prows. The population of Cartagena seethed and struggled for places in the front rows along the quays. Occasionally the monotony of waiting was enlivened by some unlucky sightseer being pushed into the harbour. The noble young volunteers who had come to follow their *arbiter elegantiarum* in his naval career were already crowding bows and bulwarks, when the roar of artillery from the forts announced the arrival of the Admiral of the Fleet. The stirring notes of bugles and trumpets, the roll of drums dominated the shrill cheers of the watching crowds.

The smoke from the big guns drifted away to sea and at

last they could see Don John on the high prow of the *Real* —a splendid figure in glittering armour inlaid with gold, the order of the Golden Fleece on his breast, high boots of scarlet Moroccan leather on his slim legs.

He stood in silence, while the Royal Standard was broken from the mast. The blue standard of our Lady of Guadelupe was run up too—a sign that under her patronage and in her service was the fleet to sail.

The flagship which he was to sail on her maiden voyage was worthy of her commander. She had been built for swiftness and strength in the shipyards of Barcelona, of Catalan pine, the finest wood in the world for ships. The famous architect, Juan Batista Castello, had drawn in Seville the designs for her decoration. Her paint was crimson (Don John's favourite colour) and white. Prow, poop and cabins were rich with paintings, carving, gilded chains of the Golden Fleece. The figurehead, above the long, sharp metal " spur," was a gigantic Hercules leaning on his club. At the stern swung the great lantern, sign of the flagship, crowned by a statue of fame—wood and bronze all a glitter of gold paint.

Vanderhammer, Don John's earliest biographer, devotes six pages to a description of pictures and mottoes in the cabins, symbolic of the qualities necessary to a great leader. How well Don John was to know all these in the next eight years when his spacious cabin astern was to be the only home he could call his own. Jason and the Golden Fleece, Mars, Neptune, Hermes, messenger of the gods with his finger on his lips, Ulysses and the Sirens, dolphins gambolling as gaily as round Dionysios in the pirate galley,

" the sea with halcyons' nests, the sky with stars and winds,"
they crowded the cabin walls, brought back memories of
old Honorato and carefree days at Alcalá de Henares, set
desire and ambition leaping forward as eagerly as the thirty-
three galleons when the west wind filled their sails and,
one after another, they drew out of the harbour, with their
white sails bellying in the west wind under the high June
sun.

The salvoes of artillery sank into silence. The town
within its red brick walls, the line of high hills sank out of
sight astern. There was no more to be seen but the endless
expanse of sea—sapphire deepening to violet like Don
John's eyes, as he stood bare-headed on the prow, with
the wind ruffling his golden hair and whipping colour into
his smooth cheeks.

That night, when he was at last alone in his big, gilded,
silk-hung cabin, he knelt before the old charred Crucifix
and prayed for Doña Magdalena at Villagarcia, for the sick
Queen in the shade of the elms of Aranjuez. Sails were
furled, anchors dropped, the scarred, chained, miserable
slaves freed from the rowing benches and asleep in the
foul stench of the crowded hold. For the first time Don
John lay listening to the whisper of the wind in the rigging,
the soft lap of little waves against the stern. Overhead the
four huge candles in the swinging lantern sent out their
gleam to the anchored fleet. In the cabin the silver lamp
shed a soft light on the young, golden beauty of Alexander
and the gilded motto : " *Feliciter omnia.*" As he drifted
into sleep Don John wondered. Like Alexander he too
was young, ambitious, daring. Would he too pine for

new worlds to conquer, for God, His Divine Majesty, for his lord the King—and for his own glory ?

South to Malaga and Cartagena, round the rock of Gibraltar to Cadiz, and not a corsair sail to be seen. Then, coming up on the western horizon the battered, storm scarred galleons, low in the water with their cargoes of gold and indigo, sugar, tobacco, cocoa, bark and hides from New Spain. Up the Guadalquiver sailed the Indies fleet to unload at the *Casa de Contratacion*, at Seville, where the customs claimed by the Crown were one fifth of the total value.

Back again through the Straits of Gibraltar sailed the Admiral with his fleet, and still without a sight of the pirates reported from Porto Rio. At Porta Santa Maria Don John landed, inspected the fortifications and reviewed his own men. Already he showed the thoroughness and grasp of detail which were later to count for so much in his victories. He planned next to slip across to the African coast and surprise the Moorish stronghold of Fagazas, but the current rushing in from the Atlantic swept the fleet out of its course and the attempt had to be abandoned. At the Spanish outpost of Peñon de Velez, where the fleet put in to water, Don John first set foot on African soil. He visited the castle, famous in annals of Christians and Moors, and rode out with the alcayde to chase a band of marauding Arabs who had come down from the hills. Further east along the African coast two corsairs were pursued and their prey, a Christian merchantman, rescued.

All along the African coast the Spanish forts were visited

and inspected, complaints investigated and injustices righted. Then the fleet sailed north to the Balearic Islands, a favourite haunt of corsairs. From there a squadron was sent to strengthen Doria, as a hundred Turkish ships had been reported off the Italian coast, and so back to Barcelona. Here fortifications, dockyards and stores were inspected and checked with the Viceroy, the Duke of Francavilla, who had been so kind to the runaway three years ago.

Here too Don John received the news of the death of Don Carlos two months before (July 24, 1568). The poor prisoner had made a good end, sanctified by the rites of the Church. It was the best fate for him. But youth's first experience of death among its contemporaries comes as a shock, because of the sudden realization that death may strike next at oneself, when life is so full of possibilities and ambitions, when, as Napoleon said : " Nothing is done, while something still remains to do."

The remembrance of that dark presentiment touched Don John with the sharp chill of bare steel. It was not till he had knelt to kiss the Queen's hands that he could believe that all might yet be well. Yet, as he watched her, the chill was still there. The young beauty was ravaged and destroyed. Her cheeks were flushed by fever, but all strength and vitality were drained by the mad folly of doctors whose only idea of the science of healing was frequent and drastic bleeding. Barely twenty-two now, Isabel had been married as a child of fourteen to an over-amorous husband more than twice her age. In the last ur years she had had two daughters and a miscarriage and now expected the birth of the much-hoped-for son.

Not only her husband and her devoted Don John, but
all the people were praying fervently for an heir to replace
the dead Don Carlos. God answers prayers in His way,
not in ours. Within a few days the Queen was delivered
of a still-born child and followed it (in her own pathetic
words to Torquevaulx, the French ambassador) " on the
road out of this unhappy world into a better one. . . . To
go to my Creator where I can serve Him better than I can
here. I would much rather go and see what I hope very
soon to see."

So passed Isabel *de la Paz*, a very lovely lady, and not a soul
in Spain but shed a tear and said a prayer for her gentle soul.

At midnight the King came to pray beside her bier,
alone but for Don John, the Prince of Eboli and Ferdinand
de Toledo. The King knelt at his dead wife's head,
frozen into marble immobility—as he kneels by the High
Altar of the Escorial, immortalized for all time in the
magnificent gilt bronze of Pompeo Leoni.

Don John stood behind him, as, ten years ago, he had
stood behind Luis Quijada at the Emperor's death-bed
and had seen death for the first time. But then death had
seemed fitting and right, the crown to a long life, crammed
with danger and action. This was different—a lovely
flower broken almost before it had bloomed, leaving its
fragrance in the darkness.

In the yellow light of the forest of candles the waxen
face under the dark hair had a remote and unearthly beauty,
a fleeting shadow of that immortal beauty for which man's
soul is sick and which, in this world, he pursues for ever
in vain.

A fleeting shadow. Already the shadow of corruption had touched that young body—or so Don John fancied. With a sickening horror he remembered the life-sized statue of Death by Gaspar Becerra, which he had seen as a child and which had haunted his dreams for long afterwards. That grinning skull with its empty eye-sockets, the dried flesh and skin splitting to reveal sinews and withered intestines, huge worms crawling from heart and brain—was this ghastly corruption the end of all human loveliness, all man's passion, dreams and ambition?

He had just taken the first step along the road to what he had felt sure was his high and predestined work. Now his world lay shattered into fragments at his feet. Within a few days he was riding over the Guadarramas into the teeth of the north wind on his way to the Franciscan monastery of the Scala-Coeli at Abrojo.

X

ENTR'ACTE

(October, 1568—April 12, 1569)

The pull that all ardent and vital natures feel between the material and the spiritual, the active and the contemplative, is perhaps specially strong in the case of the Spaniard. The realism of his outlook is not blurred by confused northern sentiment. He sees outward things and facts clear-cut and definite. Because he sees them so clearly and without illusion he realizes that they are transient, not permanent, that, only by penetrating beyond appearances will he find truth. The terrible and the splendid, the realistic and the mystic, fatalism and intense individualism, pride, generosity, courage and ruthlessness —all these typically Spanish qualities were combined in Don John of Austria.

Even to those who have an inborn knowledge of their own destiny, however, there comes at times a period of indecision—as when the compass needle swings uncertainly to and fro before pointing directly and consistently to the magnetic north.

Don John had sailed on that first voyage of four months in the full conviction that it was only the dress rehearsal for the great drama in which Fate had cast him for the role of hero. He had returned to a double tragedy, the deaths of the Prince of the Asturias and of the Queen. It was inevitable, considering his heredity, that he should turn from his crumbling world to the security of the cloister. There he could find peace and solitude in which to readjust the values of life. There too, for Abrojo was only half a league from Valladolid, he was near enough to visit his Doña Magdalena at Villagarcia.

The weeks passed. The Month of the Holy Souls was over. Advent was drawing on towards Christmas. There was solitude, except for the brown-habited friars about their business—silence but for the flap of sandals along stone-flagged passages, the chant of Office, the moan of the wind. Among the friars was an old friend of Don John's, Fray Juan de Calahorra, who had known him long ago at Villagarcia, had heard his childish confessions and had probably prepared him for his first Communion. The boy had always been drawn to the friar, but only now did the young man recognize the Franciscan's extreme holiness, combined with wisdom and gentleness, the gifts of the Holy Ghost which were the reward of advancement along that way of mental prayer which leads ultimately to union with God.

These months of November and December the two spent much time together. De Quiroga, the Prince's secretary and only worldly companion, would watch the pair pacing up and down along the cloister—the friar with his brown hood shadowing his gaunt, dark face, his work-worn hands hidden in his wide sleeves, the long brown Rosary swinging from his hempen girdle—beside him the young Apollo, slim and graceful in silk and velvet, his crimson cloak muffled tight, his yellow hair ruffled by the icy wind, head bent, face grave, one hand on sword-hilt, the other swinging the Golden Fleece under his cloak.

The talk was of other-worldly things, of friends and contemporaries of Fray Juan's, most of them unknown to Don John. There were Iñigo de Loyola, dead twelve years before in Rome—Francisco Borja, whom Don John remembered at Yuste, now General of the Society of Jesus —Juan de Avila, admirer of Iñigo, now preaching in Andalusia the evergreen truth that the true reform in the Church must be founded on the right training of youth and the thorough instruction of priests—Juan de Dios, the Portuguese shepherd-soldier, converted at Granada by Juan de Avila, and founder of the great hospital there— the Franciscan Pedro de Alcantara, whose hunger for penance was insatiable—his penitent and disciple, Teresa of Jesus, the Carmelite of Avila, who had set her own order by the ears through the strictness of her new foundations. Already she was called saint, and the friar predicted canonisation for all the rest.

" It seems to me that I live in a dream and, when I wake, I see that it is all nothing."

The words of Teresa of Avila woke an echo in Don John's heart. To turn from the world, that is to turn to God, it was for that Christ had praised Mary, saying that she " had chosen the better part."

Then, on the stillness hardly broken by the low murmur of voices, would come the noise of a galloping courier. Presently de Quiroga came out with a bundle of letters and, as in the magic mirror of Shalot, the silver circle would be filled by the moving shadows of the world.

It was best to tackle the news from the Netherlands first, for that was always bad. Alessandro was living in Brussels with his wife, Princess Maria, but his mother had gladly escaped, a year ago, back to her castle at Aquila in the high Abruzzi. Horne and Egmont, the rebel leaders, had fallen on the scaffold by order of the Blood Council and the Duke of Alba. The latter was now entrenched in the new fortress of Antwerp, planned under his supervision, by the famous Italian engineer, Gabriel Cerbellini. The Queen Dowager of France, Catherine de Medici, had asked him for a reinforcement of two thousand Spanish soldiers. He had answered bluntly " that it was better for her to ruin her kingdom by war for God than keep it in peace for the devil." The subtle, elusive Prince of Orange had at last unmasked and declared himself the champion of Protestantism and his rebellious people. In his recently published " Apologia " he had not hesitated to accuse Philip of the murder of wife and son. Alba's reply to this had been to erect in Antwerp a colossal statue of himself : " For having extinguished sedition, chastised rebellion, restored religion, secured justice, established peace." No bronze of melted cannon ever bore an inscription of bitterer or more poisoned irony.

How Don John hated that country of mud and blood and grey skies. Whether his mother was German or Flemish—he knew that she had been summoned to cheer away the Emperor's melancholy by her sweet voice— her Nordic blood had been swamped in him by Spanish. He had nothing from her but his brilliant fairness, a strain of romance and a fondness for animals.

He turned away quickly from the dark tale of blood and cruelty to news of Madrid. The Archduke Charles (the Emperor's brother) had arrived there to beg the recall of Alba and the Spanish tercios, a greater clemency in dealing with the rebels and a pardon for William of Orange. Knowing Philip he might have known that this would be a wasted journey. He brought, however, another suggestion, the offer of a fresh bride for the King, his niece-cousin, Ana of Austria, who, like Isabel de Valois, had once been proposed as a wife for Don Carlos.

Strange things were happening in England, that other northern land where men's blood ran cold and thin. The red-haired Queen had shown hospitality to her fugitive cousin, Mary of Scotland, by clapping her into prison and, at the instigation of Cecil and his party, bringing an accusation of husband-murder against her. The thought of the hapless Queen, whose loveliness and fascination were to draw all who loved her into the dark shadow of her own fate, can hardly have failed to stir the mind and heart of Don John, ambitious, reckless, romantic, chivalrous. She had been married a year before his beloved Isabel and the two had been friends in the fair land of France which the young Scots Queen wept so bitterly to leave. "A hundred times more lovely than a goddess from heaven," the old gossip Brantôme had said, and he was a connoisseur in women. Don John had seen the portrait of her when she had been promised as a bride for Don Carlos—the long hazel eyes under the plucked eyebrows, the chestnut hair, the gay laughter in eyes and lips. Vaguely he dreamed of a rescue after the fashion of Amadis de Gaul, himself as the gallant knight.

Then happenings in Southern Spain put everything else out of his head.

It was just seventy-seven years since his great-grandparents, Ferdinand and Isabel, had entered Granada (1491), and the silver Cross, with the banners of Santiago, Castile and Aragon, had replaced the Crescent on the Torre de Vela. The wisdom and tolerance of Hernando de Toledo, the first Archbishop, had been rewarded by innumerable conversions, but the warlike old Franciscan, Cardinal Ximenes, had advocated sterner measures. The Moors were given their choice between baptism and exile, and the result had been a revolt in the Alpujarras, the mountains south of Granada, only suppressed after several years of guerilla war. In 1526 Charles V issued a decree ordering the Moors to discard their native dress, language and baths. This effected nothing, but proved a fruitful source of income to the Inquisition, whose coffers benefited greatly by bribes known as the " traffic in toleration." Now, a year ago (1567) Philip resolved to enforce the edict which had long become a dead letter. Workmen began to destroy the world-famous baths of the Alhambra. Turbans, silk trousers and tunics were to be replaced by hats, breeches and doublets, Arabic by Castilian. All manuscript books of Arabic history, science and philosophy were to be publicly burnt. The books blazed. Moorish hatred smouldered. It was suddenly fanned into flame by the petty extortions of some Spanish tax-gatherers, who augmented their Christmas fare by commandeered farm produce. Aben Farax, a dyer of Granada, of royal blood, collected a band of disaffected Moors and fled with them to the mountains, thus turning discontent into open rebellion. Hernando de Valor, a brave, beautiful and dissolute young man, descended from the Khalifs of Cordoba, joined the rebels and was proclaimed King, under the title of Aben Umeya. The whole of the Alpujarras was in arms within a week. The last Morisco revolt had begun.

To Don John, at Abrojo, the appeal of Mary Stuart—faint and far as the horn of dying Roland at Roncesvalles—was drowned by the clarion call from Granada. It had taken eight centuries of ceaseless warfare to drive back across the Straits of Gibraltar the tide of Islam which had threatened to submerge western Europe. Old men still lived in the south of Spain who had heard the cry of the muezzin from the minarets of Granada, had seen the green banner of the Prophet flying on the Alhambra. Every yard of territory reconquered for the Cross in Castile and Aragon, in Valencia, Murcia, Andalusia, Granada had been watered by Spanish blood. The great names of knights and nobles and kings—the Muy Cid Campeador, Fernando I, Alfonso el Valiente, Fernando III of Castile and Jaime I of Aragon—were indelibly stamped on hearts and memories. The tales of their battles against the infidels, their hard-won victories, were sung by the hearths of hidalgos and peasants from Compostella to Valencia, from Barcelona to Cadiz.

Now, once again the clang and bellow of Moorish cymbals and horns, the promise of paradise to all who died fighting for Islam, rang in Spain. Down all the eastern coast ranged the corsairs of Aluch Pasha, renegade Calabrian and Turkish Viceroy of Algiers, insolently sure of secret help from their fellows in Granada.

Only thirty-nine years ago the victorious armies of Suleyman the Magnificent had swept over western Europe, and now his son, dreaming of conquests even greater, had set the dockyards of the Golden Horn working overtime to launch the mightiest fleet of the as yet invincible Turkish navy.

Day and night there sounded in Don John's ears the call that he had heard as child, boy and youth. He heard it as he dictated to his devoted secretary, as he rode along the wide, windswept valley, as he talked to Doña Magdalena.

He knelt in the friars' icy chapel while they chanted Compline in the darkness pierced only by one candle flame, sharp as a spearhead.

" *Procul recedant somnia, Et noctium phantasmata,*" sang the friars :

" *Hostemque nostrum comprime, Ne polluantur corpora.*"

He lay awake in his narrow cell, while all the rest slept. The cold silence was unbroken but for the crying of the wind, blowing from further north than the prison of the fated Queen, southward to the sharp peaks of the Alpujarras, where the snow was stained with blood. How to reconcile the two calls, to be sure of choosing the right ? " Far off let idle visions fly." Were dreams of war against the infidel only lures of the tempter, vain " phantoms of the night ? " " Curb Thou our raging enemy," though, that peace and security might return to the land.

De Quiroga, naturally, was all for action. Doña Mag-

galena used words which pointed in the same direction
and showed her deep and loving understanding of her boy's
character.

" Luxury and idleness will always be dangerous to your
youth.   Only the dangers and action of war will be able
to control the wild fire of your heart."

But it was Fray Juan who must give the final advice this
Christmastide.   He it was who showed Don John that, in
his case, the two calls were really one, that his vocation was
to serve God in action, an action to be sublimated and
inspired by contemplation, by prayer, vocal and mental.

" To ask grace of God our Lord that all my intentions,
actions and operations may be ordered only for the service
and praise of His Divine Majesty."

The words of Ignatius of Loyola were the advice of the
friar to the young Prince.   Then, in answer to a question
from him whether a letter should be sent to the King
asking to command against the Moors, Fray Juan uttered
the prophecy : " Not only shall you obtain what you ask,
but it will make your name greater than any in Europe."

The die was cast.   Don John, with his secretary and two
servants, rode south to Madrid and there dictated to de
Quiroga the first letter of his which we possess.

" I have heard of the seriousness of the rebellion of the
Granada Moriscos," he writes after the usual punctilious
beginning : " As this closely touches both my desire for
fame and the dignity and greatness of Your Majesty, which
are offended by the insolence of these rebels, I cannot
restrain myself from offering myself unreservedly to Your
Majesty's will.   The favour you have always shown me

emboldens me to ask this . . . and, since I owe everything to Your Majesty, I beg you to use me as your weapon of punishment. I know that you can trust me more completely than anyone else, and that no one will chastise this rabble as I shall. . . . You must send someone to do this. Such work is natural to my character and I am as obedient to your royal will as clay is in the hands of the potter. I feel that my love, my desires and all I owe to Your Majesty will be grievously wounded if I am not appointed to this command. But I know well that he who serves Your Majesty and places himself in your royal hands is entirely secure and needs to plead no further. . . . If I obtain my request I shall consider myself sufficiently rewarded." (Madrid, December 30, 1568.)

The letter won the day. The King was anxious over the growth of the revolt, sick of the bickerings and inefficiency of the Marques de Mondejar and the Marques de los Vélez. He determined to send his brother to command in Granada, but, with his usual delays and meticulous arrangements, kept him at Madrid and Aranjuez for three months. It was not till April 6, 1569, that Don John of Austria, followed by Luis Quijada and his household, set out across the plains of la Mancha and the mountains of Jaen, to the seat of war.

PART II

XI

FALCON IN LEASH

(APRIL 13—JUNE 24, 1569)

Granada was *en fête*. Every balcony was hung with garlands, gay draperies and eastern rugs. Women were busy before their mirrors, adjusting red carnations in blue-black hair, crimson roses at the breasts of silk and velvet gowns. Men were no less eager, for it was high time that the bungling and half-hearted conduct of the campaign should be ended by the action and ardour of youth.

The Count of Tendilla, Mondejar's son, had ridden out early with two hundred knights, half in crimson cloaks, plumed hats and glittering cuirasses, the rest dressed like Moors in turbans and loose silk tunics. They had gone toward Hiznaleuz, where the young Commander had spent the preceding night. The Archbishop of Granada, Don Pedro Guerrero, with four of the cathedral canons, Diego Deza, President of the Chancery of Granada, with four of his officials, the *regidor* (mayor) with four of the city council, all in full pomp, were waiting under the high walls and noble façade of the Hospital Real outside the Puerta Elvira.

At last there was a blare of trumpets, a clatter of hoofs, a confused cheering. Tendilla and his troop swept down the northern road and drew up in the square. Then riding

between the Count of Miranda and old Luis Quijada, came
the hero of the day, followed by long columns of infantry
and cavalry. Archbishop and President advanced, step
by step so that neither should presume to take precedence
of the other. The Archbishop's face was less grim than
usual, Deza's suave and smiling mask even more affable
than ordinarily.

Don John dismounted, kissed the episcopal ring, stood
bareheaded between the two ecclesiastics, his greetings
delicately adjusted so that neither could indulge in heart-
burnings over imaginary slights. The breeze ruffled the
yellow hair whose waves were the envy of all young dandies.
It fluttered the plume of ostrich feathers fastened into the
small velvet hat by a huge emerald clasp. The doublet
was crimson, shot with gold and silver, fringed with pearls.
The cuirass of dull steel over it was inlaid with gold.
Over the scarlet silk stockings were pulled up high boots
of soft white leather, gold-spurred. Ruff and cuffs were of
finest Flemish lace. The collar and badge of the Golden
Fleece hung on the Prince's breast and the scarlet scarf
which was the badge of his command was tied round his
left arm.

It was a scene of glowing colour in the brilliant April
sunshine. Ecclesiastical purple, crimson of doublets and
cloaks, scarlet turbans, the flutter of banners and pennons,
the gleam of armour and bare swords, and beyond all this
the " rose-red city," the red towers of the Alhambra on
its hill, the snow peaks of the Sierra Nevada to the south.
But, behind the tall, windowless walls of their houses in the
Albaicin (the old " Quarter of the Falconers ") the Moriscos

were gathered in sullen silence or peered down from the flat roofs with fear and hatred of the golden youth who was come to sign the doom of their race.

The Prince remounted and, between Archbishop and President, moved towards the city, between the ranks of the garrison drawn up on parade, ten thousand strong, to the continuous volleys of musketry which startled horses and frightened children. Suddenly a long procession appeared from the Puerta Elvira—a startling contrast to all the pomp and glory. Hundreds of women, in filthy rags, with wild, dishevelled hair and ravaged faces, surrounded Don John with loud cries and lamentations.

" Justice ! Justice ! " they shrieked, crowding about his horse : " Justice is all we ask ! We heard the clash of steel which slew our fathers and brothers and husbands with less woe than we hear the promise of forgiveness to their murderers ! "

Don John murmured a few words of non-committal sympathy in reply to this unchristian pronouncement, promised that justice should be done. He realized that this was a demonstration staged by the opponents of the Marques de Mondejar, who was considered to have shown too much leniency to the rebels. Mondejar, who no doubt had been forewarned, had withdrawn to the Alhambra, after having welcomed the new commander last night at Hiznaleleuz.

The long and flower-strewn progress, along the Calle de Elvira, under the tall tower of Sant Andres and the wide-eaved church of Santos Pedro y Pablo to the quarters prepared in the Audiencia, was long and tiring. The smiles and charm with which Don John acknowledged the lovely faces and the white hands which showered roses and carnations on him were a mask. All this eager, warm loveliness was no more than the petals which fell on his horse's mane and were trampled under prancing hoofs. He was here to do man's work, to carve out the beginnings of his high fame and destiny. Already he had begun to realize the bitter truth that " a man's foes shall be those of his own household," that his worst enemies here were not the rebels in the mountains but the King's men, with their petty jealousies and divided councils.

Alone at last in the gorgeous rooms prepared for him in what the Moors had nicknamed " The House of Ill Luck," he reviewed the situation. There was the Marques de Mondejar, Captain General of Granada, as his father and grandfather had been before him, ever since the conquest. He had seen the rebellion brewing, with his lifelong knowledge of the Moors, and, six years ago, had issued an edict forbidding any Moor to own or carry arms except those licensed by him and stamped with his blazon. He might have guessed that such a measure, far from being a preventive, would only prove an irritant to a warlike and subject race. He had journeyed to Madrid in 1567 to protest against the new royal edict and had returned with orders for its ruthless enforcement. To stamp out Arabic, to make the Moriscos change turban and *marlota* for hat, doublet and breeches, to abjure baths, to let their women go unveiled—as well hope to make the leopard change its spots. The rebellion had broken into open flame with the coronation of Hernando Valor as Aben

Umeya. The Captain General had taken the field at the beginning of the present year, 1569, had relieved the beleaguered garrison of Orgiba, captured Jubiles and Guajaras.

Meantime the hereditary enemy of his house, Luis Faxado, Marques de los Velez and Viceroy of Murcia, crossed the frontier into Granada and began a campaign in the eastern part of the mountains. An old soldier of Charles V, he was fierce, haughty and ruthless, considering that Mondejar had been far too merciful and conciliatory to the rebels. Mondejar naturally resented interference in his sphere and forwarded a series of complaints to the King, leaving the war to look after itself. Blunt, hot-tempered and too conscious of his own importance, he would have been more than human if he had not looked sourly on the inexperienced youth who was now in command over him, but less than human had he not realized the singleness of heart and purpose of that ardent youth.

The Marques de los Velez was far from Granada, so could not express his very low opinion of his fellow Marquis's conduct in field and council chamber, but the Archbishop and President made no secret of their feelings. For them Mondejar's clemency and compromises were traffic with the powers of evil. Don John had to listen to tales of Moorish atrocities that would have brought colder blood than his to boiling point. Not only were there incidents inseparable from any war, old men and wounded murdered, women raped, children killed or taken for slaves, but there was sacrilege such as brought any Spanish hand to sword. Churches, Hosts, altars and sacred statues desecrated and defiled in the vilest ways that the imagination of a subject race, loathing the Christianity forced on them, could invent. Priests tortured to death, old men, women and children burnt alive in the churches where they had taken refuge—he heard them all.

Hardly were the dust and fatigue of his long ride from Aranjuez gone than he was summoned to receive a deputation of influential Moors from the Albaicin. Suave, crafty and complimentary, the bearded, dusky emissaries salaamed and began a long recital of oppression, injustice, lawless robbery and rapine on the part of the troops quartered in their part of the town. They ended at last, but their dark eyes saw no softening in the fair, haughty young face of the Prince. Courteously but uncompromisingly came the answer:

" My lord the King has sent me to this kingdom to quiet and pacify it. Those of you who have been loyal to God and the King will be rewarded by keeping your goods and freedom. Those who have not will be punished with the utmost severity. Send me the list of your grievances that I may investigate and remedy them. But I warn you that any untruth or inaccuracy will damage your cause severely."

Meantime the days slipped by. Nothing could be done without a Council. A Council could not be held without the Duke of Sesa, the only member who had experience of foreign service. The Duke of Sesa had not yet arrived.

Smiling and outwardly calm Don John listened to interminable talk. The Archbishop and President Deza, with their complaints of Mondejar's weakness and incapacity—

Don Luis, old and creaky in the joints, fussy and irritable
with responsibility, full of trite maxims as Polonius—
Mondejar brooding in the Alhambra—Don John felt like
a boy at Alcalá de Henares again, listening to Honorato's
verbose lectures on the classics. But at Alcalá there had
been Alessandro, with whom to talk and ride and fence,
and now Alessandro was an old married man living at
Brussels.

He would sit dreaming under the orange trees of the
Alhambra, his mind far away while Mondejar went again
over the early months of the year, then suddenly out of the
drone something would catch his wandering attention
like the flare of a beacon on a hill, and the scene was set
indelibly on his memory.

That morning of January 10, the yawning ravine at
Tablate, spanned only by the swaying cobweb which was
all the enemy had left of the bridge, the Moors on the far
side, yells of triumph, clash of cymbals, braying of horns,
on this side the Christians under Mondejar checked in their
advance by the impassable gulf. Then, from the sullen,
baffled host strode the Franciscan friar, Cristobal de
Molina, his brown habit pulled up through his rope girdle,
a shield over his shoulder, Crucifix in his left hand, naked
sword in his right. The breathless silence of suspense was
broken by his voice, "invoking the powerful name of
Jesus," and he started across the frail broken thread that
no one thought would bear a man. He was over, and the
men after him, though one went down and was smashed
on the rocks far below. The Moors retired. The bridge
was repaired and the Christian advance resumed.

The story was interrupted by news of the arrival of Gonçalo Fernandez de Cordoba, Duke of Sesa, heir of the Great Captain, Gonsalvo de Cordoba, and former Viceroy of Naples. Don John sprang to his feet. A Council, and then to march !

The Council met the next day (April 22, 1569) ; it consisted of Sesa, Mondejar, the Archbishop, the President, a representative of Luis de Requesens (at sea with the fleet bringing reinforcements) and Luis Quijada, the Prince at the head of the table. Mondejar suggested three alternatives for the prosecution of the war : to encourage the submission of the villages in the Alpujarra Mountains, strongly to garrison points of importance in the mountains, or to ravage the valleys and so starve out the rebels. Don John then called on Deza who, after humbly disclaiming any right to express an opinion before so many military experts, proceeded to express one in no uncertain terms. He denounced all the Marquis's suggestions, said that severity, not compromise, was needed, the first thing being to evict the Moors from the Albaicin, the centre of disaffection, and then to make a signal example of such a village as las Albuñelas, full of desperate rebels who were preparing a descent on Granada itself.

The President was supported by de Sesa and Requesens' deputy and, after days of argument, gained the Archbishop and Quijada, so that Mondejar was left without a single supporter and reverted to his usual custom of sending a son to lay his case before the King at Madrid.

Nothing could be done without the royal consent. Weeks crawled by. Don John reviewed troops, inspected fortifications, went into the state of army and commissariat, gathered information about the various forts and strongholds in the kingdom and their commanders. He dictated letters to the cities of Andalusia demanding men and supplies, to different veterans authorizing them to raise men for the King's service, to the King, who replied nominating los Velez as successor to Mondejar (May 10) and forbidding his brother to leave Granada on any rash expeditions or adventures (May 20, 1569).

Los Velez, now that his old rival was swept from his path, started into the Alpujarras from his headquarters in the east, with the intention of winning some spectacular success for himself before his new rival could take the field. His course was stayed by a peremptory order from the Prince, who explained that the only result of this unauthorized advance would be to drive the whole of the Moorish forces against the comparatively weak Christian force at Orgiba, thirty miles south of Granada and cut off from it by the Sierra.

Weeks passed. Days grew hotter. In the long afternoons work was impossible. The air was heavy with the scent of fading roses, of lilies, wax-white orange blossom and syringa. The nightingales were silent. The only sounds were the chirping of the cicadas, the plash of fountains in the Court of Lions. The red towers of the Alhambra burned above the cool dark green of the stone-pines. In the south the snow-peaks were sharp against a sky as hard and bright as steel.

Don John dreamed in the silence, as he had done through Mondejar's drone. Not of love, though in this hot southern air it bloomed and died as quickly as the roses, though dark eyes melted and white breasts throbbed with desire for young Apollo. Not four leagues away, among those snow-peaks, flew the red banner of Aben Umeya. Marauding bands came down, like hungry wolves, from their mountain fastnesses, burning and plundering almost within sight and sound of the city walls. Outside the walls not a Christian was safe a league away along the valley of the Jenil. Don John dreamed, but not of love and women, as did Aben Umeya, with his smooth, beautiful face and his large eyes lustrous under the black brows that met above the aquiline nose. Don John longed to ride out, as Christian knights had done seventy years ago, when his great-grandparents had captured Granada for the Cross, ride up into the wild steep valleys, with their grey, fragrant scrub, past *El Ultimo Sospiro del Moro*, to the secret place where the crimson banner fluttered above Umeya and his women. There, hand to hand, steel against steel, he would bring the renegade to the dust.

It was a mad dream and he knew it. There was the King's command that he should remain here. His place was at the helm. But how sick he was of talk, of cowls and greybeards—lonely too, because in his position familiarity with any of the young nobles was impossible. Carlos was dead and Alessandro a thousand miles away. He was chafing like a falcon in leash and then, when at last permission came for active operations to begin, he was still to stay in Granada, directing from headquarters the campaign which he wished to lead in person.

He had yet to learn that life consists of endless anticipation and interminable retrospect, separated only by those instants of intense action and emotion which are brief and vivid as a lightning flash.

Divided command and Philip's dilatory caution played into the hands of the rebel king. By midsummer the whole of the country, from Granada south to the sea, from the Almanzora valley on the east to Malaga on the west, was in revolt. Bentomiz too had joined Umeya—a valuable addition as its inhabitants had furnished the old Sultans of Granada with their best troops, while the country was one of the richest in the south, famed for its silk and wool and fruit.

Requesens, after a stormy and disastrous passage from Naples, had arrived at last, landed his battered veterans in the valley of Bentomiz and crushed the revolt there by a brief and bloody campaign. This success, however, was counterbalanced by the loss of Seron, a strong key position in the valley of the Almanzora, to the west of Granada.

Don John had despatched a strong force to the relief of the besieged garrison when, under orders from the King, he was compelled to recall them and send word to los Velez to march to the relief. Los Velez showed no alacrity in obeying the young commander whom he hated. As a consequence of his delays the garrison was forced to surrender (July 11, 1569). Every male over twelve was massacred, women and children taken away as slaves. The Marquis flattered himself he had amply preserved his prestige by refusing to carry out the directions of the young upstart. The death of a hundred and fifty prisoners, among them two priests, murdered in cold blood, and the fate of the wretched women dragged to harems and the slave market were indeed a small price to pay for the soothing of his wounded pride and jealousy.

Luis de Marmol, in his history of the rebellion in which he himself fought under Don John, says of the Marques : " It was impossible to judge which was greater, his strength, courage and discretion or his arrogance, his thirst for fame and cruelty of disposition." In the Morisco rebellion he certainly showed more of the latter than of the former qualities.

Meanwhile things had been moving in the city, though scarcely in the way Don John would have wished. The place was seething with rumours about the Moors of the Albaicin, the money and information they supplied to their rebel kinsfolk, their young men who stole away to enlist under Umeya. The King at last consented to the President's continual requests for the evacuation of the Moorish quarter north west of the Alhambra. An edict was proclaimed on Midsummer's Eve ordering every Moorish male between the ages of ten and sixty to repair to the church of the parish to which he belonged and there to await the royal commands as to his future fate.

Terror and despair reigned in the prosperous houses beyond the river. Ruin and exile seemed the most any could hope for. Swift death appeared far more likely. The reassurances of Mondejar were powerless. President Deza's written promise that no lives were in danger was equally ineffective. It needed the presence of the Prince himself, the spoken pledge of his royal word that no harm should befall any, before the terrified Moriscos consented to be herded into the churches. The doors were shut and barred. A strong guard was posted before each one. The short summer night was passed in misery and fear by the wretched prisoners.

The next morning (June 24) a long procession was formed and marched to the Royal Hospital outside the Elvira Gate. " It was a heartrending sight to see so many men of all ages, with bowed heads, bound hands, and faces wet with tears, suffering and sorrowful, forced to leave comfortable homes, families, country and position and possessions." (Marmol.)

Don John and all the members of the Council were present to see that order was kept and no attempt at rescue made. One over-zealous infantry captain had a Crucifix veiled in black carried at the head of his company. The captives, seeing this sinister emblem of *auto-de-fés* as they were hustled along the Calle Elvira, cried out in horror :

" O miserable men, driving us bound like sheep to the slaughter ! Why did you not slay us in the homes where we were born ? "

Just outside the gate a soldier struck a young Moor who, goaded beyond endurance, knocked him down with a brick. The youth was instantly cut down by the halberdiers. A cry went round that the Prince had been killed because the wounded soldier's tunic had been the same colour as the Prince's doublet. In another moment there would have been a general massacre of all the prisoners if Don John had not been on the spot. He drove his horse into the struggling mob shouting at the infuriated soldiery.

" Let no one dare to break the word which I pledged !
If he does and God delays judgement, *I* shall not delay
but shall make a terrible example by his punishment."

The danger was averted, but he took no risks. The city
gates were closed by his orders, the bleeding soldier
smuggled away, and he himself did not leave till the doors
of Isabel the Catholic's hospital had closed behind the last
Moor.

The next day three thousand five hundred men and many
more women and children were marshalled in the square
between the hospital and the gate, divided into companies
and, under strong escorts, marched off to the destinations
assigned to them in bleak Castile and Estramadura. " Many
died by the way, of work, exhaustion, misery, hunger,
by the hands of their guards, were robbed or sold as
slaves," tersely records Mendoza, who, like Marmol, was
an eye-witness of this miserable exodus.

The rich and flourishing quarter of the Albaicin became
a desert. The soldiers, instead of the luxurious billets to
which they had been accustomed, found themselves now
in empty houses, tenanted by rats and vermin. They made
up deficiencies by plundering neighbouring Christians, so
that insubordination in the ranks and continual quarrels
between soldiers and civilians made things more difficult
than ever for the Commander.

" By the destruction of this rich and beautiful city,"
moralizes Marmol, " one saw that the loveliest and most
splendid of human things vanish most swiftly under the
strokes of fortune."

In the gorgeous rooms of the Audiencia, amid silks and

bronzes and marbles, the lonely young Prince, beating
against the golden bars, thought too in his darker moments
that " the loveliest and most splendid of human things,"
success, fame and glory, were but a mirage receding from
sight and touch.

XII

MOUNTAINS AND MOLEHILLS

(Late July—December 24, 1569)

The hot summer days dragged on. Los Velez, an elderly Achilles, sulked within the walls of Calahorra while his troops, starved and unpaid, deserted in companies. He complained that effort was useless in teeth of the Council's opposition. Mondejar complained of Los Velez's inaction, of the Council's refusal of his own suggestions. The Council complained impartially of both marquises. The war of tongues continued unabated—the only war carried on with energy and determination. Aben Umeya, elusive as a fox, swept down from his mountain covert, ravaging and massacring, now here, now there. He kept more than royal state. His personal guard was four hundred strong. Another sixteen hundred surrounded his quarters and his crowded harem.

Within the walls and between the high, huddled houses of Granada the burning sky was like a copper lid pressed down on a simmering pan. Don John's charming smile and tactful words became more and more of an effort. The mask of diplomacy and caution, never natural to him, began to wear very thin. That his nerves were near breaking point is obvious from letters of the King in answer to his impassioned tirades against Los Velez and enforced inaction for himself. In one letter he had actually forgotten his almost worshipful respect for his brother, who quietly rebuked him.

" It is not fitting that you should write to me as you did at the end of your letter, but I forgive you, because of the great love I bear you." (Philip to Don John, May 20, 1569.)

In July breaking point was reached. The Prince went down, probably with the fever to which he had always been subject and which in every war took a higher toll of lives than did the enemy.

" I am specially grateful to Your Majesty for your anxiety over my health and for your commands to me to be careful of it. I will be as far as is possible with all the business and worries here, for, when ill, I cannot serve Y. M. as I wish to and should do. This place, as everyone knows, is so unhealthy and insanitary that the wonder is I kept well so long."

The note of affectionate anxiety recurs again and again in Philip's letters. After Isabel *de la Paz* and their daughter Eugenia—his favourite child—he seems to have been fonder of his half-brother than of anyone. Men love and admire most in others those characteristics lacking in themselves. It is probable that in this handsome, popular, ardent, recklessly courageous young brother Philip the Prudent enjoyed just those qualities which nature and training had denied to himself.

To the King alone, and to Ruy Gomez, could the Prince pour out his difficulties and irritations—want of money, insubordination of troops, bickerings, jealousies and enmity between commanders. In the answers from " *Vuestra buen hermano, Yo el Rey* " (your affectionate brother, I the King) he was sure of cautious and carefully thought out advice, prudent, even if it did not suit his own desire for instant action.

" I believe all you say of the Marques de los Velez, since I have had to see and manage him for years past . . . but your best way to serve me is to treat him with dignity and respect and not show your anger and disgust. . . . I am distressed to hear that you yourself went out with a raiding party the other day. It is not your place to do this, but rather to attend to the safety of the city. It would be disastrous if the enemy attacked you in force as they might easily do. . . . I hear too that it is your custom to make the rounds yourself to inspect guards and sentinels. . . . Let Luis Quijada or the Duke do this." (Philip to Don John, September 7.)

Early in September de Quiroga died. Philip named as his successor Juan de Soto, who had been at sea as secretary to Garcia de Toledo, so was an expert in naval matters. He did not arrive till the following spring to take up work but was to serve the Prince with the faithful devotion of all his subordinates.

August and September passed uneventfully in Granada. In the green valleys of the Alpujarras, which a Moorish poet had called " the gardens of paradise," a new jewel adorned the harem of Aben Umeya. This was Zahara, whose beauty, grace and charms moved even Christians to poetry. Umeya was to pay for this precious pearl with his life. Alguazil, a kinsman and lover of Zahara, mad with jealousy, began to plot against the rebel king, whose warlike zeal was melting fast in the warmth of her embraces.

One element of discord had been removed from Granada early in September by the departure of Mondejar to lay his grievances before the King. Philip listened, soothed, committed himself to blame neither of los Velez nor the Council, appointed Mondejar Viceroy of Murcia and later of Naples, thus effectually soothing his wounded feelings while preventing him from returning to the seat of war.

The burden of Don John's letters now consisted of appeals for money and demands to be allowed to take the field in person and end the rebellion with swiftness and determination.

"I would reply otherwise if I had already gained experience, but how much better shall I succeed in Your Majesty's service—in which I hope to live and die—if I can seize every chance of perfecting myself in the essentials of my profession. These occur every day and it is to your interest that I should not be so imprisoned by my youth nor any other reason." (Don John to Philip, September 23.)

"I must reserve you, and you must reserve yourself," came the inexorable answer, "for greater things. It is from such that you will learn, and in my way, not in your own." (Philip to Don John, September 30.)

"I desire nothing so much as to please and satisfy Your Majesty in all things and in every way possible. Yet, seeing my age and the position to which you have appointed me, I consider it only right that, during raids and feats of arms, the troops should find me at their head. It is most certainly fitting that, at the very least, I should be there to encourage them to do their best, since they will know that I am with them by Your Majesty's wish." (Don John to Philip, October 4, 1569.)

In late October Don John writes with delight to acknowledge the permission which his importunity had at last forced from the King. Earlier in the month an edict had been published banishing those Moors who still remained in Granada, announcing that the war would now be carried out " *a fuego y sangre* " (to fire and blood) and passing sentence of death on the rebel kinglet.

But Aben Umeya was already dead. A letter he had written to Don John to ask for clemency on his father and brother roused a suspicion that he was treating with the enemy. Alguazil fomented these suspicions and by a plot of typically Oriental treachery, gained entrance to the " royal " bedroom with some Turkish guards he had suborned. The faithless Zahara twined her lover so tightly with her arms that he could neither escape nor reach his scimitar. He met death with the courage he had shown before women and luxury had rotted his youth and, to the amazement of his murderers, declared that he died a Christian. His body was flung, like a dog's, into a dungheap, where it remained till Don John, hearing that the rebel had died a Christian, had it disinterred and buried with Christian rites in consecrated ground at Guadix.

Hardly had the news of Aben Umeya's death reached Granada than his successor, Aben Aboo, with over ten thousand men, laid siege to Orgiba (late October, 1569). He was in every way a contrast to his predecessor. He lacked his youth, charm and adventurous spirit. Severe and grave, he showed foresight in making plans and competency in carrying them out. Arrogance perhaps was the only quality he shared with Umeya. At his coronation on the mountain side he carried a banner with the motto: " More I could not desire, less would not have contented me."

Four furious assaults were repulsed by the garrison of Orgiba under Francisco de Molina, and Aben Aboo settled down to starve them out. Food and ammunition ran low. Two messengers sent for help were taken by the Moors. At last news was got through of Orgiba's desperate straits. Don John sent out a strong relieving force under the Duke of Sesa. Aben Aboo attacked the advance guard and only the heroic efforts of the Duke prevented a general rout. De Molina evacuated Orgiba. A repetition of the Seron tragedy was avoided. Sesa withdrew to Granada and Aben Aboo entered the empty stronghold in triumph, drums beating, flags flying.

News of his success spread like wildfire along the mountains. All the country south of Granada, except Malaga and Ronda, was now up under the banner of the Prophet, and it seemed only a matter of days before the rising tide of revolt spread over Murcia and Valencia as well. Such was the result of seven months of divided authority, personal jealousies, incompetence and over-caution.

At last the King moved. Permission to take the field reached the Prince, who was to succeed los Velez in command of the eastern front of the Almanzora, while de Sesa, under his orders, was to move into the mountains south of Granada with a force strong enough to protect the city.

If the news of Aben Aboo's success had flashed through the Alpujarras, still more swiftly spread through southern Spain the word that at length Don John was allowed to go into battle. Nobles who had not stirred before now seized their arms and called up their men. Hidalgos, knights and soldiers came hurrying to Granada in such numbers that Philip had to issue an order forbidding recruits to join without his permission.

The result of Don John's hard and steady work during these months of seeming inaction was now apparent. Discipline had been tightened and order restored among the troops quartered in Granada. Drastic measures had been necessary to remedy such a state of insubordination " as had never been seen nor heard of in past times of war " (Mendoza). Out of forty-one captains, for instance, thirty-two had had to be cashiered.

Discipline had been restored among the veterans by the end of October, and luckily the bulk of the new volunteers were well trained, anxious rather for honour and glory in the " Holy War " than for plunder.

Beacon fires blazed along the mountain tops. The Moors, gone to earth in their caves, came down for raids on the vega, carrying off women and children and leaving behind them mutilated corpses and burning farms. Bands of Christians rode out of Granada bent on revenge and came thundering back swinging aloft on their lances bearded, turbaned heads that left a trail of blood along the cobbled streets.

Don John was busy with last preparations before he led out the Christian army in force. One thing was most necessary, to take Guejar, a hill town three and a half leagues east of Granada, a hornets' nest of rebels.

A night march was to be made, in two divisions, one under himself, the other under de Sesa. The town was to be attacked at dawn from opposite sides and taken by surprise. The plans were carefully laid. Guides were procured who knew the country well, Diego de Quesada being allotted to the Prince's division. This, two thousand strong, with Don John at its head, left Granada in the afternoon of December 23, taking a route through the mountains so as to reach Guejar at dawn from the north-east. De Sesa, with three thousand men, marched a few hours later, up the valley of the Jenil, with orders to light fires when they reached the mountains as a signal to the other division of their arrival.

Don John, at the head of his column, topped the eastern heights just before sunrise and, to his amazement, saw the flag of Castile floating on the tower of Guejar. The work was already done and victory gained before he had entered the stage. At the gate the Duke met him with an explanation. His advance guard had come unexpectedly on a Moorish outpost which had fled. The troops had swept after them, through the pass and into the town, meeting with no resistance except at the ford through the Jenil. There a small band of Moors had made a gallant stand while the townsfolk, women and children fled to the hills. By daybreak the place had been captured.

Don John listened with courtesy and outward calm, though (says Marmol, who was present) " his eyes were blazing with anger like live coals." He then turned to de

Quesada asking why he had delayed them by leading them such a long way round. Quesada was forced to exonerate himself by saying that not only had he been ordered by the Council to safeguard the Commander-in-Chief, but had also received private instructions from Luis Quijada, who had accompanied this division, to delay it as long as possible.

Sesa could not be blamed for circumstances beyond his control, nor could old Luis be publicly reproved. Don John, still white and furious, put the captured town in charge of Juan de Mendoza, turned his horse and, refusing to touch a mouthful of food or drink, rode back in unbroken silence to Granada.

It was his first attempt in person against the Moors— except for unimportant raids. The laurels which he had hoped to win had been snatched by another. His own failure was due to the over-care of Quijada, who had " meant well." Angry and bitterly disappointed, he rode through the snowy mountains in silence that seemed the only alternative to childish tears of rage.

The towers of the Alhambra were black against the stars as he entered Granada, stiff after almost twenty-four hours in the saddle, faint after twelve hours without food or drink. In the cathedral the Archbishop and canons were chanting the first Vespers of Christmas Day.

" The King of Peace is exalted above all the kings of the earth."

XIII

GALERA

Preparations were at last complete and the army was to march tomorrow. Discipline had been rigorously reinforced. Men had been hanged for insubordination on several occasions. A paper of careful and detailed advice (probably written by Ruy Gomez, Prince of Eboli, at the King's dictation) had been received by the Commander-in-Chief. This gave minute instructions as to commissariat, billeting, checking of arms and equipment, care and reward of the wounded, daily personal inspection of troops, their food and lodging.

" Your Excellency should always carry a purse with two or three hundred gold scudos," was a recommendation easier to make than to practise, considering the chronic shortness of cash. " If you find the soldiers at a meal Your Excellency might stop to see what the food is like and have a mouthful with them." " It is well for Your Excellency to be plainly dressed when in the field, without buttons, chains or ornaments of gold."

The last remark shows that reports had reached the court about Don John's care and splendour in dress. No doubt the old greybeards in their shabby black had seen with a jaundiced eye the plumed hat with the emerald buckle, the huge, puffed, slashed breeches which made the silk-clad legs look still more slim, the pearl-sewn doublet, the fine lace at neck and wrists, the gay crimson of the cloak, so noticeable amid the general sombreness. They were apparently unaware that courage need not be dowdy nor holiness unwashed.

President Deza and the Duke of Sesa were to remain in authority at Granada with a garrison of four thousand. Later the Duke was to strike at the enemy in the western Alpujarras. Three thousand foot and four hundred horse were to march tomorrow under the Commander, and with them would ride a large number of young volunteers of noble birth, the majority from Andalusia, eager to distinguish themselves in the Holy War.

The Prince himself, on the eve of departure, did not forget that this materialization of his boy's dream was, before all, a crusade. Here, indeed, everything reminded him of it. Less than ten miles to the west, visible from the heights of the Alhambra, was the town of Santa Fé, built by Ferdinand and Isabel for their besieging army. On the slope of the Alameda, below the Alhambra, rose the tower of la Vela, on which seventy-eight years ago the crimson banner of Castile and the Cross had replaced the green, crescent-strewn flag of the Prophet. In the middle of the Alhambra, amid its horseshoe arches, glittering honeycomb and rainbow tiles, rose the palace of Charles V.

Don John knelt alone in the December dusk in the royal chapel of the cathedral as, five years ago, he had knelt in the dark little sanctuary of the *Virgen del Pilar* at Zaragoza. Then he had stolen away to pray for the success of a boy's mad escapade, now for that of his manhood's first great adventure. Before him lay the marble figures of his grandparents, Philip the Handsome and Joan the Mad, gorgeously dressed and jewelled. His great-grandparents, *los Reyes Catolicos*, armed and plainly garbed, lay side by side on the great alabaster monument carved with the four doctors of the Church and the twelve Apostles—the only figures the Genoese sculptor considered great enough to commemorate their conquest. The sword of Ferdinand was here too, with its strange half-circle guard to the hilt, keeping safe the heart of the kingdom he had won after so many years at the point of the sword.

The short December day had ended. Within the splendid iron *reja* all was silence, except for the faint distant chant of the canons in the cathedral. It was the eve of the feast of St. Thomas of Canterbury—a good omen to march at dawn under the protection of a high-hearted dauntless fighter who fell in defence of the Church's rights.

It was four days' hard march, a rough track over mountain passes and flooded valleys, to reach Baza, where Luis de Requesens waited with heavy artillery, supplies and reinforcements which he had brought up from Cartagena. He reported the inefficiency of Los Velez, who was besieging Galera, a strong Moorish town, with his usual half-hearted dilatoriness. Don John needed no urging to push on at once to Galera, before the Marques should break camp and release the Moorish garrison. Before attacking, however, it was necessary to concentrate men, guns and stores at Guescar, on the further (north east) side of Galera. De Marmol (the historian) was sent on with seven hundred waggons and fourteen hundred mule-loads of stores, with an escort only three hundred strong, as it was supposed that the blockade of the town rendered more protection unnecessary.

Los Velez, however, reserved for the young Prince a more deadly hatred than he had ever shown to " the enemies of God " and, on hearing of his advance, broke his camp and retired, leaving the Moors free to attack the convoy. Luckily Marmol heard in time of this manœuvre, sent back for reinforcements and managed to reach his destination in safety.

Two days later Don John with the main body made a forced march to Guescar, twenty miles over rugged mountains and through valleys flooded by the Moors who had opened the irrigation sluices of the network of streams and rivers. If stores and guns had not gone in advance it would have been impossible to get them through the morasses of mud. Word had been sent on for quarters to be got ready in the castle for the Commander. Los Velez refused to move from the best rooms, miserably damp and chilly as they were. Not till he was mounting to ride out and meet his successor did he tell his servant to pack and remove his belongings.

The meeting took place about a league outside the town. Don John, soaked and mud-splashed from the long ride, no doubt felt as murderous as did Los Velez, and with more reason. " Treat him with dignity and respect and do not show your anger and disgust." It was necessary silently to repeat the King's words to maintain an outward control. If the blue eyes were " blazing like live coals "

Los Velez was too full of his own hurt pride to see anything else. He kissed the Prince's hand without even taking the trouble to get off his horse, but probably did not appreciate the sarcasm of the speech made to him.

"I am delighted to make the personal acquaintance of one so famed for courage and brave deeds. My soldiers shall show you the obedience they owe me. As for me look on me as a son who will always rely on your advice and experience."

The Marques's reply was blunt.

"It is not fitting for me, at my age, to be an inferior officer in command of a few men, so I shall retire to my own home."

He was kind enough to accompany the Prince to the town gates, then, wheeling his horse, he rode east with half a dozen men to his castle at Velez el Blanco. His departure was a gain, as it removed the chief cause of bickering and delay. In his case Spanish individualism, pushed to its extreme limits, rendered him incapable of making self secondary to God and King and made him sacrifice loyalty and service to a base, mean jealousy.

The next day Don John rode out with Requesens and Quijada along the heights on both sides of the vega of Galera. A thorough examination of the ground was made by him personally so as to gain knowledge of the enemies' defences and to decide on the best places for his own camp and batteries. The town appeared impregnable. Built on a long steep height between two rivers it was named because in shape it resembled a galley. The only approach, where this height joined a spur of the Sierra, was protected by the castle, on whose highest tower grinned the bleaching skull of a captured officer of los Velez' force. The houses were built up the side of a hill so steep that, like those of a Cornish fishing village, the roof of one was level with the foundations of the next. Every wall was loopholed and every flat roof commanded the one below.

The main camp was now pitched to the east, behind a ridge which protected it from the fire of the garrison. Three batteries were constructed to south, east and north, the last housing two of the heavy cannon which had been dragged from Guescar along a road and over two bridges constructed for them in a night. These two opened fire at dawn and before long battered a breach in the walls. The Moors were incapable of putting them out of action for their only artillery consisted of two " falconets " (light cannon) captured from los Velez.

Thanks to the big guns, castle and church (on a lower slope) were captured and trenches toward the centre of the town begun. In order to dig them it was necessary to protect the men from the fire of the defenders above. The Moors had burnt every bush on the vega which could give cover, so broom branches had to be cut on the mountain sides, tied in bundles and carried down on the men's backs—a wearisome business and, when the line of fire was reached, a dangerous one. The task was highly unpopular until Don John himself joined the workers, cutting and carrying bundles like the rest. It is not easy to imagine what Philip's feelings would have been if he had seen his sacred brother sweating and mud-plastered engaged on such a menial task.

A new battery was constructed. The outer walls of the houses were smashed. Not till the attack was launched were the full difficulties realized. Every house was a fortress. Every yard of street became a shambles, commanded by the fire of Moors on roofs and in upper rooms. One young knight of Santiago, who had only ridden into camp two hours before, and was conspicuous by his red Cross, was surrounded and literally cut to pieces. After heavy losses the attacking party was forced to retreat.

Seeing the uselessness of such attempts Don John resolved to mine the city wall, a difficult business as it was built on the solid rock. It was done at last and a feigned attack was made at that point to draw the Moors there. Six hundred of them were sent flying into the air, with huge lumps of rock, walls and roofs, as the mine exploded. The Spaniards attacked without waiting for orders, or discovering that the hole in the wall itself was only big enough for one man to get through at a time. The few who did penetrate into the town were cut down and the breach was blocked by the defenders.

The Moorish fire from roofs and windows prevented the capture of a single house on the eastern side of the castle, where Don John commanded in person. Four hundred Spaniards were killed, five hundred wounded, a large percentage of officers among them, and nothing had been gained. As night fell a Council was called. The Prince strode in, booted, spurred and grimed from the long day's fighting. He spoke at once, quickly and bluntly. (January 19, 1570.)

" I am here not to ask advice but to give orders. Today's

defeat must prove only a step on the road to victory. As for the inhabitants I will punish them mercilessly for their bloody resistance. Everyone shall be put to the sword, Galera razed to the ground, the site sown with salt. The engineers will work day and night till the wall has been destroyed. If we all help as we should His Majesty should hear the news that we have taken the town as soon as he hears of today's reverse." (Marmol.)

The fresh mines were finished by February 10. New batteries opened a furious bombardment. Cavalry was stationed in the vega to cut off enemies trying to escape. Infantry was ready to attack as soon as the breaches were made. The first mine again failed to destroy the wall. The second, at the west end, blew up a large number of houses right in the town and caused a panic among the defenders. Don John sent forward a reconnoitring party which captured the enemies' flag and drove them down the hill till their flight was arrested by another party advancing through the lower town. Two thousand Moors fled to the market place where they were cut down. Others were shot in the houses through holes made in the roofs. Two thousand four hundred men of fighting age were killed and hundreds of women and children massacred. Four thousand four hundred women and children were taken prisoners. Large booty was captured—silk, gold, and jewels, which were divided among officers and men, and wheat and barley enough to feed men and horses for a year, which were annexed by Marmol for the commissariat.

A large number were massacred in cold blood. Accounts differ as to Don John's responsibility for this. Marmol

says that the order was given : " No prisoners." Another
chronicler says that the slaughter was due to the fury of
the soldiery and that, as soon as Don John rode into the
town from the vega, where he had been with the cavalry,
he called off the troops at once.

A courier galloped with news of the success to Philip,
who was spending the beginning of Lent in the monastery
at Guadelupe. He received the news with the same *sang-
froid* as he had heard that of the previous defeat. " He
allowed no rejoicings, only gave thanks to God and the
glorious Virgin Mary . . . being of a nature which preferred peace and concord to a bloody victory." (Marmol.)

Such feelings were not shared by his brother. Don John,
a young lion who had tasted blood, knew he had taken his
first stride along the road which, Fray Juan had promised,
would lead him to fame " greater than any in Europe."

Don John was a sixteenth century Spaniard. He
belonged to a race which with its vivid realization of the
eternal verities often fails to set due value on bodily life,
which, for eight centuries had fought to the death with
" the enemies of God," had seen the end of their kingdom
within the memory of living men. He belonged to an age
when life was too short and too crowded for time to be
wasted on fruitless sympathy with the sufferings of others,
which saw, without a qualm, men and women burned
alive, or hanged, disembowelled and quartered while still
alive. He would have agreed with Napoleon, that it is
better to pay for victory with a hundred men than to waste
a thousand by cautious humanitarianism. The Moors, in
his eyes, were rebels and apostates. The final assault on

Galera had cost him heavily both in officers and men. "*Si Africa llora, España no rie*" (if Africa wept, Spain did not laugh). Hardly a noble house of southern Spain but mourned the loss of one of its sons who had enlisted under the banner of the Cross and the Prince.

If Don John indeed ordered the ruthless destruction of the Moors of Galera—as it is possible that he did—he was to show later a care and generosity towards his own wounded which were rare in his day.

The bloody day of February 10 had begun at nine in the morning and was barely ended when nightfall was hastened by the heavy masses of clouds which blotted out the lurid glare of sunset but threw into higher relief the flames from burning houses. Every square and street of the doomed town were piled with corpses. The gutters ran with blood. Not a living Moor was left. The Christian dead and wounded were collected for burial and attention. Before Don John broke camp and rode through the night over the mountains to Cullar he repeated his orders to Marmol, who remained behind. Every house was to be destroyed. Every wall was to be razed to the ground, not a stone left upon another. The place was to be strewn with salt. To this day nothing marks the site of the once strong and wealthy city except a few mud huts straggling in the vega.

"*Delenda est Galera.*"

XIV

"FIRE AND BLOOD"

(FEBRUARY 19—MARCH 10, 1570)

The clouds that had blackened the red glare of the sunset over burning, bloodstained Galera broke that night in a fierce storm of thunder, lightning, snow, hail and torrents of rain. The Christians looked on it as little short of a miracle that the weather had held up till the siege was over. It would have been as impossible for them to remain in camp as it was now for artillery and baggage to follow the main body to Cullar. Guns and stores were compelled to turn north along the main road to Guescar while Don John rode south through flooded valleys and over snowclad mountains to Baza, which he made his head-quarters for a few days.

The little town, which had resisted all the efforts of Ferdinand but had surrendered at once on Isabella's arrival in 1480, rose from a plain so strangely scarred with grotesque ravines and gigantic furrows that it resembled a corner of the Inferno. It was strongly fortified, and the memory of Isabella's victory was kept green by a battery of her cannon parked in front of the cathedral. The castle lacked all the amenities of life. The big open fireplaces of Villagarcia, Yuste and Madrid were unknown here. The dark, gaunt stone rooms, with their narrow, unglazed windows, were icy cold and damp. The snow had crept down to the lowest spurs of the Sierra. Vega and valleys were a sodden mixture of flood and mud. Sickness was general. Numbers of officers and men died of plague and fever. Don John alone appeared immune. All that week he was out, riding through ice and mud, through snow, hail and rain, discussing commissariat with Marmol, reconnoitring south beyond Caniles towards Seron, which was to be the next point of attack. Old Quijada preached care and caution. In vain. There was nothing for him to do but to add his prayers to those of Doña Magdalena anxiously waiting in Madrid for news of her husband and boy. The slender young body, which had never been robust, seemed made of steel. The red wine from the vineyards of the *convento*, reported to be the best in Granada, was as little appreciated as the beauty of the women, said to be the loveliest in Spain, with their proud carriage, small dark heads and their slim sandalled feet under their full green *sayas*, black-striped, red-edged. There was no room in Don John's yellow head for anything but plans for the recapture of Seron, to wipe out the memory of Los Velez' criminal inaction, to avenge those massacred Christians, those women dragged to harems seven months ago.

On the evening of February 18, 1570, Don John marched from Caniles (seven miles south of Baza) and by dawn his advance guard had occupied the hilly ground near Seron, which was built on the southern slope of a hill, crowned by the castle and looking east down the valley of the Almanzora. He sent cavalry under Francisco de Mendoza to occupy the pass on the south and so prevent the arrival of Moorish reinforcements. Two infantry detachments, under de Requesens and Quijada, were to attack the town from opposite sides, while the remainder of the cavalry advanced along the river bed. The alarm had been given and an appeal for help made to the rebels by the beacon fires which blazed along the hill-tops as the shepherds' fires used to blaze across the valley from Villagarcia. It was urgent that a successful assault should be made at once before the enemy was strengthened or a counter attack launched from the mountains.

The Prince, from a neighbouring hill, saw the cavalry compelled to take shelter on the river banks, saw Quijada's company take an old watch tower and drive back the enemy to the walls of the castle. Then discipline snapped. Quijada's men, thinking the day won, broke ranks to plunder and were joined by Mendoza's cavalry who hurried down for their share of loot. Hardly had they left the pass unguarded than six thousand Moors swept through it and into the town.

Panic seized the infantry. A body of horse sent to their help caught the infection. Panic degenerated into rout and men fled, throwing away not only their plunder but also their arms.

Don John galloped furiously down, pulled his horse across the narrow path in a vain attempt to stem the stream of fugitives by words and blows.

"What is this, Spaniards? Where is the honour of Spain? I am with you. Whom and what then do you fear? Withdraw in good order with your face to the enemy like men and these savages will soon fly from you."

Little by little the flight was arrested. A bullet struck

the Prince on the head. He reeled in the saddle and would have been killed if his steel helmet had not deflected the bullet. Near him Quijada, who was re-forming a body of infantry, was shot in the shoulder and fell from his horse. Don John hurriedly detailed a party to carry the old man to his billet at Caniles and, when he had restored some order to the broken troops, he led them back over the mountains to Caniles. All the way the enemy hung upon their flanks and rear and, only when in sight of Caniles, returned to Seron in triumph. There they celebrated the victory which had cost the Christians over six hundred men, " as well as honour and more than a thousand swords and muskets." (Marmol.)

That very night the Prince sent Philip his report of the rout and of Quijada's wound.

" I assure Your Majesty (with deep shame and disgust at the cowardice of the troops) that veterans with experience of many wars have never seen such panic and terror. For myself, if I had not actually seen it, I could never have believed that a few Moors could throw soldiers into such confusion. Nothing would induce them to turn and face the enemy—not angry words, encouragement nor even blows with the sword. If Don Garcia Manrique had not enabled us to retire along a track he had discovered only the day before . . . we should indeed have been on the edge of a terrible disaster. . . . Just then Luis Quijada, doing his best to make the men stand their ground—as all should have done—received a bullet in the left shoulder, a very dangerous wound. Today they have made five incisions where the ball entered and one behind. They have found the shot but have not succeeded in extracting it, which is most unfortunate. The loss to Your Majesty's service is already deeply felt. His military experience, his care and thoroughness have been of such help to me that I realize keenly how important he is to Your Majesty's service. I beg you to thank him for all he has done and to order him to be more careful of himself. I hope to God he may recover, though his condition is now dangerous." (Don John to Philip, Caniles, February 19, 1570.)

The same courier, riding through the night, took a letter to Doña Magdalena, and for the next six days every moment that could be spared from duty was spent by her " son " at the bedside of the old man, often so fussy, irritable and hot-tempered but always " *el cristiano viejo y rancioso*," upright, loyal, faithful and honest.

On February 20 Luis realized that the end was near and demanded the last sacraments. A small, shabby little priest came in answer to Don John's message to the Franciscan friary at Caniles. This insignificant little person was Fray Cristobal de Molina, the hero of the famous exploit at Tablate bridge. When he had gone Luis turned to Don John with a flash of the old " rusty " spirit.

" It worries and distracts me to keep wondering how such a mean-looking little man could have done such a daring deed ! "

News came on February 23 of Doña Magdalena's approach. Don John rode out to meet her and led her to her husband's bedside. The dying man was in a high fever and delirious, so did not recognize her, but on the evening of the next day recovered consciousness and was able to talk to her. He weakened gradually and on the night of February 25, with his wife and pupil kneeling by him, Fray Cristobal and de Requesens behind them, Luis slipped out of life " as gently as passing from mortal to eternal sleep."

For one moment, worn out with her hurried journey and long vigil, Doña Magdalena broke down. She clung to her " Jeromin," his arms round her, her face hidden on his breast. Then she regained control and, stooping over the body, closed the dead eyes, while her boy dropped onto the lids the wax from the blessed candle which sealed them in their last rest.

The body lay in state all the next morning, a brown Franciscan habit over the armour, flags draped round, while the troops defiled past it. Then, in the afternoon, the funeral cortège filed over the hills to Baza, arms reversed, drums muffled. The passage of any wheeled vehicle was impossible, so the coffin was carried by relays of old soldiers. Don John rode behind it on a black mule whose mourning trappings swept the ground. He was muffled to the eyes in his cloak, the hood pulled forward to hide his face. " Keep your tears for when you confess your sins," the harsh old voice had barked at him that morning long ago at Villagarcia. But Luis's pupil would have been more or less than human had tears not blurred his sight of the long cavalcade that wound up the steep narrow path under the snowpeaks flaming in the sunset.

For three days after the burial in the Hieronymite friary at Baza Doña Magdalena remained with Don John at Caniles. He arranged a comfortable litter for her homeward journey, becomingly draped in black, and rode for several miles beside her. "*Partire è un po mourire*" says the Italian proverb and, in this parting, both tasted something of the bitterness of death. It was worse for her, on her way to the convent at Abrojo. She left behind her in these cruel mountains all her human love. For the rest of her life her love, her thoughts, her prayers—those that were not given to God—centred in that slim figure, with bare head gleaming in the wintry sunshine, sitting on his horse without stirring till a turn of the path hid her from sight.

The day of Luis's death Don John had written to the King.

"Your Majesty has today lost one of your most faithful servants by the death of Luis Quijada. His loss will be specially felt just now for, as I have already written, the campaign has been directed by his advice and opinion. Your Majesty will understand how lonely I feel and how much I need someone to help and advise me. The attack on Seron will entail great risks and dangers and, in my opinion, should only be attempted with much care and prudence. It needs someone with more military experience than I or the Grand Commander possess. . . . God knows, I assure you, how deeply I feel my responsibility as well as the misfortune of being left alone." (Don John to Philip, Caniles, February 25, 1570.)

He wrote to Cardinal Espinosa in the same strain : "I love him as dearly where he now is, with God, I firmly believe, for certainly he died a most Christian death." Philip, who had moved to Cordoba to be nearer the seat of war, showed genuine distress at the loss of his old friend and servant.

"I have heard with grief about the behaviour of the troops but with greater grief the news of Luis Quijada's wound. . . . Keep me informed of his progress. I know I need not tell you to take the greatest care of him." (February 24.) "I think I never received a letter which grieved me more than yours of the twenty-fifth. . . . I know how much we shall both of us feel his loss. It is impossible to speak of him without sorrow and you have every reason to mourn him as deeply as you do." (Cordoba, March 3, 1570.)

Once again Don John was obliged to defend himself against an accusation of rashness. No one, he wrote, could have done otherwise than he had done at Seron. "Under God, only my flinging myself into the path of the fugitives prevented the total destruction of the greater part of our army. . . . I see plainly, Señor, that, as God made me different from other men, I must be the more careful to be better than they." (March 12.)

"Your Excellency," wrote the Prince of Eboli, in fatherly reproof, "is reputed to be reckless, desirous of winning fame as a soldier rather than as a commander. Let this be changed and allow yourself to be restrained." (Cordoba, March 4.)

Time pressed. War allows no pause for regrets, and youth looks forward, not back. The Prince completed the preparations for a fresh attack on Seron and, at the end of February, sent forward a party of cavalry under de Aguilar to reconnoitre. The Moors, hoping to catch the Christians in the same way, withdrew to the mountains. But " in vain is the snare set in the sight of any bird." After receiving de Aguilar's report the main body advanced on Seron, only to find that the enemy had set fire to the castle and evacuated the town.

Don John sent two strong forces to guard the passes and hardly were they in position when the Moors appeared in strength under El Habaqui, their commander on the eastern front. De Aguilar was restrained by the Prince who ordered up the artillery and so checked the enemy advance. El Habaqui executed a quick flanking movement and attacked the force in the upper pass so furiously that the troops broke and their flight was only averted by the arrival of reinforcements sent by Don John. Certainly Spanish soldiers, famed all over western Europe for their splendid fighting qualities, did not show to advantage against the Moors.

The fight raged for an hour in the pass without either side gaining any definite advantage. Then the Prince ordered de Aguilar to take the enemy in the rear. So steep was the ascent that even the catlike Andalusian horses were baffled. Of a hundred only forty reached the top, but they gained the day. The Moors hearing hoofs and trumpets in their rear, which they had thought safe from attack, caught the Christian panic, broke and fled. Seven standards were taken. El Habaqui, who had ridden gallantly into battle at the head of eighty picked horsemen, barely managed to escape on foot into the mountains.

Don John occupied the town, and the next few days were occupied in burying the dead who had been killed ten days before and in strengthening the defences. Then, leaving a strong garrison in Seron, the Prince marched against Tijola a league away, perched on a steep spur of the hills and only to be entered by one narrow path.

A new town had grown up along the river banks, among gardens and orchards, but war had driven the inhabitants once more to the almost impregnable stronghold of their old walled town on the hill. The Christians occupied the new town by the river, but to the surprise of the inhabitants days passed and no attack was launched.

These ten days of apparent inactivity were spent in cutting gun emplacements on a high rock overlooking the town and in raising to them, by means of wooden cranes and rope pulleys, some new brass cannon of eighteen cwt. each. These engineering feats were personally superintended by Don John, who wrote to the King in despair at the license and lack of discipline among the troops.

"Their shamelessness is insufferable. Today there are eight thousand. Tomorrow two thousand may have vanished. Neither the gallows nor the galleys will stop them from deserting. The day I arrived here two were hanged and four sent to the galleys. The rest behave as if nothing had happened. . . . The officers are largely to blame for the men's insubordination. . . . The chief reason of this cowardice and evil is the dissoluteness and carelessness of the men about their souls and consciences. . . . Every man needs a chaplain to himself, and a confessor as well." (Tijola, March 12, 1570.)

Meantime El Habaqui had issued orders to all inhabitants of Moorish towns to evacuate them and take to the hills.

The people of Tijola were to regret that they had not fled while escape was still possible. The batteries on which so much thought and work had been expended, opened fire on March 22 and a breach was soon made in the old walls. Terrified and deafened by the thunder of the big guns and the crash of falling masonry, the Moors began to steal away through the rain as soon as night fell. But Don John had foreseen this and posted pickets all round the town. A few fugitives escaped, thanks to troops, as usual, rushing in for plunder, but the majority were driven back and captured with the town next day. They, with women and children, were left in the castle in charge of a garrison commanded by Luis de Marmol's brother.

On March 25, Easter Eve, Tijola was destroyed as Galera had been and Don John marched seven miles down the fertile valley of the Almanzora against Purchena. This fortress—granted to Boabdil as a home after the capture of Granada—was also perched on a rocky height, and a long siege seemed in prospect. The only garrison, however, was found to be some old men too infirm to fly to the hills, and a few women. Purchena was occupied without firing a shot. The same thing happened (early April) at Cantoria and Padules, where Don John made his head-quarters for the next few months.

The last six weeks had seen the capture by the Prince of Galera, Seron, Tijola, Purchena and Cantoria, the subjection of the Almanzora valley, which had been the main seat of the rebellion in the east. A new phase was now beginning, for negotiations with El Habaqui had been opened before the fall of Tijola. A new era in war, too, had been begun. The mines at Galera, the big gun emplacements at Tijola had marked the end of the old chivalrous war and hand-to-hand fighting and the dawn of the age when war would consist of engineering and chemistry, and men would be blown to pieces or asphyxiated like rats in a trap.

XV

"THE ENEMIES OF GOD"

(Early April—June 7, 1570)

The three months' campaign between Christmas and Easter had completely changed the outlook. The Moors had seen all their strongholds in the east captured. They had lost the Almanzora country, the most fertile and wealthy in the Kingdom of Granada, as well as hundreds of fighting men and quantities of gold, riches and provisions. The Christian forces no longer lay inactive or moved in dilatory, half-hearted fashion under the command of old men who were incompetent, cautious and jealous. The rebels realized bitterly that the new Commander-in-Chief was young, ardent, ambitious and ruthless, that he combined the reckless courage of a soldier with the foresight of a general, a care in planning and preparing with a deadly swiftness in striking. The guerilla war which was the Moors' only hope had been successful here and there, and the winter was over. But the Christians now held plains and valleys, orchards, vineyards and cornfields, and had taken large quantities of corn and barley in each captured town. Food was going to be a problem in the coming months.

El Habaqui, the rebel commander in the east, had a wider experience and outlook than his fellows. He had crossed to Algiers to raise reinforcements. They had been annexed by the wily old fox Aluch Ali for his own use and El Habaqui had returned with promises, some arms and the sweepings of the corsair's prisons. Algiers and Constantinople had received the appeal of their co-religionists with an Oriental blandness which was barren of results.

After the loss of Seron, El Habaqui, seeing that the end was inevitable, had decided to turn from force to diplomacy. Negotiations had been opened while the batteries were being constructed before Tijola (March 11–21, 1570). Don John despatched a personal friend of the rebel commander to a secret meeting with him in the mountains. El Habaqui frankly acknowledged that he and many Moors, seeing the uselessness of prolonged resistance, were anxious to make their submission. Francisco de Molina, who had commanded the garrison of Orgiba and had been in charge of the mines at Galera, arranged another meeting with El Habaqui outside Purchena. Molina, when governor of Guadix, had lived in El Habaqui's house and had been on terms of great intimacy with him. He now urged him, by their old friendship, to give up a hopeless struggle. El Habaqui promised to evacuate the towns in the Almanzora valley and to explain to Aben Aboo and the other leaders the folly of further resistance. An answer would be received in a few days' time. Tijola, Purchena and Cantoria, occupied by Don John's forces, added weight to de Molina's arguments.

Don John, on his side, was anxious to bring the campaign to a successful close and to end the rebellion quickly and completely by the submission of Aben Aboo and his men. In the last three months he had recovered all the ground

lost in the preceding fifteen months. A long drawn out
guerilla warfare would not only entail heavy expense but
would bring no more glory to his arms. He was already
looking farther afield for greater fame than could now be
won by the hunting down of an already discouraged
enemy.

The year 1566 had been an eventful one. It had seen
the death of Suleyman the Magnificent, the succession
of Selim II, who boasted that his conquests would exceed
his father's, and the election to the Chair of Peter of
the grim old Dominican, Michele Ghislieri, as Pope
Pius V. This winter and spring of 1570 the men in
the Sultan's shipyards were working furiously in preparation for an attack on Cyprus. Venice, which had
been at peace with the Turk since 1538, was straining
every nerve to avert war, in spite of the menace to her
island.

Pope Pius V, with a Crusader's zeal, the fire of youth
still burning in his veins in spite of his sixty-eight years,
considered that the time had come to unite Christendom
against the infidel and so to guard Europe from the tide
of Turkish conquest which had reached Vienna forty
years ago. Meanwhile the Venetian envoys hurried from
court to court imploring help, but the Adriatic Republic
was disliked and envied and everywhere a deaf ear was
turned to their prayers.

Cosimo di Medici, two years ago, had pointed out to
the Pope that the only hope of a Christian triumph over
the Turk lay in a league between the Holy See, Venice an

Spain, so now, the Pope, in his turn, sent out an appeal to
the Catholic sovereigns. The Vicar of Christ received
the same excuses as had been given to the Venetian envoys
—except from Philip of Spain. To him, accordingly was
sent Luigi Torres, Clerk of the Apostolic Chamber, to
press the cause of the proposed Holy League. He met the
King on his way from Cordoba to Seville, which was
entered in state on May 1, 1570, to celebrate the
King's first visit there. Philip received the nuncio and
the Pope's letter with respect but, cautious as ever,
postponed an answer. He too felt doubtful about
binding himself to Venice, which, as someone wrote, had
a good large piece of fox's tail sewn onto the skin of
St. Mark's lion.

Don John, waiting in camp at Padules for the result of
his offer to El Habaqui, was in touch with his brother's
negotiations over the suggested League. His horizon was
not bounded by the snowpeaks of the Alpujarras. He
was burning to leave this backwater and take his place
in the main struggle between the Cross and Crescent.
The direction of his thoughts and desires is shown in
a letter to the King written after the publication of the
amnesty pardoning all rebels who should submit without
delay.

"Your Majesty knows of the interest I take in your
orders to the fleet at Messina. . . . It is now to Your
Majesty's interest that I should serve you elsewhere [than
here], where I may win the success I desire. . . . This last
week I believe this business practically finished and, within
four days, I hope to have the Moorish chiefs in my power

so that I shall be able to hand over their arms and goods to Your Majesty." (Padules, May 1, 1570.)

Hopes and desires were indeed leaping ahead, but six months were to " drag their slow length along " before these wild mountains were left behind.

The amnesty, proclaimed on April 17, had promised pardon to rebels who submitted within twenty days, but liberty only to those males between the ages of fifteen and fifty who should give up their arms. Those who had surrendered were to wear a large red Cross on their left shoulders to protect them from the soldiery—a necessary but hardly successful precaution.

The amnesty was also published by the Duke of Sesa at Adra on the south coast. He had started his campaign successfully by the relief of Jubiles, but the capture of his whole baggage train by the Moors had reduced his men almost to starvation. By the middle of May disease, hunger and desertion had reduced the ten thousand which the Duke had led from Granada to a bare four thousand, and these shattered fragments were absorbed into Don John's main force on a spur of the mountains near Padules, surrounded by a fertile vega, well wooded and watered.

The days of waiting were not spent idly. There were foraging and reconnoitring parties to be sent out, despatches to be dealt with and answered. April had gone. Ascension and Whitsuntide were over and May was drawing to a close, but still the answer had not come from El Habaqui. Don John was in the saddle all day on his Andalusian horse, with its fine, silky mane and tail, deep shoulders, long legs. The tireless " *paso castellano* " was faster than a walk, smoother than a trot, and the beast sure-footed as a cat on the steep, slippery mountain-sides. The supper would be set out on a trestle table in front of the tent— fine white bread, hare or partridge stewed in an earthen " *olla*," savoury with saffron, garlic and red pimentoes, one of the famous Trevelez hams, pickled for eight days with little salt and much sugar, hung for another eight in the snow of the Alpujarras, and strong ruby-red wine from Baza, the city of beautiful women.

Supper done he might sit on, comfortably tired and lazy. De Soto, the new secretary, was at work in the long, silk-hung tent, on despatches for the courier who was to ride at dawn to Granada and on to the King at Seville or Madrid.

The lower slopes, from which the snows had withdrawn, were dark with stone-pines, ilexes and bay-trees. The rocky wastes above were fragrant with thyme and myrtle, and lavender, feathered with tamarisk, gay with golden broom, pink and yellow cistus, with mauve and crimson rhododendrons. Down in the vega violets and narcissi, the blossom of almond and peach and cherry were over, but red and white oleanders gleamed like fairy lamps among their dark, burnished leaves. The sun set. The swift southern twilight veiled the valley. In this clear, high air the stars glittered so near that it seemed as if an out-stretched hand might pluck them from the sky. The men were chanting fitfully round the camp fires, endless songs with a queer Eastern beat in their age-old rhythm. The air was full of nightingales' notes, of the heavy scent of waxwhite orange and lemon blossom, of the hoarse croaking of frogs among the rushes, of the chirrup of cicadas.

It was a night made for love, but Don John had resolved that there was no place in his life for women. The patient protective tenderness of Doña Magdalena, the living, romantic memory of the dead, lovely Queen—that was all. It was enough. That brief, fierce passion for Maria, that had so soon burnt itself out, had taught him one lesson. However easily a man slips into sin, however lightly he may forget it, the dead thing, which he has fancied so deeply buried, rises and confronts him with its spectral reproach.

Yet he was lonely. Physical content and well-being are not enough to still the longing of the human heart. Greatness entails loneliness and Napoleon's dictum that " he goes farthest who travels alone " is as hard as it is true. Don John thought of Alessandro and the happy days when, free from old Honorato, they had ridden and tilted by the yellow Henares. The story of Alexander of Macedon was one of the few he could still recall, because it had struck an answering note in himself. The young conqueror had swept like a whirlwind across half the known world, had pined for fresh worlds to conquer and—till he met Roxane —had never loved a woman. A bright, bright life, swift and dazzling as the falling star that had just blazed a trail down the eastern sky—what more could man hope or pray for ?

News came at last of El Habaqui's return, and orders were given that his reception on May 20 was to be a full dress affair, so as to give him some idea of the power and resolution of the King of all the Spains. He arrived escorted by an officer in command of three hundred musketeers. His troop of Moors was marched in a long column, five abreast, guarded by four companies of infantry. The entire army was drawn up in parade order on each side. Bands played and salvoes of musketry lasted for a quarter of an hour.

El Habaqui dismounted and entered the tent where the Prince awaited him, surrounded by his staff and all the noble volunteers. De Soto followed, carrying Aben Aboo's banner. El Habaqui prostrated himself at Don John's feet.

" Mercy, lord, mercy ! " he cried. " In the name of the King let your Highness forgive our offences which we confess have been great."

Still on his knees he unbuckled his finely damascened scimitar and handed it over while de Soto cast under his master's feet the rebel flag.

Courteously, but haughtily, he was bidden to rise, take back his sword and use it henceforth in the King's service.

The scene was unforgettable. Outside, the blare of trumpets and glitter of arms, snow peaks and green valleys brilliant as enamel under the May sunshine. In the dim richness of the tent, draped with red and gold, the young Prince, his fair face grave and stern in the shadow of his gilded helmet, the Lamb and chain of the Golden Fleece over his gleaming cuirass, at his spurred feet the bearded Moor in red turban and flowing white robe, under his feet the crimson banner with its proud motto: " More I could not desire, less would not have contented me."

The three hundred Moors were marched off to Andarax. Their commander remained for a couple of days in the enemies' camp before returning to discuss with Aben Aboo the final details of the capitulation. He was back in three days (May 25) with the consent of the rebel kinglet and chieftain to the royal terms, " and especially of the common people who desired nothing more than to see themselves again in peace and quiet." (Marmol.)

He had to wait till the end of the Corpus Christi celebrations for which the whole camp was *en fête*. High Mass was celebrated outside a tent embowered in branches and pennons. The route of the procession had been marked out by a double alley of young trees. Priests and friars, officers and nobles, each bearing a lighted candle, moved slowly between the long lines of infantry and cavalry, who presented arms, while drums were beaten and trumpets blown. Don John of Austria and Luis de Requesens, the Grand Commander, were two of the canopy-bearers and the Bishop of Guadix carried the Host. The proceedings ended by an emotional sermon from a Franciscan, " who, with many tears, praised our Lord for the great good and mercy He had shown the Christian nation in bringing this people [the Moors] to a knowledge of their sins." (Marmol.)

The negotiations were now complete. El Habaqui had brought the final submission of Aben Aboo and all the rebel chiefs. Don John accordingly signed a proclamation extending the time of grace, owing to the difficulty of news reaching the remoter mountains. He then allotted the various districts to the emissaries who were to receive

the submission of Moors willing to surrender and ruth-
lessly to stamp out any attempts at further resistance.
El Habaqui took his leave in order to carry out the work
assigned to him of arranging the embarkation of the
Turkish troops and the Berbers who had crossed from
Africa in hopes of plunder.

All was apparently in order and the end in sight. Don
John was pining to be gone.

" Every hour now seems as long as a year," he wrote to
the King. " I am waiting the end which, please God, will
be soon and complete." (June 4.)

Three days later there is an indignant outburst.

" I must emphasize another point strongly—the abuse
with which friars and other religious publicly denounce
from the pulpits here Your Majesty's kindness and clemency in dealing with this people. Certainly it is a terrible misfortune, misery and scandal that we should be
reduced to such a pitch. Soldiers whose duty it is to pursue
and attack the enemy spend their time robbing and deserting as fast as they can, while priests and religious, instead of
pleading with Your Majesty for the miserable creatures
who for the most part have sinned only through ignorance,
use their power to denounce mercy and meddle with other
people's business when they do their own so badly."
(June 7, 1570.)

The same day he writes to the Prince of Eboli begging
him to hurry on the appointment of a successor, " so that I
may leave as quickly as possible, please God."

The fighting was over and, " since God has made me
different from other men," he had no wish to linger where

his special gifts had no scope. The Mediterranean, seen from the higher peaks of the Sierra Nevada, glittered blue in the June sunshine. Beyond the eastern horizon, where the Turkish fleet was gathering at Rhodes for the final assault on Cyprus, there lay his true destiny.

XVI

TIDYING UP

(Early June—November 30, 1570)

After the ceremonies of Corpus Christi Don John disappears from the pages of Luis de Marmol in the last sixteen chapters of the *Historia del Rebelion de los Moriscos*. He had hoped soon to be gone, as he had written in those letters of early June, but six interminable months were to pass before he rode north—months empty of military triumph or spectacular success.

The weeks crawled by. El Habaqui was busy in sending away Turks and Berbers. Every day bodies of men came down from the mountains to make their submission, hand over swords and muskets and go home with the hated sign of the Cross on their shoulders. Then, about mid-July, news of or from El Habaqui was silenced. The steady trickle of submissions ceased. An envoy sent to Aben Aboo returned with an evasive answer. At the end of July the mystery was solved by an Arabic letter from Aboo found in a captured galley. In it he boasted of the execution of El Habaqui as a traitor to the Moslem cause and begged help from Algiers to carry on the war.

Once more the rebellion flared up, though it must have been obvious even to Aben Aboo that there was less chance of success now than ever. A strong body of Moors on their way to rouse again the country round Velez (east of

Galera) were defeated and killed. In revenge Christian hamlets were sacked and burned, the inhabitants massacred. Another envoy sent by Don John to beg an end to the renewed misery of war was received by the rebel leader with insolence and the uncompromising words : " If I were left alone in the Alpujarras, with nothing but the shirt on my back, I would live and die a Moor rather than accept the greatest favour King Philip could offer me."

The Prince was now (early August) at Guadix which, between Granada and Baza, was a good centre. He was busy raising and organizing fresh troops, garrisoning and strengthening castles and towns. De Requesens (September 2) advanced from Granada by order of the King, into the western mountains, devastating the country and burning fruit trees and crops as he went. For the next few weeks the wretched Moors, innocent and guilty, were hunted down, the men killed at sight, women and children taken slaves. The red Cross of submission proved little protection from the savagery of the soldiers. Large numbers, who had taken refuge in caves, were smoked out or smoked to death in their earths. As always, the common people paid with lives and goods for the folly and ambition of their leaders.

The rebellion, which had spread even to Ronda (north of Gibraltar), was however crushed there by the Duke of Arcos, who had immense estates in the district.

Since the beginning of August Don John had made Guadix his head-quarters. During the next three months the only glimpses of him are found in his letters, especially in those to the Prince of Eboli, to whom he wrote more

freely than he could do to the King. He received Ruy
Gomez's often frank criticism humbly and generously,
with the words that since Luis Quijada's death there was
no one whom he trusted more or could more rely on to
criticize him and his conduct like a father. Again and
again in his letters to the minister, as in those to the King,
is the appeal for money and, at the moment, money was
pouring out of the royal treasury much faster than it was
trickling in.

The Netherlands, once " the Indies of the North," were
now a ceaseless expense. The galleys laden with pay for
Alba's troops, borrowed at exorbitant interest from the
Genoese bankers, had been forced by storms to take refuge
in English ports. Their gold had proved too much of a
temptation, and no protests on Philip's part had obtained
its restitution. Elizabeth had inherited all her grandfather's parsimoniousness, and William Cecil, ruthless
and astute, saw beyond the immediate gain to the English
exchequer the difficulties of Alba faced with a mutinous
soldiery whose pay had vanished. The Morisco rebellion
was another sieve of Danae into which money had to be
poured continuously. Now the Papal envoy, in his
endeavour to persuade Philip to join the Holy League,
opened up yet another vista of expenditure and debt.

" The Wealth of the Indies," which tradition has exag-
gerated to fabulous proportions, actually consisted in
imported gold and silver whose value varied from one to
two million pounds sterling annually. The King's share
of this was one fifth. The year after Charles V's death the
interest on the national debt was seven million ducats (a

gold coin worth about nine shillings). The debt itself was five and a half times the amount of the total royal revenues. No wonder that, in 1575, Philip wrote in despair : " The financial muddle is irremediable. . . . I do not know how I shall live tomorrow. I do not even know how I manage to survive today with all the load of these worries."

Considering all this, and the fact that he had inherited none of his father's carefulness about money, it is not surprising that the burden of Don John's letters—from the Alpujarras, from Messina, from Naples, from the Netherlands—was always to be the same appeal for the two most " necessary things, money and men."

During these summer and autumn months of 1570 the note in the letters of May and June is repeated again and again, the desire to be in the centre of the world's stage, not lingering in a corner at work better done by experienced and cautious old men. Patience was never one of Don John's virtues. Like everyone of ardent and ambitious temperament he wanted things badly and he wanted them at once. Philip's decision to join the League (taken after three days of prayer at Seville) had naturally filled his eager brother with delight, but it was followed by the inevitable long drawn out arguments as to who had the right to appoint the Captain General of the League. The Venetians were afraid that Philip might name Giovanni Doria, whom they hated and distrusted. The Pope did not join in the discussion, though the Papal Admiral, Marc Antonio Colonna, had every qualification for the post. The matter remained undecided, and Don John remained in the Alpujarras.

"I shall be thankful to be quit of this place," he writes to Ruy Gomez from Guadix, "and to be able to serve His Majesty on this other business, which seems to me to be a glorious war, where one will learn something. But I will obey orders and remain here, since it has been judged advisable that I should do so. I agree that it is my duty only to think how and where I can best do that which is my particular end and work. I rejoice that my youth enables me to do it with ease. As for my authority and the place and position I am called on to fill. . . . I shall certainly be as careful of them as I am to serve with all possible vigilance." (August 14, 1570.)

There was one person to whom he could unburden himself even more freely than to the Prince of Eboli—his more than mother, Doña Magdalena.

"Whatever I am, wherever I may be, I shall owe it to him by whom I was formed, or rather begotten, in a nobler birth. Dear, sad, widowed Mother, I only am left you. To you indeed I belong by right, since it was for my sake that Luis died and you have been so stricken. . . . If only I were with you now to dry your tears or to mingle mine with them. Goodbye, dearest and best of Mothers. Pray to our Lord that He will send your son safe back to your arms." (Stirling Maxwell's *Cloister Life of Charles V* from MS., National Museum, Madrid.)

This letter is one of unselfish love and consolation, but a later one has all the signs of impatience, discouragement and frayed nerves.

"Things have got to the stage when, if one decides to do something one moment, one has to change at the next.

One can only drift with the times. I shall be obstinate over one thing, if I am sent to Flanders. It is too far away and too dreary a country to please me. . . . This black war still drags on. It has reached the stage when, if no fresh outbreaks occur, I may have finished my work by the end of October. I long for the end so keenly that, even if I saw it, I should hardly believe it ! " There is an angry denial of rumours that he had visited Granada for pleasure. " If I go to Granada it is because it is easier to make decisions there than in such a god-forsaken place as this. I did not undertake the expedition on my own opinion but with the consent of those who help me and know what is best to be done " (the Duke of Sesa and de Requesens). " In your love for me you bid me be careful how I behave, because all eyes are now fixed on me. You tell me not to be reckless but, when possible, to avoid danger. Once more I kiss your hands for all you are doing for me and I beg you not to tire of doing so. I answer you, Señora, with the simple truth which I value so much. Since my uncle-and-father was taken from me I give our Lord infinite thanks that I always try to live rightly while absent from him who did so much for me. I dare to believe that no one can say that I have lost my self-control nor neglected my work. As to splendour of dress, however much I should enjoy it the work of nine months' campaigning has given me no chance of doing so. Also, Señora, times and conditions are different. Reasonable men, who are not mere brutes, change with age, but there are others in the world who will seize on anything to speak evil. I am not surprised that they speak and whisper against me. They would against God Himself. Nor that you should write that things have got to such a state that you hardly dare ask about me. The saints themselves are not free from the troubles of this world. I will try to follow your advice as much as possible when I know it. I pray you always to hear me, for there is no one I wish to please more than her to whom I owe my education and my position. I shall acknowledge this even from the grave. Forgive such a long letter, but one never knows what will happen, such are the inventions of this world. . . ." (Probably Guadix, end August or early September, 1570. MS., Real Academia, Madrid, Jesuit Miscellanies, Vol. 72.)

The end was at last in sight, and on November 11, feast of the soldier saint, 1570, the Prince made his entry into Granada with the Duke of Sesa and the main body of troops. Once again the Archbishop, President Deza, the civil authorities, the garrison and the people received him with acclamations—this time not of hope but of congratulations to the victor in a long and hard campaign. Once again windows and balconies, gay with tapestries and silken hangings, were crowded with black-haired southern beauty. If the young god with his gilded armour and golden hair acknowledged their cries and glances and flowers with a smile that hardly lightened the severity of his face, there were plenty of other young gallants who were not so abstracted. "Soft eyes looked love to eyes that spake again" and the clear air under the wintry stars was musical with serenades.

There was ruin and desolation in the Albaicin. From Guescar to Almeria, from the Almanzora valley to Ronda

" the land was left unto them desolate." All the Moors in the Kingdom of Granada who could be collected had been marched to Granada, Guadix and Almeria early in November, and from these centres they were despatched under guard to the various places of exile assigned to them. Orders had been issued, with Don John's sanction, if not at his suggestion, that the exiles were to be well treated and that families were not to be separated. Nothing, though, could lessen the misery of the wretches torn from their homes in this fertile country and soft climate to be sent to the barren uplands of Castile or the wild forests of the Estremadura. It was a harsh fate and Nordic historians have lamented that, with the Moors, departed the glory and riches of southern Spain. They have forgotten that the glory had faded long before the capture of Granada by Ferdinand and Isabella, that riches are not only material. As long as the Moors remained still Moslem at heart, as well as Arabic by speech, dress and customs, a united and Christian Spain was impossible.

More than twenty-one thousand Moriscos had fallen in battle during the twenty-three months of the rebellion. Of the fifty thousand left a large proportion of the younger fighting men remained hidden in the mountains and a good number managed later to escape to Africa.

There were still nineteen days of work for the Prince, who was too busy to be impatient. Troops had to be paid off, officers to be rewarded, garrisons and outposts to be strengthened and provisioned for the winter. A miracle would have been necessary to multiply the funds enough to satisfy officers and men. The charm and gracious personal thanks of the young Commander were badly needed to supplement meagre gratuities. The smiles which had been angled for in vain by feminine beauty were lavished on war-worn veterans who went away with feelings of loyalty and satisfaction, if with thin purses.

One of the last letters from Guadix to the King is full of warm recommendations and generous praise of de Requesens, de Sesa and others who had served His Majesty so well as to deserve special personal thanks from him. Particular mention is made of the new secretary, Juan de Soto. " Not only has he fulfilled his duties as secretary with the greatest honesty, care and vigilance, so that he relieved me of much business, but he also efficiently superintended all the arrangement of the commissariat."

It was the Eve of St. Andrew. At dawn Don John was to ride out of the Elvira Gate on his way to Madrid. There was only one shadow on the glowing anticipation of his return. When he had come back from his Mediterranean cruise his dear and lovely Isabel *de la Paz* had welcomed him home. Now there was a new Queen, Ana of Austria, who had landed in Spain six weeks ago. He had never seen her, though her brothers Ernest and Rodolf had been at court for six years. It would be hard to find her in Isabel's place, but the need was imperative for an heir to the empire on which the sun never set.

He lay in the cold winter night, watching through the high windows of the Audiencia the brilliant glitter of the changing stars above the unchanging snow. It was nineteen months since he had first slept here. In that time he had gained experience of war, both in fighting and in organization. He had had his baptism of fire and blood and that bitterer initiation into the quarrels, jealousies and malice of mean spirits out for their own ends, not for the Cause. He himself had not been blameless, he knew. He had been impatient, reckless, hot-tempered, ambitious, cruel, but was not ruthlessness the greatest wisdom in the end? He had "kicked against the goad" both of men and circumstances, but at any rate God and the King had come first. He had remained true to his work, to conquer "the enemies of God and the King."

Every morning, when possible, had begun with Mass. However long and arduous the day he had never lain down without the prayers which he had first learnt at Doña Magdalena's knee, under the little old charred Crucifix which had hung in his room or in his tent all through this campaign.

The work was done, he thought as he fell asleep. Aben Aboo's capture was only a matter of time. The rebel chief was now deserted and powerless.

In a few weeks Aben Aboo's head was over the Rastro Gate, where it grinned down sardonically on Granada a generation after his brilliant young conqueror lay dead in the ruined dove-cote by Namur.

XVII

"IF IT BE A SIN" . . .
(December, 1570—June 6, 1571.)

It was good to be back again in Madrid after nearly two years of absence, after the long ride of two hundred and fifty miles into the teeth of the north wind, through driving sleet and rain. The palace in the little Plaza de Santiago, which the King had assigned to Don John after the fire of 1560, was conveniently near the Alcazar, with its wide view over the valley of the Manzanares to the snows of the Guadarramas. It was a fine building of two stories, the ornate facade flanked by two towers, like the Torre de Lunes, where Francis I had been imprisoned after the battle of Pavia. The place felt oddly quiet and lonely without old Luis's heavy step and harsh voice. The rooms that were always ready for Doña Magdalena were empty too, for she was at Villagarcia.

Early as it was, the King was already at his piled writing desk. There was much that he wanted to hear by word of mouth about the rebellion, about quarrels, inefficiency and the slanders against the young Commander. But to Don John these were an old and boring tale. The Morisco rebellion was over and done with. It had been only a trial flight in which the young eagle had tested his wings. The Holy League and the Turk were all that interested him now—every move that had been made or was going to be planned.

The last year (1570) had been a record of quarrels, dissensions and ineffectiveness before which that of Granada paled. Gianandrea Doria, in command of the forty-nine Spanish galleys, had been a fortnight late at the rendezvous at Otranto with the Papal fleet of twelve galleys under Marc Antonio Colonna. The Venetians (a hundred and fifty-four galleys) started with a cordial dislike of Doria, which was not lessened by his refusal to sail at once for the relief of Cyprus. The result of delays and arguments was the capture of Nicosia by the Turks (September 9, 1570). Dissensions between the leaders came to a head in a conference on the Venetian flagship which nearly ended in blows. Doria announced his intention of returning to Messina with his fleet, in defiance of Colonna's orders. "If you had the powers of Don John of Austria I might obey."

The King had received the report in which Colonna (Hereditary Grand Constable of Naples, so one of the greatest of Philip's Italian vassals) had pointed out the unanswerable reasons of his differences with Doria. It was impossible for the King to have signed contrary orders (a clever argument even if its writer did not believe it). It was as important, if not more so, to keep up the Spanish reputation as to be careful of the fleet's safety. The Pope, not content with writing his disapproval of Doria's behaviour, sent to Madrid Pompeo Colonna, Marc Antonio's lieutenant and nephew, to make strong verbal representations. Cardinal Pacheco had put the matter in a nutshell when he remarked caustically that Philip would always be ill served at sea so long as the Spanish fleet was commanded by a private shipowner, for it was hardly likely that the Turkish fleet would be destroyed by one whose daily bread depended on the safety of his own galleys.

It was only human nature, if human nature on its baser side, that Doria's chief interest should be not the glory of Spain nor even the victory of the Cross but his own interest in preserving the ships which he hired at a high rate to Philip. Venice had not forgotten Prevesa, when the escape of the Turkish fleet had been due to the great Doria's anxiety to keep his own ships safe. Nor would Venice forget this new manifestation of self interest on the nephew's part. The Lion of St. Mark, regardless of that hidden bit of fox's skin on his own tail, condemned treachery in others without mercy. Gossipers in the Piazza di San Marco cursed the alliance with those old enemies, the Papacy and Spain. It had only repeated the story of Doria treason and humiliation for the Adriatic Republic. " Better trust the Turk," they grumbled, " than Philip of Spain."

All this did not make very cheery hearing for Don John. He had escaped from slanders and quarrels at Granada only to find the same evil spirits where he had hoped to see enthusiasm and desire for glory. The fate of the Holy League, not yet formally ratified, seemed likely to be that of the house built on sand.

There was an ordeal to be got over, which for a moment made him forget Turk and Venetian. The King led the way to the Queen's apartments where everything spoke of Isabel *de la Paz*, held the echoes of her soft voice and gay laughter, the memory of her lovely face.

The Queen was sitting by the window, bent over her

eternal needlework. When he had kissed her hand Don
John watched her while the King related the exploits of
the Alpujarras. She was pretty, in a fair foolish way, her
hair, inclined to be sandy, drawn unbecomingly back from
a high forehead, her rich dress, with its long, tight bodice,
ill worn and accentuating her awkward figure. But she
was there solely to provide an heir to all the Spains and,
if she did that, where her three predecessors had failed,
what did it matter that she was in every way the antithesis
of Isabel de Valois ?

The weeks slipped by, every day occupied. The new
year had begun, the year of 1571, which Don John felt
sure would bring the fulfilment of his dream, the crown of
his destiny. The Eboli palace was still a centre of gaiety.
The Princess had lost none of her wit and vivacity, though
the first bloom of youth had gone after thirty years of life,
eighteen of marriage and the birth of many children.
Don John was no longer afraid of *la Tuarte*, for all the
alluring gleam in that one black eye. His heart was
armoured against women, but he enjoyed her sharp tongue,
her fascinating manner, her shrewd insight into men and
affairs. She could listen too, unlike most good talkers,
and would sit silent while her husband and Antonio Perez
talked business and politics with Don John. Sometimes
Pompeo Colonna was there and then the talk was all of
ships, crews, soldiers, provisions and the slaves without
whose toil on the rowing benches the great bulk of the
galleys would have been inert. Don John's eyes blazed at
tales of insubordination—as Marmol had seen them blaze
before Guejar. His hand clutched his sword-hilt, that

strong, masculine broad-palmed hand whose long slender fingers glittered with rings. Antonio was an expert at casting oil on troubled waters, suave, subtle, very much the intimate of the house but close as an oyster when the King's business was discussed. Don John respected his brains, with the frank admiration of the unintellectual for the clever; liked him in spite of curled hair, dandified clothes and scent.

Twelfth Night was kept again with games and dancing. Don John remembered that Twelfth Night five years ago when he had first noticed Maria. Little Ana was over three now, with Doña Magdalena at Villagarcia. He had not seen his Tia yet. It was impossible for him to get away from Madrid and the centre of things, even more impossible to ask her to face the long winter journey over the snow-bound mountains.

In February things looked like being settled at last. The Dominican Pope chose the feast of St. Dominic (March 7, 1571) and the great Dominican foundation of Santa Maria sopra Minerva for the final signing of the treaty by the representatives of the three powers, after solemn Pontifical High Mass. De Granvelle had been raising difficulties ever since the Committee had begun to sit nine months ago, whether at Philips's suggestion or merely in accord with the royal passion for procrastination. Even he had at last been talked down.

March drew on. Don John, in a fever of impatience to be gone, waited for news of the ratification to make his final preparations. Already he had been busy discussing organization, orders to the fleet at Messina, to the dockyards at Barcelona, details for the refitting of the *Real* which was again to be his flagship.

At last the courier arrived from Rome, late in March. The whole house of cards had collapsed. All chance of laurels and glory vanished. As the Treaty was being read, before signatures were affixed, de Grenvelle had again, to everyone's amazement, raised obstacles. The hot-tempered Pope had flared up, ordered him from the room. Argument and discussion ended in the meeting breaking up with nothing done. Instead of a triumphal progress back to the Vatican His Holiness drove home, head bowed, eyes red with weeping, the bitterness of failure in his heart.

If Don John did not weep when the news came, yet his future looked as black as when the shadow of the Red Hat had darkened it. His whole life had been a training for one end, his whole ambition had been the desire for glory in war, honour as the soldier of Christ. "And if it be a sin to covet honour," then was he "the most offending soul alive."

The expected happened. The Venetians, knowing that Mahomet Sokoli, Selim's Grand Vizier, wanted war as little as they did, sent Ragazzoni on a secret embassy to the Porte. He started four days after the collapse in Rome and, when he reached Constantinople, got some home truths from the Grand Vizier.

"As for your League, we know well how little the other Christian powers love you. Mistrust them. Hold by the Sultan. Enjoy constant peace. Do what you like in Europe."

Arguments were unnecessary to convince one already converted and Ragazzoni started home delighted with the results of his mission and expecting no difficulty in obtaining the consent of the Council of Ten to the proposed terms of the treaty with the Sultan. Before he reached Ragusa the Holy League was already signed and ratified.

The apparently final disaster of March 7 had only stiffened the old Pope's determination. Marc Antonio Colonna was sent to Venice, Cardinal Alessandrino (the Pope's nephew) to Madrid, Francisco Borja, now General of the Society of Jesus, travelling in his train.

The Cardinal Legate arrived at the Dominican house of the Atocha, just outside Madrid, where he was visited by Don John and the young Archdukes (May 14, 1571). At the formal reception two days later it was Don John who brought him in a royal coach as far as the city gate, then rejoined the King to ride with him through the streets, with the hundred noble archers and the Spanish and German guards. Streets, windows and balconies were crowded to watch the long and gorgeous procession, after the meeting at San Martin, thread its way to the church of Santa Maria opposite the Alcazar. For once there was a riot of colour. Horsemen, guards and royal officials a blaze of red and gold, the purple of prelates, and,—after the sombre group of grandees,—came a protonotary, purple clad, surrounded by a guard with tall blue lances, bearing the Papal banner of white damask, embroidered on one side with a Crucifix, on the other with the triple tiara and the Keys. Once more the Roman Fasces were borne in state in Spain,—symbol of strength and unity,—and behind them, crimson and gold on his big black horse, rode Don John of Austria. Twenty paces behind him came the Legate on a crimson caparisoned mule, gift of the city, in full cardinal's scarlet and beside him the King, dressed as always in black, rich though sober, with the Collar of the Golden Fleece.

Twenty paces between Don John and the two ; but, long before Santa Maria was reached, he was riding abreast of them, on his brother's left, and talking eagerly to both. Such a thing, in a court of iron etiquette, was startling. Everyone was agog with surprise and curiosity. Was it chance or intention ? Had the King approved ? What did it mean ?

The King took ceremonious leave at the porch but Don John accompanied the Legate into the church. In all that crowded congregation there was certainly no heart more attuned to the splendid triumph of the " *Te Deum* " than that of the Generalissimo of the Holy League.

The ceaseless efforts of the Pope won at last and the League was signed, sworn and proclaimed (May 25, 1571). But before that Don John's preparation for departure was already in train. He was little concerned with the actual articles. The fact that the Vicar of Christ had nominated him as Supreme Commander of the Holy League, both on land and sea (with Colonna as second), was enough.

Probably most cynics—and the majority of sixteenth century men of affairs were cynics—saw the treaty with eyes very different from those of the crusading Pope. The League was to be perpetual, to fight every year against the infidel. No member was to make a separate peace with the Turk. . . . All bore the hall-mark of a Dominican saint rather than that of practical politics.

The Generalissimo, never a cynic, had neither time nor inclination for speculations as to the remote future. Twenty-one days only separated the state entry of the Legate into Madrid from Don John's departure. Such hurry seemed impossible in Spain, the land of *mañana*, in the sixteenth century, the age of interminable delays and pompous procrastinations.

The Legate had gone on to Lisbon, to enlist the aid of the wild, chivalrous, reckless young king Sebastian, who had much in common with his cousin Don John, " the last of the paladins," but lacked his masculine genius for war. The court was at Aranjuez. Don John was to and fro between it and Madrid. There was a new household to appoint, worthy of the Commander-in-Chief of the League : Major-domos, Gentlemen, Grooms of the Chamber (among them the faithful Jorge de Lima), a Master of the Horse, Don Luis de Cordoba, the Secretary, Juan de Soto, jesters, cooks, caterers, servants, grooms, couriers. The royal chaplain was Fray Miguel de Servia, a Franciscan of Mallorca.

Orders were despatched to governors of ports and garrison towns. Santa Cruz was to bring the fleet from Naples to embark at Cartagena the troops no longer needed in southern Spain now that the rebellion was over. German and Italian troops in Milanese territory were to march to Spezia and be shipped there. The Archdukes Ernest and Rodolf were to accompany their uncle as far as Genoa on

their way home to Vienna. Young noblemen and gentle-
men crowded to enlist as volunteers on this new adventure.
Antonio Perez was most popular; his influence as the
King's private and confidential secretary was invaluable.

"His Highness" was of course the idol of the hour at
the Eboli palace as in every house in Madrid, large or poor.
It was no use for Ruy Gomez to insist on the authorized
title of "Excellency." His wife, the Legate and everyone
else, except a few strict and old-fashioned royal servants,
considered that nothing short of "Highness" was good
enough for the Generalissimo.

Philip began to grow uneasy, in spite of "the deep love"
he bore his brother. It was only natural that suspicion
should insinuate itself into his cautious and tortuous mind,
—fostered perhaps by the subtle hints of Antonio Perez.
A young Prince, beautiful, brilliant, charming, with military genius, already a popular hero, likely, if successful on
sea as he had been on land, to be the hero of Christendom
too, son of the great Emperor Charles V,—he would appear
to be the obvious choice as successor to the crown of all
the Spains, since a wise Providence had mercifully seen fit
to take Don Carlos to a better world. True, the baby
which the Queen was expecting in six months' time might
be a son, but a long and bitter experience of daughters,
miscarriages and deaths in childbed had taught Philip not
to build any too certain hopes of a male heir of his body.
His fourth wife might prove luckier than his other three.
Time enough to act if this last effort also proved feminine.
Meantime he fancied that his brother's head was a little
turned with adulation and power. Perhaps the dream of

the succession had entered his mind too, or been hinted at by de Soto who, far from being a restraining influence, had fallen under his master's spell and fostered his ambition and love of glory. Philip made a note to remind himself to write careful and detailed instructions to all his representatives in Italy that the title " Highness " was forbidden. It would be better to delay till the young hothead was at Barcelona and could not expostulate in person.

Unconscious of all this, Don John was pushing furiously ahead, with his usual impatience. There was so much to do, so little time in which to do it. The drama of life is oddly inartistic. It alternates between long stretches of monotonous and uneventful delays and fierce attempts to cram an impossible amount of action and intrigue into a breathless hour. But, whatever else was deferred or omitted, there was one thing which absolutely must be done. It was incredible that Don John had been back for six months and had not yet seen his Tia. Now she wrote that she was coming to Madrid to say goodbye and bringing with her all his old friends who could be spared from Villagarcia : Doña Petronila, Luis de Valverde, and Juan de Galarza, who had been so delighted with his pupil's horsemanship.

Strangely enough when two who have loved dearly meet after a long absence there is almost always a barrier of constraint which chills the loving words and greetings so eagerly looked forward to. Now both found the other changed. For a moment Don John fancied his Tia a stranger. He had always seen her in black, like all women of her class, but in satin or velvet with long " angel " sleeves which swept winglike about her, with gossamer lace ruff and cuffs, the milky lustre of pearls. Now she was in deepest mourning, from black veil to the hem of her dull cloth skirts, no lace nor jewels, the white wimple that bound face and chin like a corpse cloth accentuating the pallor of her face and the redness of her lids. She was angry with herself for having wept, she who so seldom shed a tear, but it was the first time she had been here since Luis's death and every corner held memories of his burly figure, his booming voice, his grumbles—memories which habit had dulled at Villagarcia.

This splendid, arrogant young man, brilliant in red and gold, with pearl-sewn, jewel-belted doublet, was a stranger to her too. His hand was on his sword-hilt, his face grim as he flung a curt order to a servant who had forgotten an order. His face was thinner, the line of the jaw more sharply marked, the well-cut mouth harder and stronger under the little fair moustache. There was an air of authority, of sharp command, of the pride and ambition which she had always feared for him.

Mercifully all the old Villagarcia friends were waiting eagerly. Doña Petronila bent her creaking knees with difficulty as she knelt to kiss the ringed princely hand, then, as she was pulled to her feet, she forgot ceremony and royalty and in ecstasy hugged the "Jeromín" whom she had so often scolded and smacked. The ice was broken. Constraint vanished.

There was much to do and talk about during these short last days. Visitors came to pay their respects to Doña

Magdalena—the Princess of Eboli and Antonio Perez among them. She had to pay her own to the new Queen. There was one subject which Don John could only discuss freely with her as with the King, a most distasteful one, that of his mother. The Emperor had left Barbara Blomberg a meagre annuity of two hundred florins a year. When her husband had died in Brussels in 1569 the Duke of Alba had written to Philip saying that she was poor and in distress as one of her two children had recently been drowned. Philip had provided her with a pension and a household at Ghent, but her incurable frivolity and extravagance made her a continual source of scandal. Philip wrote to suggest that she would be best in a Spanish convent. Alba replied that it was impossible to make her leave Flanders and her numerous cavaliers. Altogether the situation was a mixture of the ludicrous and the scandalous which was more than galling to a sensitive, ambitious young Prince on the eve of his first international command.

This was not the only tale of woe which he poured into his Tia's sympathetic ears. He talked of the future, his determination ruthlessly to stamp out delays and insubordination such as had been due to divided command in Granada. He talked of Mondejar and los Velez, his enemies rather than those of the rebels. Then she slipped in a word of unexpected warning. Antonio Perez. Antonio? Why his influence was great, his friendship greater. She repeated an Italian proverb which Luis had been fond of quoting, " Who knows not how to pretend friendship knows not how to be an enemy." The subject was changed. She hoped the seed would germinate.

There was one promise which he gave her before they parted : that, on the way to Barcelona, he would visit the great Benedictine monastery of Montserrat, as his father had visited it before starting on the Tunis expedition in 1535. She felt that the antidote was needed, a breathing space in peace essential, even if only for a few hours, " the world forgetting, by the world forgot."

XVIII

PAX INTER SPINAS

(JUNE 6—JULY 26, 1571)

Their attitude toward time was one of the things which revealed most clearly the difference between the two brothers. Philip regarded it as a faithful ally and servant, " I and time " against the world. To Don John it was a galley slave, to be whipped to speed and effort. Fond as he was of his stable and his stud, like all his family, he never spared his mounts. A journey with him was a nightmare from which his household prayed to be delivered. His progress now from Madrid to Barcelona was a race whose various stages were marked by the collapse of exhausted competitors.

It was three in the afternoon of Wednesday, June 6, 1571, when he left his palace with de Soto, Luis de Cordoba and a dozen servants, but the thirty-five miles to Guadalajara were covered before night. Here the Duke of Infantado, head of the Mendoza family, entertained the Prince and his party for two days in the gorgeous palace, with its plateresque façade, arcaded Patio of the Lions and lofty rooms with their gilt *artesonado* ceilings. Here Isabel had first seen her elderly husband and had been silenced by his gravity. There was one relic in the church of Santa Maria which thrilled Don John, the Virgin of the Battles, the old statue of painted wood which had accompanied

Alfonso III in all his campaigns against the Moors. His own *Cristo de sus Batallas* was with him now, as always, a continual reminder of the cause for which he was setting out, and everywhere in this magnificent palace there met his eye the motto of its founder, Cardinal Mendoza, friend and counsellor of the Catholic rulers and known as " the third king of Spain "—a grim assertion of the transience of earthly hope and ambition : " *Vanitas vanitatum.*" All is vanity.

Dinner done on Friday the order was " To horse." All that afternoon and evening under the blazing June sun, all that night, with its welcome coolness, they pushed north-east, up the Henares into the mountains, through Sigüenza where a halt was made to change horses, clattering through the streets of sleeping Medina Celi. High-perched castles on the rocky hills were black against the stars and, as dawn broke, the little party rode into Arcos, stiff and weary after eighty miles of riding and fifteen hours in the saddle.

Whatever his companions thought, Don John had no intention of lingering. It was fourteen months since his spectacular success in the Alpujarras had ended and he had written to the King that " every day seems like a year." It was twelve months since the delegates had first met in Rome to discuss the ratification of the treaty. If more time were lost, if more delays occurred, it would not be Don John's fault. " Whom the gods love die young." Perhaps in those so favoured there is some obscure instinct, some unconscious knowledge of the necessity to push ruthlessly forward to that " one crowded hour of glorious life" which is a fate desired by all but the mere clod.

" Push on " was certainly the order of these scorching June days. Sleepy and aching Luis de Cordoba and Juan de Soto climbed into the saddle to cover the thirty-eight miles to Cataluyd after a few hours' halt. At Cataluyd the courier from Rome was met on his way to Madrid and handed the Prince a number of letters from Italian rulers and one from the Pope in his own hand (Rome, May 24, 1571).

" Greatly do we rejoice to see you embarking that, with the other fleets of the Holy League, you may prepare the destruction of our common enemy. Therefore We entreat and warn you, in Christ our Lord that . . . you do your utmost to provide everything necessary for the success of the campaign, avoid delays and use that speed which is so important and so valuable in war."

The Holy Father's plea to "avoid delay" was as unneeded as the letters from Colonna and de Granvelle (now Viceroy of Naples) urging the Prince's arrival at Messina where the three fleets were to meet. There was one letter which gave greater pleasure than any except the Pope's. Alessandro was to sail with Don John as the representative of his father Octavio Farnese, Duke of Parma.

Hardly were the letters read, a hurried dinner gulped down and fresh horses saddled, than Don John was off again, "with more swiftness and endurance than his followers cared about "! (Vanderhammer.) Sixty miles separated Cataluyd from Zaragoza, the scorched, scarred mountains like blood-stained steel, which had merged into a feverish nightmare on his last ride this way, a country desolate and cruel as a glimpse of the Inferno. Then, after the burning sun had sunk at last behind a spur of the Sierra de la Muela, crowned with the jagged battlements of its ruined Moorish castle, before swift night fell, there broke on eyes aching with dust and glare a welcome view of the wide green plain of the Ebro, running east to the sea, and the sharp, high minarets of the Aragonese capital.

It was two hours after dark when the Prince and his exhausted suite galloped past the Castillo de la Aljaferia. The narrow streets were a glare of flaming torches. Balconies, windows and streets were crowded with cheering, excited spectators,—past the cathedral of the Pilar, the wide-eaved Lonja and so, at last, to the palace where the Archbishop, Don Maximilian of Austria, was waiting in the full pomp of ecclesiastical purple to welcome his dusty, grimy young cousin, who had ridden a hundred and seventy-six miles in the last thirty hours.

Once more Don John awoke in the great room looking down on the seven-arched Puente de Piedra and beyond the sluggish, yellow river to the silver green of willows and olives, the dark spears of cypresses, and, on the far horizon, the snow-peaks of the Pyrenees. Sunday was no day of rest. It was difficult to snatch a few minutes from ceremonious receptions and speeches to slip into the cool dimness and kneel before the *Virgen del Pilar*. Perched on her silver pillar above the forest of flickering candles, she looked down with pitiful yet serene tenderness on the poor, foolish, sinful, sorrowful children whom her divine Son had given into her care at the foot of the Cross.

" My expedition is for the service of God and my lord,

the King, and for the sake of my reputation I cannot give it up." The words of the truant boy six years ago were as true now as when they had first been spoken, and the old Catalan prayer again went up. "*Virgen Santa, Madre mia, Trono de Gloria, Tú a la victoria nos llevarás.*" Thou wilt lead us on to victory. Again, as on that first cruise from Cartagena, she would be protectress and patroness. The blue banner of Guadelupe would again fly at the mast of the *Real*.

The fever which so often burned and froze his body burned now in mind. On Monday Don John rode out to meet the Archdukes, attended their reception and left Zaragoza in the afternoon. Soon after dawn on Wednesday after having ridden all night he dismounted at the gate of the great Benedictine monastery of Montserrat, perched high above the rushing Lobregat on those queer, haunted mountains.

Don John had been here before, six years ago, so it was like coming home, to be greeted as an old friend by the black monks. They offered the traditional hospitality with which, says St. Benedict, the guest should be treated as "if he were Christ Himself." Even in this high sanctuary there was noise and stir, for workmen were busy on the new church which was to be the gift of the King. But, away from hammering and stone-cutting in the cool clear air, in the dark shadow of pines and ilexes, under the piled, tumbled peaks that were like the fantastic battlements of an enchanted castle, in the caves of the hermits, in the Gothic cloisters, there was peace, "the peace which the world cannot give," the Benedictine "Pax."

As he listened in choir to the wavelike beat of plain chant Don John caught again the echoes of the call he had heard so clearly at Abrojo, a call drowned for so long now by the strife of tongues, by action and danger, by business and organization, by ambition and desire for fame. He walked to and fro on the terrace behind the church in the cool and quiet of evening. There was musing talk, alternating with long stretches of silence. The Abbot told his guest about Iñigo de Loyola, of whom Fray Juan had talked at Abrojo, how the Basque nobleman and soldier had stripped himself of all his rich clothes and, dressed only in a shapeless garment of sacking, had hung his sword and dagger on the Lady altar and, the last night before he left for Manresa, had kept vigil all night before her.

The sun set. Twilight fell. The bell rang for Compline. Don John knelt on in the darkness after the last plaintive notes of the "*Regina Coeli*" had sunk into silence, after the low rows of black-habited monks had filed out. To-morrow at dawn he would ride to Barcelona. Yet he had been reminded that, in the midst of bustle, organization, action, danger, perhaps death, he might still carry with him the Benedictine peace, even though it were "*Pax inter Spinas*," peace encircled by the Crown of Thorns. Like Ignatius of Loyola he knelt before the old statue of our Lady, "making a generous offering of himself for the Divine Service and imploring the help of the Queen of Heaven."

For the second time Don John saw below him the famous capital of Catalonia, which boasted that all its

houses were castles, all its women beauties. West of the
mole which circled the wide bay, rose the slope of Mont
Ivic, the tall watch-tower of its castle with a far view to
sea ; the Mediterranean, dreaming silver and sapphire in
the late afternoon sunshine, as Don John had seen it a
year ago from the heights of the Alpujarras. It was like
the decorations in the cabin of his beloved *Real*, " a sea
with halcyons' nests." Soon he would be afloat under
" the sky with stars and winds."

There was the usual ceremonious reception at the city
gates, the Viceroy, Don Hernando, the nobility, Luis de
Requesens, the magnates of Barcelona, who vied with
each other in their wealth and material splendour (Friday,
June 15). There was a motley crowd in the streets on the
way to the viceregal palace, soldiers waiting to embark,
sailors on leave from their ships in the harbour, traders
and merchants from other ports and countries whose ships
were loading and unloading at the quays, fishermen and
poor people. The sound of hammering and sawing in the
docks was drowned by the roar of cannon, the rattle of
musketry and excited cheers. There was the inevitable
mass of local beauties leaning from windows and balconies
to add their shrill applause and admiration of the young
hero whose black horse was too tired to prance at the
deafening din.

After Mass the next morning Don John summoned de
Requesens (his lieutenant in this campaign), the Viceroy
and de Soto. No need now of Councils. The Generalissimo could act on his own initiative. Orders were despatched to the Marquis of Santa Cruz to bring his galleys

from Cartagena ; to Sancho de Leyva at Mallorca to get ready to sail at once ; to the commander of the ships in harbour to complete his supplies of provisions for crews and troops. Juan de Soto was kept hard at work ; despatches to the King, to Colonna, to de Granvelle, letters to the various Italian princes who had sent their congratulations or promised help. Don John was busy inspecting ships, sailors, soldiers, slaves, docks and forts.

The young Archdukes arrived on June 25 and the next night the Mallorcan squadron came into harbour in line of battle. The three princes watched from the balcony of the viceregal palace the lovely sight as the long line of galleys, all dressed and illuminated, came round the lighthouse, greeted by thunder of cannon from the forts. The next few days were crammed with consultations with the newly arrived officers, the launching and arming of new battleships, after High Mass and solemn blessing, the overhauling and refitting of the *Real*, on which Don John entertained the Archdukes and officers to a banquet (July 1).

Preparations were well in hand for embarking the households, horses and baggage of the three princes, as well as two regiments of infantry. Don John hoped to be off towards the middle of the month. The sky seemed incredibly serene, when a courier arrived from the King. There was a long and complicated manual of instructions to Don John, with proper methods of respect and address to be used to every class of person, from Pope and Emperor to such unimportant entities as municipal councillors and the priors of small orders. Then came the dagger thrust,

forbidding the use to the Commander-in-Chief of the Holy
League on land and sea of the title with which practically
everyone addressed him. In future " Highness " must
invariably be superseded by a mere " Excellency."

Naturally a proud and sensitive nature was wounded to
the quick. Duty and glory were temporarily submerged
in anger and hurt feelings. There was a passionate outburst to the Prince of Eboli, " to tell you how hurt I was
and am about this, as it is only natural I should be. . . . I
was living in the surest confidence that His Majesty would
proclaim to the world his love for me and his great pleasure
in the honour which has been shown me. I confess I am
broken by the unjust treatment which lowers me to an
equality with everyone else, now when the world's eyes
are on me. I have several times thought of resigning . . .
since I have been shown so clearly that I am considered
unfit for my high command. . . . My services may not
deserve a laurel crown but what I have done seems to be
thought so little that it has lowered rather than raised me
in His Majesty's eyes." (July 8.)

Three days later he wrote to the King to reproach him
for the slight and for not dealing direct with him by word
of mouth. " God has made me Your Majesty's brother
so I must be forgiven for my plain-speaking and for
feeling deeply hurt that I am considered so little. I am
wondering whether it would please Your Majesty better if
I found some other way of serving you, since I am so much
out of favour in my present command." (July 11, 1571.)

Like most hot-tempered people Don John was not a
sulker. The storm blew over. Wounded feelings were

soothed. More pressing business and cooler consideration pushed the slight into the background. No one could suspect that this was the first prick of the poisoned blade which, in Antonio Perez's treacherous hand, was later to deal a mortal blow to de Escovedo and to his master's hopes.

The fleet weighed anchor at last. The long line of forty-seven galleys stood out to sea, headed by the *Real* with the three princes on board (July 20). The great golden Hercules shone above the sharp steel " spur." The tall gilt-bronze Admiral's lantern, with its four candles as thick as a man's wrist, swung above the high stern. Once more Don John was in the big stern cabin, with the little charred Crucifix above his berth and, round the walls, linked by gilded chains, the song of the sirens and the inspiration of golden young Alexander : " *Feliciter omnia.*"

XIX

ON THE WAY

(JULY 26—SEPTEMBER 16, 1571)

Don John's luck in weather at sea was almost always to be bad but for once halcyons ruled supreme and in six days' time the Italian coast was sighted. He stood on the bow of the *Real*, saw the bay of Genoa, with its background of low, bare hills and, behind them, the snow-peaks of the Ligurian Apennines. He recognized the long semicircle of white buildings, the jutting mole, with its tall campanile that protected the harbour as thickly fringed with masts as a pond with reeds, the taller tower of S. Pier d'Arena. His childish vision had been the memory of Genoa as he had seen it when, a child of four, he had sailed with Francisco Massuin and his wife with the fleet of the home-coming Philip.

Genoa was his first introduction to Italy, where he was to spend his time ashore during the next five years—except for the Tunis expedition and a flying visit to Spain. It was a complete contrast to the life he had known in Spain. A great mercantile republic, the powerful Genoese families of the city, whether they belonged to the St. Luke (" old ") faction or the St. Peter (" new ") party, owed their nobility to the success of ancestors (more or less remote) in business and to wealth made or inherited. The dominant building of the city was the Palazzo di San Giorgio, home of the world-famous bank, its three stories, with their pointed arches, topped by battlements ornamented with the red Cross of St. George on a white ground, the arms of the city too.

Culture, like that of modern Britain and North America, was built on a material foundation. Life was splendid, colourful, rich, selfish and unscrupulous. The Renaissance in Spain and Italy differed fundamentally. In Spain it sprang from a Catholic soil and remained within the frame of Catholic dogma and doctrine. In Italy it was neo-pagan, born in a corrupt society and, for all its magnificence, material and mental, showing the phosphorescence of decay inevitable in all society and culture founded on other than spiritual values.

It was in this atmosphere, so alien to all he had hitherto known, that Don John was to make his first international appearance and to spend the rest of his life but for its last two years. Not that he considered such matters. He was too much of a Spaniard and a soldier to be anything but a realist in action, dreamer though he might be over the future. His five days at Genoa were too crammed to allow time for thought or rest. He was housed in the palace of the Dorias, with its marble façade, its three stories of wide loggias, its triple pointed arches, twisted pillars and honeycomb lattices. The terrace, cooled by many fountains, looked over the sea. Halls and passages were decorated with paintings commemorating the naval exploits of the old Doge. Prevesa and last year's exploit of his nephew did not figure in these glorifications.

There was a regal entertainment on July 29. Fifty-two of the noblest beauties of Genoa, dressed in crimson and

white to honour the hero, sat down to the banquet in
honour of the Prince, the Archdukes and the Italian rulers'
representatives. The ladies were slightly reminiscent of
an animated pack of cards and, if they were disappointed
at the cool politeness with which the Generalissimo acknowledged their charms, there was nothing but wholehearted
admiration of his prowess in the ballroom. One of the
suite of Antonio Tiepolo, Venetian ambassador on his
way to Madrid, wrote of Don John : "A young man of
active and well-trained body, fair hair, a handsome and
attractive face. . . . The Archdukes danced fairly well
but everyone was amazed and delighted by the grace and
agility of his Highness."

Balls and banquets were only brief breathing spaces in
a rush of work. Envoys had to be sent to all the Italian
princes who were supporting the League. The Conde de
Priego departed for Rome, on a personal mission to the
Pope from Don John. The Archdukes started for Vienna,
with a very sad farewell on the part of Ernest, who had a
romantic devotion for his young uncle. There were receptions to welcome the princes who were accompanying the
expedition : Francesco de Medici, son of the Grand Duke
of Tuscany (who three years before had suggested the
idea of the League), Francesco Maria, heir of the Duke of
Urbino, and Alessandro, representing his father, Octavio
Duke of Parma—all with numerous suites to be billeted
and embarked.

At last Genoa was left (daybreak, August 1, 1571).
Santa Cruz, with the Neapolitan galleys, had already sailed
to take the Italian and German troops on board at Spezia.

As the fleet lay to at night Don John was free to pour out
to Alessandro all those hopes and disappointments, ambition and dreams of glory which no one else could understand
as well. Alessandro was as slim and handsome as ever in
spite of a wife and three children, with the charming, suave,
Machiavellian manner which was all the fashion in Italy,
with the old mocking tenderness and that salutary tang of
cynicism without which life is as insipid as a dish without
salt. Though not two years older than his uncle he was
so much older in intellect and knowledge of the world,
in quick judgement and a mistrust of pleasant appearances.
Don John seemed still a child to him, in spite of his twenty-
four years—a child in his dreams, in his passion for glory,
his crusading spirit, his trust in men and fate, his utter
lack of interest in abstract and philosophic speculation.
Don John was the afterglow of the Middle Ages, Alessandro the forerunner of the modern spirit.

The nights were still, with a silver, heavenly beauty,
the sea a gleaming wonder of phosphorescence, dolphins
gambolling as they had done on the Ferrarese cuirass at
Villagarcia which had been Don John's first armour.
Spezia, Elba, Civitavecchia and Ostia lay astern. Tomorrow the *Real* would make Naples. There would be the
usual state reception by the Viceroy, the usual roar of
cannon and cheering crowds. Then would come the presentation of the Banner of the Holy League to the Commander of its forces.

Robert the Wise's church of Santa Chiara was crowded
for the presentation. The banner hung at the Gospel side

of the altar, its blue folds weighted by great silk and gold tassels. On the altar lay the baton, three bound in one by golden chains, the handle jewelled. Both had been specially blessed by Pius V in person. On a high brocaded throne on the altar steps sat Don John, in full armour, his silver-steel cuirass elaborately ornamented with gold relief, the Collar of the Golden Fleece over it. By him were Alessandro and Francesco Maria. When the Pontifical Mass was over Don John advanced into the sanctuary and knelt to receive the tokens of command from the hands of Cardinal de Grenvelle, Viceroy of Naples. The Cardinal's sonorous voice rolled through the church as he repeated the words in Latin, Spanish and Italian.

"Take this symbol of the Word made Man. Take this living sign of the Holy Faith of which thou art defender and champion in this holy enterprise. May it bring thee a glorious victory over the enemy that by thy hand the power of the infidel may be broken."

"Amen." Don John's answer rang clear. "Amen. Amen," thundered choir and congregation.

The procession rode down the splendid street of Pedro de Toledo to the harbour, in the burning midday sun. The banner was borne by a rider on a white horse. Two other riders held out the sides of the banner so as to display the great golden Crucifix surrounded by the arms of Spain and Venice, of the Pope and Don John, all linked by golden chains. Don John rode behind it in his golden armour and helmet, his big black horse armed too in steel and gold, with trappings of crimson and gold that swept the dusty ground.

A little breeze fluttered the banner as it was carried on board the *Real*. The big guns of ships and forts, the crews of the galleys, the soldiers on the quays, saluted. The Holy War had begun.

On the evening of August 23 the fleets of the Papacy and Venice cleared the harbour of Messina to welcome the Commander and his thirty galleys. The twelve ships of the Papal fleet were black from topmast to waterline, sails, rigging and hulls all in deepest mourning for Colonna's daughter, the Duchess of Mondragone. The superstitious Sicilian populace set up a wail of horror at such an evil omen but, like most omens, it was to prove false. It would be Veniero, the Venetian leader, not Colonna, who provided the dark shadow in the future.

The next morning the three admirals met on the *Real*. Colonna, eleven years older than Don John, had wide experience both in war and diplomacy and united good judgement to tact and courteous manners. He knew the Venetian character and methods, having served last year in conjunction with their fleet and then gone on an embassy to Venice. Sebastian Veniero, the Venetian leader, was a complete contrast. He was old, bad-tempered, jealous of his own authority and of the interests of his native city. He was also ugly and untidy, with straggling white hair and beard, and his Venetian dialect sounded uncouth to the Roman Colonna. Veniero gives an account of the meeting in a report written later to the Council of Ten. Don John evidently wasted little time on preliminaries.

" His Highness told us that the first thing to be considered was the force at our disposal. For his part he had eighty-four galleys, seven thousand Spanish and six thousand Italian troops, all in good trim. Marc Antonio Colonna said that he had few galleys but all in good condition."

Veniero did his utmost to put a good face on his own report but was forced to confess that his fleet was only forty-eight strong and that he was expecting reinforcements both of men and ships. Don John, who had already heard something of the shocking state of the Venetian fleet, put the pertinent question: "How many soldiers do you allow for each galley?" Veniero, unwilling to disclose that his man power was fifty per cent. below par, shuffled: "Forty to fifty, for our slaves can be trusted with arms." As the proper number of troops for each ship averaged a hundred Don John offered some of his soldiers to make up the numbers and asked for a written statement of provisions and stores required and suggestions from the two leaders for the conduct of the campaign.

Business over for the moment, there was the inevitable reception to be faced, even more gorgeous and flattering than usual. He mounted the magnificent horse with silver trappings which was the gift of the city and, as he rode under a triumphal arch which, in a rich riot of pagan gods and Christian saints, represented his triumph over the Turk, he turned and exclaimed angrily to Requesens, who was riding just behind him.

"This premature boast is disgusting. Please God I shall not have to pay for it."

Like the Queen of Sheba, Don John found that " the half was not told him " about the disgraceful state of the Venetian galleys, which he inspected after he had reviewed the twelve Papal ships and the three from Malta. He had begun a correspondence with Don Garcia de Toledo, who, as Viceroy of Sicily, had relieved (though late in the day) Malta after the famous siege of 1565. The old man was now taking a course of baths at Poggio in Tuscany for the gout which had crippled him, but his pen was still active and advice was substituted for the active service he would have preferred.

" Yesterday I boarded the Venetian flagship and inspected their galleys," Don John wrote to him from Messina on August 30. " The shocking state both of soldiers and sailors is incredible. True, they have arms and artillery but, as war needs men, I am horrified when I see with what stuff the world expects me to win a great victory. It is unlucky that fleets are judged by numbers not by condition. . . . Even worse than the disgraceful condition of the Venetian ships is the insubordination of the officers. No wonder they are not anxious to fight."

The Venetians were not the only people who showed no desire to back the Generalissimo in his determination for swift action. The Spanish officers, with the exception of Don John himself and de Requesens, favoured a policy of caution and delay. They were, of course, supported by Gianandrea Doria, who wished to preserve his galleys and the large rent paid for them by Philip in money borrowed at a high rate of interest from the Genoese bankers. Two of the Italian leaders, too, argued that the fleet was not yet strong enough to take the offensive. There was friction and discord on every side. Colonna was unpopular with the Spaniards, who thought him too favourable to the Venetians. Enemies did their best to poison the Commander-in-Chief's mind against him. Don John, with his usual frankness, told Colonna of these efforts and of their failure and the two became friendly. Unluckily some tactless expression in a letter of Philip's upset Colonna as much as the instructions at Barcelona had upset Don John. Marc Antonio poured out his feelings in a letter to the Jesuit General, Francisco Borja. " It would be a great relief to me to throw up the whole business. . . . Don John knows and will see how well I serve him, but I cannot bear to be told [by the King] to do my duty as if I and my house were not accustomed to do it."

There had been quarrels too between Spanish and Italian troops, whose mutual hatred had better have been kept for the enemy. Swords had been drawn and blood spilt in the streets of Messina before Don John's arrival, but the punishment of the gallows for members of both nations had somewhat cooled hot blood.

Spanish and Venetian reinforcements continued to arrive. Early in September the fleet was at full strength and was reviewed by Don John. It was the greatest Christian force the world had ever seen, organized and under one command. Over three hundred sail and eighty thousand men were under the orders of the Prince who was only twenty-four. The Spanish fleet numbered a hundred and sixty-four sails, the Venetian a hundred and twenty-six, the Papal eighteen. There were fifty thousand sailors and galley slaves (the average crew of a big ship being about a hundred and fifty) and thirty thousand troops.

A full Council was called on board the flagship after the review (September 10) and was attended by about seventy officers. Colonna and Veniero spoke in favour of an immediate attack on the Turk, as they had arranged with Don John to do. Two Italians, Doria and Corgnia, urged caution and delay. There was some argument and the matter seemed in the balance when Don John broke in with a few abrupt words.

"Enough, *señores*. . . . All we have now to do is to hasten our departure and to sail in search of victory."

It was Galera over again, the swift blade cutting away the tangle of difficulties and delays. All was arranged. Provisions and stores had been shipped. The garrisons of the Venetian ships had been supplemented by Spanish troops, which, as might have been foreseen, was to lead to trouble. The ships, galleys, galleasses and frigates were ready to sail. The order of sailing, the position of every ship both during the voyage and in battle, had been carefully drawn up under Don John's personal supervision. "I consider them excellent and I strongly recommend them to the attention of future commanders-in-chief," is the verdict of Admiral de la Gravière in his book on the battle of Lepanto. Every captain received a memorandum showing him his position in the order of battle and on the voyage. It had been decided by the three leaders that the three fleets should not be kept as separate entities but their units mixed together in the three squadrons of centre, right and left wings, advance guard and reserve, the right wing, distinguished by green pennants, to be under Doria, the left, with yellow pennants, under Barbarigo (a Venetian).

Not only had Don John worked out all the dispositions for going into battle and superintended the embarkation of men and stores ; he was writing frequently to Garcia de Toledo and referring to the veteran endless questions of tactics. He received detailed and practical directions in return. " Arquebuses should never be fired till you are near enough to be splashed with your enemy's blood," wrote the old man in answer to a question when to fire : " The most experienced sea-captains say that the crash of a ship's beak and the first roar of her guns should be heard at the same time. But your men must learn not to think about the enemy, nor to wonder who is to fire first, but only to fire when your Highness gives the order."

For five days after the Council a terrible storm of wind, torrents of rain and lightning made it impossible for the fleet to sail. The approach of their departure had healed divisions between men. A wild enthusiasm for the Holy War on which they were about to start, the arrival of Cardinal Odescalchi, the Papal Legate, and the fleet chaplains turned Messina into a holy city. The Nuncio brought to Don John a large *Lignum Crucis*, enclosed in a silver reliquary flanked by angels, and an *Angus Dei* for each man, as well as proclaiming a Jubilee. Six Spanish-speaking Jesuits were appointed by Father Nadal (acting General during the absence in Spain of Borja) as chaplains to the Spanish fleet. The chaplains of the Papal fleet were Capuchins, those of Genoa, Venice and Savoy Franciscans. On the *Real* were three priests, Fray Miguel Servia, Don

John's private chaplain, and two Jesuits, Fathers Francisco Briones and Cristobal Rodriguez. The last had been a captive of the Turks and, after his release, had devoted himself to work among the galley slaves at Malaga during the Morisco rebellion. He was a personal friend of the Holy Father's and brought a private message to Don John : " That he should not hesitate to go into battle, because, in the Name of God, he was promised victory." There was the rumour too that the Pope had said that, after victory, he himself would see that the young Commander-in-Chief would be provided with an independent kingdom, which he would have earned by his services to Christendom.

Astrain describes the religious fervour which swept fleet and city. Churches and confessionals were besieged. Not sailors and soldiers alone frequented the Sacraments. Even the wretched galley slaves were unchained from their benches and marched through the streets under strong escort to the Jesuit College. There the students were kept busy preparing them for Confession (ten priests being continually in the confessionals) and then for Communion.

According to the order of the day on the *Real* the men were paraded at certain hours when one of the Jesuits read prayers and gave an address or instruction. Finally, there was a general procession to the cathedral, with its unimposing flat-topped façade and its beautiful jasper pillars inside. There the Nuncio, in his scarlet robes, proclaimed for all engaged on this enterprise the same pardon and indulgence as had been granted to the Crusaders who had captured the Holy Sepulchre from the infidel.

The storm abated. On the evening of September 15 Don John ordered the cumbrous Venetian galleasses to go on, towed by oared galleys. Early the next morning the whole fleet sailed. The Nuncio, standing on the prow of a brigantine at the end of the mole, gave the Papal blessing to each ship as it passed. At the yard of each ship of Don John's squadron was a blue pennant. The *Real* herself flew the blue banner of our Lady of Guadelupe. The Pope had sent word that the banner of the Holy League was not to be flown till the fleet went into action. As the *Real* passed the mole and the Nuncio's hand was raised in blessing, crew, troops and nobles knelt, the figure of Don John in his golden armour alone on the high prow.

The snowcap of Etna glittered in the morning sun. The wind filled the sails. " The forest of masts " sped south before the favouring wind. The last Crusade had begun.

XX

BATTLE ARRAY

(SEPTEMBER 16—OCTOBER 6, 1571)

The religious revival which had swept the Spanish fleet at Messina had sent nearly every man to Confession and Communion that he might be eligible for the Plenary Indulgence proclaimed by the Nuncio. It was heightened by the story from Rome telling how Pius V had selected Don John of Austria for the leadership of the Holy League. The server of the Mass in the Pope's private chapel had been surprised by the old Dominican's sudden pause in the middle of the last Gospel. After a prolonged silence the Pope had murmured, as if in a dream : " *Fuit homo missus a Deo, cui nomen erat Joannes.*" Then, after another pause, he had repeated the words like a clarion call to battle : " There was a man sent from God whose name was John."

If the Venetians did not share this fervour their indignation was roused by relics of recent Turkish raids down the east coast of the Adriatic. When Don John landed in Corfu (September 28) after a long and stormy passage round the south of Italy, he found the remains of sacrilege which reminded him of the Alpujarras. Churches and houses had been sacked. Altars were defiled, Crucifixes smashed. Holy pictures had been used as targets for bullets or had been hacked with scimitars.

Another Council was summoned, for the Commander-in-Chief was bound, by the terms of the Treaty, to consult the leaders of the other fleets before taking any decisive action. Reports of the strength and whereabouts of the Turkish fleet varied in every detail. It had dispersed for the year after sacking Corfu. Ali Pasha, the admiral, was at Prevesa (forty miles south of Corfu) with his whole fleet. He was besieging Zante (an island south of the Gulf of Corinth). Prisoners ransomed from the Turks described the fleet as three hundred strong and said that Ali Pasha had withdrawn to Lepanto (in the Gulf of Corinth) while the corsair Aluch Ali, Viceroy of Algiers, had gone home with his squadron.

Unanimity is always the rarest of virtues in Councils and Committees. It would have been almost a miracle in this case. The usual arguments were advanced in favour of caution and delay ; enmity of various contingents in the Christian fleet, its lack of practice in combined manœuvres, the overwhelming strength of the Turkish navy, never yet defeated, the disgrace to Christendom if the disasters of Prevesa and Gerbi were repeated. Some suggested attacking Navarino. Others thought it best to besiege some weakly fortified Turkish town.

It was enough to drive a saint to distraction, and Don John was far from showing any signs of sanctity. He was impatient, self-willed, proud, sensitive, hot-tempered, as well as young and entirely inexperienced in naval warfare. But he was the champion of Christendom. His youthful dream had been realized. He knew his vocation, felt himself a torch held aloft to light the way to victory and consumed by a flame of zeal in which desire for personal glory was not the main element.

Colonna, Barbarigo and Santa Cruz supported him, and the next day (September 29) the fleet left Corfu for Gomeniza (on the Albanian coast). Here it was joined by the scouting squadron under Gil de Andrade, who brought definite news that Ali Pasha was in Lepanto harbour. Some Greek fishermen reported that there were only two hundred Turkish sail and much sickness on board so that "Victory was assured to the Christians." That they had furnished Ali Pasha with equally cheering (and remunerative) news was of course unknown. A general review of the whole Christian fleet was held. Don John sailed through it in a frigate, boarded and personally inspected the more important ships. All seemed serene, battle and victory near at hand when an event occurred which all but wrecked fleet and League.

Don John was enjoying one of his rare moments of peace and leisure on the *Real*, amusing himself and the young Prince of Urbino with the tricks of his little pet monkey. Suddenly an outbreak of shots and angry shouts from one of the Venetian galleys broke the peace of the bay. Everyone rushed to the bulwarks to see what was wrong. In a few minutes Paolo Sforza, colonel of the regiment which had supplemented the troops on the Venetian ship, boarded the *Real*. Some of the Spaniards had refused to obey orders. Veniero had threatened to sink Sforza's ship if he interfered. At that moment the bodies of four Spaniards were seen swinging from the yard-arm of the Venetian galley.

Don John went berserk at this unspeakable insult to his authority and his country. His eyes blazed. His hand clutched the hilt of his sword. He strode to and fro on the poop " like a caged lion with an arrow in its side." The torrent of fury which poured from his lips was applauded and added to by the Spanish officers with him. The cursed Veniero should be brought on board the *Real* in chains—flung into the filth of the hold with sick and dying slaves—be hanged to the mast—Spanish ships must open fire on the Venetian and send them to the bottom.

Mercifully, before anything had been done, Colonna came on board with the fat, whiskered, cautious Barbarigo. Coolly and tactfully he soothed and explained, emphasized the disaster to the League if precipitate action were taken. Don John, white and shaking with rage, turned his back and leant against the bulwark, looking out to sea. There was a breathless silence, broken only by the whimper of the frightened monkey, while the fate of the League hung in the balance. At last Don John turned and faced them, still deathly pale, blood on his under lip.

" I know, better than any of you, my duty to my brother the King and to God Who chose me for this undertaking."

He went on to say that he would not exact vengeance and so wreck the League, but that never again must Veniero dare attend a Council nor show himself on board the *Real*. Barbarigo must replace him (October 3).

Don John was alone in his cabin at last (October 6). For two days fog and contrary winds had made all attempts at progress vain. The Turks, like the English after the

Armada, might have asserted that God was arranging the weather according to their desires. News of their capture of Famagosta and the inhuman barbarity with which the infidels had treated their prisoners had only just reached the Christian fleet, two months after the events, and had roused the Venetians to a fierce desire for vengeance. Only the elements remained enemies.

Actium lay astern, the gulf which had seen the igno-minious flight of Antony, his courage and manhood rotted by unbridled lust, as Aben Umeya's had been. Prevesa too had been passed, with its rankling memory of Doria's baseness. The ships strained at their anchors in the south wind, which drove the fog before it and had baffled all efforts of the slaves who lay now, broken and exhausted, in the fetid poison of the hold. Now and again the coast of Cephalonia showed through the mist, and the hills of Ithaca, as when Ulysses had seen them but not known them for home. The moon, from behind the clouds, cast a pale spectral light on the white mist, driven north like tattered wraiths.

Don John pulled his furred gown tighter about him as he paced to and fro, once more going over the endless details which had been so carefully thought out and written down. When the fleet went into battle the six Venetian galleasses were to be towed behind the vanguard under Juan de Cardona. They were floating fortresses with heavy guns, but inert as dead leviathans without a favouring wind. The *Real* was to be flanked on the right by the flagship of Colonna, on the left by that of Veniero. The left wing (sixty-four strong) was under the command of

Barbarigo, the right (sixty-three) under Doria, the reserve
(thirty-five) under Santa Cruz. The Genoese flagship,
with Alessandro Farnese, his hundred and fifty soldiers
and fifty noble volunteers on board, would be left centre.
One cannon shot was the order to prepare for battle, a
square white pennant to be run up to the peak and the
standard of the League to be broken at the mainmast. The
Pope's request that it should not be flown till the day of
battle had been obeyed.

Don John looked again at the papers which Juan de
Soto had left in neat piles. He could think of nothing that
had been forgotten. Cannon and muskets had been over-
hauled, swords, daggers and axes sharpened. Stores of
bread, biscuit and wine were ready to be distributed.
Out-of-the-way corners had been assigned for the surgeons
with their bandages, dressings and instruments. Bulwarks
had been strengthened and heightened to protect the men
against the enemy's fire, and netted against boarders.
The Christian slaves were to have their chains knocked off,
be provided with arms and promised freedom after victory.
This was a daring innovation and another flashed into Don
John's mind now. The long steel-plated " spurs " which
protruded ten or fourteen feet beyond the ships' bows
made the galleys harder to handle, made hand-to-hand
fighting and boarding more difficult. They must be sawn
off in the morning. He made a note, knelt below the charred
Crucifix which hung over his berth. Like the thoughts of
most men in the fleet that night, his went home, back to
Villagarcia, where Doña Magdalena was in the chapel,
praying for him.

As he flung himself on his bed the Figure on the Cross seemed to stir in the shadows cast by the swinging silver lamp. The little monkey, shivering, crept into his arms. His thoughts flickered to and fro like the lamp flame. Fray Juan de Calahorra and his quiet, confident promise at Abrojo : " It will make your name greater than any in Europe." His talks since they had left Messina with the Jesuit Father Cristobal Rodriguez, in whom he had recognized the same selfless and simple directness as in Fray Juan, that mark of true sanctity which consists in the emptying out of self that the soul may be filled with God. Montserrat, its still, clear air the home of peace, which, legend said, had housed the Holy Grail, the symbol under which the Middle Ages had figured the eternal quest of the human heart for God.

Suddenly he was conscious of a change, a stir. The wind had veered. The fog had lifted. The moon shone. At two in the morning of Sunday, October 7, 1571, the fleet weighed anchor and set sail for Lepanto.

XXI

LEPANTO

(Sunday, October 7, 1571)

Very much the same scenes had been enacted in the
Turkish fleet as in the Christian. The older members of
the Council—among them Pertev, a soldier of fortune
commanding the Janissaries and Spahis on board—advised
caution : they should remain safe under the guns of the
fort. Scirocco, Pasha of Alexandria, supported him ;
Hassan, son of Barbarossa, most famous of all the Mediterranean corsairs, was all in favour of a dashing attack. Ali
Pasha, the Turkish admiral, like Don John, was young,
enthusiastic, ambitious and, with Hassan's help, he carried
the day. The policy of Aluch, corsair leader who had
risen to be Viceroy of Algeria and was the ablest seaman of
the lot, was apparently in support of Ali, provided that the
Christian fleet was not too strong. Like Gianandrea Doria,
he had his pocket as well as his glory to consider. Otherwise the Turkish admiral had none under his command
who fought for anything but the Prophet. Every man
went into battle with the sure conviction that death in
war against the infidel ensured an immediate admission into
Paradise. On the other hand victory meant a reward as
material in this world as the fleshly joys promised in the
next.

Ali Pasha, unlike most of his fellow-countrymen, was

cultured and kind-hearted, a generous foe and a sympathetic master. He had brought with him his two sons, Ahmed Bey, a youth of sixteen, fierce, fanatical and arrogant, and Mahomet Bey, a boy of thirteen, more like himself. The mother of one of them was a sister of the Sultan, Selim. Ali himself dreamed of a return to Constantinople as glorious as, though less barbaric than, that of Mustafa who had sailed up the Bosphorus after the capture of Famagosta with the stuffed skin of Bragadino swinging at his yard-arm. The great blue Banner of the League would be a worthy offering to lay at the feet of Selim as he sat drinking in his harem, hair, beard, face and hands scarlet as those of some blood-drenched idol.

The Turkish fleet weighed anchor early on the morning of Sunday, October 7, 1571, left the bay of Lepanto and, with a strong east wind in their favour, were soon passing the marshes of Missolonghi, where shallow sea and malarial land were inextricably mingled. Ali Pasha might well be proud of his fleet of about three hundred ships, many built in the shipyards of the Golden Horn by skilled Venetian shipwrights. The troops on board consisted of the famous Janissaries, said to be the fiercest, best disciplined and best paid troops in the world, Spahis, cavalry who, Pertev thought, would show to disadvantage in naval fighting, and volunteers. Selim was in the proud position of being able to call to his standard eighty thousand horse from his European dominions and fifty thousand from Asia. It had been his father's boast that he could fight for eighty years on the accumulated treasure in his exchequer, and Selim, in contrast to the Spanish rulers (tottering chronically

on the brink of bankruptcy and sometimes falling over it),
saved a quarter of his yearly income of eight million ducats
(£1,800,000). The fleet, in half-moon formation, extended
nearly from the Albanian marshes on the north to the
deeper water under Cape Papas.

The Christian fleet, which had left the Straits of Cephalonia at two that morning, had reached Cape Scrophia, at
the entrance to the Gulf, when an Italian pilot, sent out on
a swift frigate by Don John, returned with news that the
whole enemy fleet was in sight. " Out with your claws,"
he muttered to Colonna : " For the day will be a tough
one."

At once a cannon shot sounded from the poop of the
Real and the square white flag ran up to her yard-arm :
the signal to manœuvre into line of battle. This was not
so easy. The slaves had been rowing against the wind
for the last five hours. The right wing, under Doria, had
to make a wide semicircle and the centre to sweep out
from the left wing under Barbarigo to make the right turn
and face the enemy. The two fleets approached each other
in " line ahead " (every ship directly astern of the one in
front), and when within striking distance turned to form
" line abreast " (each ship turning at right angles so as to
be broadside on to her neighbour).

Even at this eleventh hour there had been talk of a
Council, silenced by Don John with the curt words :
" The time for talk is over, now is the time to fight."
Unarmed, with an ivory Crucifix in his hand, he passed
in a swift frigate along the centre and right wing, calling a

friendly greeting to old Veniero who already stood,
armed, on the prow of his ship, shouting a few blunt words
to the men who crowded the bulwarks : " Remember,
men, that we are fighting for the Faith and no coward will
win heaven." The supply of money, medals, scapulars
and rosaries with which he and de Soto had been supplied,
was soon exhausted. Even his cap and gloves were
snatched by enthusiastic hero-worshippers. Bare-headed,
bare-handed he boarded the *Real* and ran down to his
cabin to change into armour.

The " spurs " of the ships had been hurriedly sawn off.
The Christian slaves had been unchained and armed. In
many galleys the rowing benches had been cleared amid-
ships to give more room for the soldiers. The surgeons
stood by tables loaded with their gruesome paraphernalia.
Bread, wine and biscuits were ready for sailors, soldiers
and slaves. Don John appeared on the high, gilded prow
of the *Real*, a glittering figure in golden armour and helmet,
the Golden Fleece round his neck, the *Lignum Crucis* on
his breast. He knelt below the little Crucifix from Villagarcia, which hung on the mast. There was dead silence
through the Christian fleet as every man knelt at his post,
while Franciscans and Capuchins in their brown habits
and Jesuits in their black gowns, Crucifix in hand, sprinkled
ships and men with holy water and recited the General
Absolution in the Hour of Death.

From the Turkish fleet came a bloodcurdling noise,
screeches, yells, the clash of cymbals and of scimitars on
shields, the bellow of horns, the crackle of musketry.
Then it was blown away. The wind had changed, dropped

then veered due west, in favour of the Christians and against the Turks.

It was a quarter to twelve and a hot sun shone on the sea, already calm, as the great blue Standard of the League ran up to the mainmast of the *Real* and the first shot of battle was fired from one of the heavy guns on the Venetian galleasses in front of the main line. It carried away the highest of the three lanterns which marked Ali Pasha's supreme command—an omen greeted with cheers by the Christians. The fire of these floating fortresses was so deadly that Ali ordered his line to open and avoid them, a manœuvre which caused some confusion in his fleet.

The left wing, under Barbarigo, was the first to come to grips with the right Turkish wing under Scirocco, as Barbarigo's ships, being near the axle of the wheel, had less distance to sail. The two flagships of Don John and Ali Pasha, distinguished by their greater size and more elaborate decorations, made for each other. They crashed so violently that the " spur " of the *Sultana* reached the fourth rowing bench of the *Real*. The superior height of the Turkish ship was a disadvantage, for her fire went high through the rigging, while that of the Spaniards riddled the enemy near the waterline. The impact of the shock separated the ships. Ali came on again. There was a grinding roar as the ships crashed broadside on, oars snapping and bulwarks cracking. Grappling irons were flung and for nearly two hours the two ships formed one bloody battleground. Twice the Spaniards boarded the *Sultana* and reached her mainmast. Each time they were repulsed. Forces were about even, for Don John had on board four hundred soldiers, Ali three hundred Janissaries with muskets and a hundred archers.

In the thick of the fight de Requesens begged Don John to take cover. He might have known better than to waste time and words. As the Spaniards were driven back the second time, contesting every inch, and the Turks almost boarded the *Real*, Don John, sword in hand, was at the foot of the mainmast in defence of the Standard. One slash from a Turkish scimitar and the sacred symbol of the League would have been down. Ali Pasha too was fighting. From the prow of his ship he shot arrows into the *Real*, which like all the other vessels engaged was bristling with arrows, as one witness said " like porcupines with bristles up to attack."

Once more the Spaniards were on the *Sultana*, falling on gangways and decks which had been greased so as to afford no hold to their heavy boots and which were now more slippery with blood. A ball struck Ali in the forehead. He fell. A Spaniard hauled down the sacred Standard of the Prophet, green, with the name of Allah and texts from the Koran embroidered in gold. The Cross flew from the mast of the Turkish flagship. A great shout of triumph went up from the Christians. But the battle was yet far from won.

The engagement had become a mêlée of single combats, the tale of each one an epic of heroism, in which every great name of Spain and Italy was decked with fresh glory. Alessandro Farnese, with only one soldier, leapt from the Genoese flagship onto a Turkish galley and captured it. The Prince of Urbino, two years younger than Don John, fought like a veteran. Barbarigo fell, mortally wounded with an arrow through the eye. His nephew was killed going to his assistance. Michele Bonelli, the Pope's nephew and a young brother of Cardinal Alessandrino, was spattered by the brains of a man beside him and calmly went on reloading his musket. But not princes, nobles and leaders only won fame. Soldiers and sailors displayed equal heroism. One, whose eye was pierced by an arrow, pulled out eye and arrow, tied a handkerchief round the bleeding hollow and went on fighting. Another, whose hand was mutilated by the premature explosion of a bomb, seized a knife, hacked off the hand and returned to his post. De Requesens captured the Turkish galley with Ali Pasha's two sons.

On the left wing and in the centre the tide of battle ran in favour of the Christians. The Turks of Scirocco's squadron, disheartened by the death of their leader, began to jump overboard, to swim and wade ashore. Colonna had come to the rescue of the *Real*, surrounded by half a dozen Turkish ships. The *Sultana* was captured. It was now about two o'clock and ships were a terrible sight. Sereno describes them without rigging, bulwarks or oars, decks running with blood, piled with corpses, while men continued to fight and kill one another even in the sea.

Meanwhile Doria on the Christian right had all but brought disaster. He made a wide sweep to take up his position, to be longer getting into touch with the enemy, so as to save his galleys, said his enemies. Aluch, his opponent, took advantage of this in a flash, put his squadron at the gap left between centre and right, surrounded and captured the isolated galleys of the Knights of Malta and

would have taken the Christian centre in the rear had not
Santa Cruz with the reserve, and then the *Real*, come to
the rescue. After a long struggle, Aluch, seeing he was
worsted, cut the Maltese flagship adrift and escaped with
thirteen of his Algerian corsairs. He returned to lay at the
Sultan's feet the black banner of the Knights with its
eight-pointed white crosses, to be rewarded with the post
of High-Admiral and to die in his bed in his luxurious
palace at Constantinople.

If Doria gained no laurels in the battle, there was on
board the *Marquesa*, one of his ships, a poor but well-
born young Spaniard, the same age as Don John, whose
name is a household word through the world, though that
of every other combatant is forgotten. Miguel de Cervantes
rose from his sick bed saying he would rather die by the
enemy's hand than of a fever, fought all day and received
two wounds in the chest and one from which he lost the
use of his left hand. His right remained whole to write
the story of Don Quixote de la Mancha.

It was five o'clock when the battle was over. Great black
clouds were piling up in the west and the sea was beginning
to heave ominously. Obviously the sunny day with its
favouring wind was to be succeeded by a night of storm.
Don John gave orders to put about and made for the port
of Petala a few miles to the north.

The scene of the battle was a terrible sight. The sea,
red with blood, was covered with débris of oars, rigging,
plunder, and floating bodies. The glare of burning galleys
reflected the stormy sunset, which touched the low hills
too with the hues of fire and blood. The sunset was

strange as those of Toledo, when real and unreal, visible and invisible are interwoven and the stage set for immortal actors to play out the queer tragedy of human life.

Don John went down to his cabin. The cut on his ankle which he had not even noticed in the excitement of battle was still bleeding and had begun to ache. He felt glad to have shed his blood, even in so small a way, during the day which had been crowned by the triumph of Christ over Mahomet.

Up above, the flicker of lightning showed torn sails, splintered bulwarks, bloody decks piled with corpses. Down here, in the yellow light of the silver lamp, swinging with the roll of the ship, all was quiet. The tattered green Standard of the Prophet lay across a chair. The monkey was curled on the bed, fast asleep. Don John knelt before the charred Crucifix, back in its usual place, and, after his thanksgiving, remembered Montserrat. "*Pax inter Spinas.*"

XXII

LAUREL CROWNS

(October 8—end of 1571)

There was little sleep that night on board any of the battered Christian ships. The sea was crashing on the rocky shores of Ithaca and Cephalonia. The thunder was pealing. The lightning flared more luridly than the dying glare of burning galleys as they were swallowed by the blood-red sea. Men went from ship to ship, to hear and tell tales of almost incredible heroism, of apparent miracles, to embrace friends whom they had feared dead, to mutter a brief prayer for those who had won immortality.

There was the Maltese flagship, captured and rescued, nothing but the piled corpses of crew, officers and Turks on board, except two knights left for dead and the Prior, riddled with wounds. There was the big Crucifix on the mainmast of the *Real*, under the blue Standard. A Turkish ball had come straight at it. The old carved wooden Figure had swung to the right to avoid the enemy shot and remained twisted to one side, the Arms askew. Don John's little monkey had also done her part. The Villa-garcia Crucifix had been hung on the mast above the cabins. Arrows had struck all round it, then one had pierced the wood of the Cross, another below the left breast. Monecilla had dashed up the rigging, chattering with fury, had pulled out the arrows, broken them with paws and teeth and flung them into the sea. The Banner of the League too was untouched, though wood and rigging round it were bristling with arrows and torn with shot. The green banner of the Prophet, though, now on the *Real*, was shot nearly to ribbons, so that the verses from the Koran and the thirty thousand names of Allah were all but indecipherable. How suddenly too the wind had changed in answer to Christian prayers. " He blew with His winds and they were scattered," murmured some of the chaplains, not knowing that they were anticipating the boast of Drake's men seventeen years later. Old seamen discussed the sawing off of the " spurs " and were forced to acknowledge that the young Commander's iconoclastic inspiration had proved successful not only in making the ships easier to manœuvre but also in rendering the fire of the guns in the bows far more effective.

Losses and gains were discussed, though it was impossible as yet to give an accurate account. (It was to remain impossible, for individual accounts of eye-witnesses varied fundamentally as each saw only his own corner of the tangled whole.) Nearly fifteen thousand Christian slaves had been freed from Turkish benches, scarred with lashes, verminous, naked, half-starved and exhausted, but free men and with friends. There were about ten thousand Turkish prisoners to replace the Christian slaves who had been unchained and armed by Don John's orders, and those who, in the confusion, had managed to jump overboard and swim or wade ashore to the Albanian marshes. Eight Venetian galleys had been sunk, one Papal one was so badly damaged that it would have to be destroyed.

One of Savoy and two of Sicily and Doria completed the toll of Christian loss in ships.

Don John had taken Ali's two sons and their tutor onto the *Real* and assigned the two boys the cabin of de Soto, one of the best on board. The captured *Sultana* had been ransacked to supply them with the pick of the robes of silk and gold. The loot on her had been immensely valuable, not only hangings and clothes of silk and cloth of gold heavily embroidered and jewelled, but golden armour, golden sequins to the value of seventy thousand pounds, wonderful brocade hangings and Persian carpets, carvings and gilding. There were hoards of gold on nearly every ship and the following days men were busy fishing up floating bodies to strip them of silk garments, gilt chain armour, heavy belts and pockets of gold coin, the jewelled aigrettes of Pashas' turbans, the tall plumes of Janissaries' helmets.

The day after the battle was a busy one for Don John. He had to inspect the fleet, congratulate the leaders, visit the sick and wounded. He himself had escaped scot free but for the wound from a Turkish scimitar which had slashed his high boot and cut his ankle. In the rush and excitement he had not even noticed it and, as he wrote to the King, did not even know how it had been done. It seemed, as far as was possible to estimate the Christian losses, that about seven thousand had been killed and double that number wounded. A number of wounded died later from wounds of poisoned arrows and spears, and probably as many others from the brutal and incompetent hands of the surgeons. The Turkish loss in ships was guessed at two hundred and fifty, including those captured; their killed at thirty thousand. The wounded, except on the corsair ships which escaped, were negligible. The battle had not been fought in kid gloves and little mercy had been shown on either side.

There was wild talk of sailing on Constantinople. Even Don John, reckless though he was often inclined to be, saw the folly of such an idea, with his battered and under-manned fleet. It would have meant wiping out in disaster the wonderful victory which had crowned the prayers of the old Pope and the efforts of the three Allies.

Critics have doubted the great results of the victory, pointing to the fact that the wily Aluch was afloat again within eight months as admiral of a Turkish fleet of a hundred and fifty galleys. They forget the moral results. The Turkish navy had never been beaten. Much more than Philip's Armada did it deserve the name Invincible. It could no longer claim that title. The spell of Islam was broken, the day of Turkish supremacy was past its zenith. Lepanto marked the first step on the downward road of decadence for the Porte.

It marked too another milestone in history : the end of that Mediterranean warfare which had not changed its essential character since the first oared boats had ventured beyond the shelter of bay and inlet. The era was over which had lasted for nearly three thousand years. The oared galleys of Egyptians, Myceneans, Greeks, Romans, Phœnicians, of the great mercantile republics of Italy and the great empire of Spain were to vanish from the scene and be replaced by the small, mobile sailing ships of Drake and his English pirates, the forerunners of modern naval war.

On arrival at Corfu at the end of the month the enormous spoil was divided: half the captured galleys, artillery and slaves to go to the King of Spain, the other half to be divided between the Pope and Venice, as had been settled by the treaty. The Generalissimo was entitled to one tenth. Loot taken on Turkish ships was left to those who had won it. The account was drawn up in Spanish, the native language of the Commander. Veniero refused to sign the agreement because he did not understand Spanish. It took all Colonna's tact and diplomacy to induce the cantankerous old Venetian to sign, on assurance that the Italian translation was identical with the original document. He had forgotten the generosity with which Don John had addressed him before the battle, visited him after it.

From Corfu, too, Don John sent home the tutor of the two sons of Ali, to reassure the widowed mother of their safety. There were not wanting tongues poisonous enough to whisper that this was done in hopes of a larger and speedier ransom for Ahmed and Mahomet, who were Don John's slaves by right of capture. The elder of the two boys maintained an air of stoic arrogance which masked a deadly hatred and a broken heart. Told the reason of young de Cardenas' tears for his dead father he exclaimed scornfully: " Is that all? *I* have lost father, freedom and fortune, but I do not weep." He was proof even against Don John's charm and kindliness—to which his young brother soon fell a victim. On one occasion, finding Mahomet playing with the monkey, he tore her roughly away with furious words : " Have you forgotten that her master, accursed infidel, is our father's murderer ? "

Don John entered Messina harbour on October 31, 1571, at the head of his fleet, towing the Turkish flagship whose flags and pennants trailed astern. The green flag of the Prophet was not on board. It had been taken to Spain two days after the battle by Don Lope de Figueroa who had been wounded in the fiercest fighting on the *Real*. He carried too Don John's autograph letters to his brother and Doña Magdalena and de Soto's official account of the whole naval campaign.

Messina was mad with enthusiasm and excitement. The state reception on the quay, by Archbishop, clerics, nobles and municipality, the procession to the cathedral to the thunder of the *Te Deum*, the pontifical High Mass of All Saints' Day, were followed by a gorgeous banquet and a present of thirty thousand gold escudos. The money was at once distributed to the sick and wounded in hospital by Don John himself. By his generosity and personal care of them he won their undying admiration and love. This act of reckless generosity was true to character. He had the attitude of the typical aristocrat to money : it existed only to be spent and given away, not to be put out to usury, nor to be laid away to breed more filthy lucre. If he had had the treasures of Selim at his disposal he would still have been hard up. As it was, life was a perpetual and unsuccessful struggle to get even the bare necessaries from Philip, whose finances consisted mostly of overdrafts on Genoese banks.

The wild Sicilian enthusiasm which greeted Don John's victorious return was not as soon forgotten as his generosity had been by Veniero. The great gilt bronze statue of him by Andrea Calamech, which still stands in front of the church of our Lady of the Pillar at Messina, was finished and erected within a year of Lepanto. It is perhaps the finest and most vital of the few genuine representations of the hero. He stands on a high marble plinth, in full armour and huge trunk hose, the Collar of the Golden Fleece round his neck, as he appeared at Lepanto. His lifted right hand holds the triple Baton, the left rests on his sword-hilt, the left foot on a Turk's head. The face is framed in the small, close ruff above the gorget. The head turns a little to the left in that position long imitated by admirers. Thick wavy hair and small moustache are close-cut. The deepset eyes have the far-away look of a sailor. The whole expression is stern and tragic.

The generous admiration of Messina was the first wave of a tide of hero-worship which swept over Catholic Europe. Philip received the news of the victory not from de Figueroa, who had been delayed by his wound, but from one of the gentlemen of the Venetian ambassador. The King was at first Vespers of All Saints (not, as legend relates, in the Escorial church, which was not finished till fifteen years later, but in the friars' chapel there or that of the Alcazar at Madrid). He did not move a muscle when the "news of a great victory" was whispered to him. Only when Vespers were over did he send a request to the Prior that the *Te Deum* should be chanted in thanksgiving.

De Figueroa wrote an amusing account of his reception to Don John, when he did at last get to Madrid. The King, the Queen " with all her old duennas round her " (she was within a few days of her confinement), bishops, priors, grandees were all eager for a personal account of the battle (November 22).

" I never expected to arrive at all, for in Italy and France I was nearly torn in pieces to be distributed as relics of your Highness's messenger ! When I reached the Escorial, still not recovered from my bullet wound, I was received by the King as well as your Highness would be by the Pope. For the first half hour it was nothing but : ' My brother, is he really well ? ' with all the questions you can think of. Then he told me to relate everything from the very beginning and not to leave out a single detail. Three times he made me repeat things, and other times made me go back after I had finished. He wished to know all about your care for the wounded and how you had given them your share of the prize-money, which delighted him. I had two interviews with him and finally he said he prayed that God would give you health and strength to do next spring all that still remained to be done, that if all went who wished to join your Highness he would have to build a thousand new galleys ! . . . All are anxious to leave wives and children, wishing for no better fate than to die in your service. . . . The Bishop of Cordoba swears he would rather be your Highness's chaplain than take possession of his bishopric. . . . I have had more feasting and visitors than your Highness had the night of the battle, and my fare has been better than the dry biscuits and scant food on that occasion ! I told the King of your wound, as you said. Celebrations are being prepared. I do not know if they will be like those at Avignon, where there were more processions than there are saints' days in Andalusia ! " (Rosell.)

The warmly affectionate letter in Philip's own hand must have given his brother great pleasure. In it he expresses the anxiety he had felt till news had come of Don John's personal safety and his pleasure in all that de Figueroa had told him.

" What delighted me most of all, so that nothing could have enhanced my joy, were the details he gave me of the great courage you showed that day and the way you personally had planned everything by your own brain and labour. This was fitting in so momentous a matter. So it was that you, by doing your own part, should have shown others how to do theirs. Without doubt this was the chief cause and part of the victory. So it is to you (after God) that I give the credit and thanks for it, as I do. Some credit is due to me too, since it is by the hand of one so dear to me that so great a business has been successfully accomplished, so much honour and glory won in sight of God and of the world, to the benefit of Christendom and the humiliation of its enemies. Though I long to see you and congratulate you in person you will understand the reasons why I have found it necessary for you to winter in Messina." (Rosell.)

The Bishop of Cordoba, an old friend, wrote reminding

Don John how, when the Crucifix had been saved from the fires at Villagarcia and Madrid : " I took it for a sure sign that God had marked your Highness as His standard bearer. . . . I shall be useful to your Highness by breeding horses at Cordoba for the campaign in Barbary, where I hope to be your Highness's chaplain."

For the rest of the year congratulations poured in, from the Pope, from Venice, Genoa, Parma, Urbino, Milan, the Emperor. Philip had foreseen truly that a triumph over the Turk at sea would make his brother the hero of Christendom as he had already been of Spain. The King, however, could face the fact now with more equanimity, thanks to his present glow of affectionate pride in his brother's prowess and the successful birth of a son to his wife and himself. Titian (then ninety-five), in the picture he painted to commemorate the Christian triumph, represented Philip, in a mood of unwonted emotion, offering his remarkably large and ugly son to an angel descending from heaven in an undignified hurry, head downwards.

The Pope, who was said to have had a miraculous knowledge of the victory at the very hour when the blue Standard was hoisted, wrote a letter in his own hand to the " man sent from God, whose name was John," as well as sending him presents to Madrid of a magnificent black marble table, inlaid with an intricate pattern of captured Turks, lions, terrestrial globes, etc., in many coloured stones, and a large silver-gilt shield with a Crucifix in relief surrounded by the words : " *Christus vincit, Christus regnat, Christus imperat*," words commemorating the

triumph of Christ the King, afterwards engraved on the
tomb of His servant at the Escorial.

The winter at Messina was a long pæon of glory, inter-
spersed with hard and steady work : repairing the damage
to ships and personnel and preparing for next year's
campaign. Venice and Rome gave their commanders a
delirious welcome. Indeed the Spanish ambassador in
Rome was annoyed at the almost imperial triumph accorded
to Colonna. Don John had no need to be jealous. " Let
Marc Antonio have his triumphal entry with all the splendour he wishes, it does not disturb me."

The praises and exploits of " Don Zuane " were sung
in every language and dialect from the lagoons of Venice
to the slopes of Etna, from Perpignan to Cadiz, in sonorous
Latin hexameters, polished Italian sonnets, in homely
Provençal, Catalan and Mallorcan ballads. Even the
pedantic Presbyterian, James VI of Scotland, added some
dreary doggerel, entitled " Lepanto," to his " Poetic
Exercises at Vacant Hours."

" The world rang with his heroism. Princes, nobles,
magnates and prelates vied in praising him. His victory
was celebrated in hymns and epics, immortalized in bronze
and marble, by brush and chisel." (Rosell.)

The crowns of Albania and Morea (a somewhat uncertain
quantity) were laid at his feet by bearded, kilted emissaries,
refused with the diplomatic regret that he could do nothing
without his brother's permission. His dreams and ambitions had leapt far beyond petty and half barbarous Dal-
matian states. There was the Pope's promise of a sovereign

state. There was his old hope of emulating Alexander the Great—but in Africa, not Asia. " The campaign in Barbary," of which the bishop of Cordoba had written, was already taking shape in the young Prince's head—for next year or, at latest, the year after.

There was another old hope which had come again to his thoughts : the romantic adventure of rescuing the imprisoned Mary Stuart and after that perhaps the crown of England, though he could not fancy himself in the position of King Consort. However, sufficient unto the day the honour and glory. Ruler of a Christian empire in Northern Africa, he would no longer be an empty-handed wooer—empty as his pockets invariably were now. He was at the zenith, the high water mark which no man touches more than once in life, most never at all. The motto of the banner of Aben Aboo, which had been under his feet, might have been his motto now : " More I could not desire, less would not have contented me."

PART III

XXIII

WILD FIRE

(November—Christmas, 1572)

The *Real* rounded the Punta de Campanella, called after
the big bell which Charles V had had hung there to give
warning of the approach of corsairs. The Banner of the
League and the blue standard of our Lady of Guadelupe
flew at the mast. The castle of Sant' Elmo and the heights
of Posilippo were already in sight ahead. The smoke of
Vesuvius rose into the cloudless sky like a straight black
plume. The ruins of Pompeii, the Torre del Greco, the
houses of Sorrento, white amid their pines and orange
groves, shimmered above a sea of sapphire and amethyst.

Don John leaned against the bulwark scowling and
unconscious of all this beauty. In a few hours he would
have to face another triumphant entry and ceremonious
reception by Cardinal de Granvelle, Viceroy of Naples.
He was sick of such empty shows and their vain repetition.
There was only one that remained unshadowed in his
memory : when he had entered Messina harbour towing the
captured *Sultana* at the head of his victorious fleet after
Lepanto. That high water mark of triumph and glory
was a year ago, a year in which, far from fresh laurels
being added to them, those of Lepanto had grown a little
dusty and withered. He reviewed the twelve months
bitterly.

The winter at Messina had been busy and happy enough. After his visit to Palermo in the spring he had hoped for leave from the King to sail and join the Papal and Venetian fleets. The permission had only arrived in July, when he had been at Palermo again, for the marriage of de Soto to the Sicilian heiress whose hand he had obtained for him. Philip had distrusted the Venetians and had feared that the Dominican Pope, who had died in the spring, might be succeeded by one of the French, anti-Spanish factions. His fears had not been realized, for the new Pope, Gregory XIII, was Spanish in sympathy and showed himself as determined to push on the war against the Turk as Pius V had been.

Don John had sailed within a few days of his receipt of the royal permission and had reached Corfu with his fleet only to find that Colonna and Foscarini (Venetian commander in succession to Veniero) had gone south after Aluch Ali, in disobedience to his orders. There was a stormy scene on their return, even the usually conciliatory Colonna threatening to resign his post. September had been wasted in trying to tempt Aluch from the safe shelter of Modon, a strongly fortified port near Navarino, in the south of the Morea. There had been an equally unsuccessful attempt to take Navarino, but torrential rains and bitter cold made it impossible to leave the four thousand infantry under Alessandro out in the open.

On October 7, 1572, it seemed as if the triumph of Lepanto a year before would be repeated. Aluch came out as if to give battle but, apparently considering the Christian fleet too strong and well ordered, he withdrew again into safety after some clever manœuvring. Don John wanted to force the narrow channel even if several galleys were lost in so doing and then bombard the forts and destroy them as well as the trapped Turkish fleet. Cautious counsels prevailed and nothing was done. So back to Corfu, back to Messina and another year wasted in delays and quarrels. He had seen in Venetian action a warning of something worse than greed and had written to the Spanish ambassador in Venice that no trust was to be placed in their promises and that he hoped that they would not secretly conclude a separate peace with the Turk.

He thought of Alessandro and smiled, rather grimly, as he remembered how he had reproved him for reckless exposure of himself during some unimportant foraging expedition in search of water. It was funny that he, who had always been in trouble in the Alpujarras for his own mad daring, should now be playing mentor to his elder. It has been good to have Alessandro this summer. He had said to himself last year that Alessandro was just the same. It was not true. Each autumn, when the campaign had ended, he had landed at once to go home to wife and children.

Don John was a little envious. He had armed himself invulnerably against women, he told himself; had no intention of falling into any toils. There was that old dream of rescuing the captive Scottish Queen, who, her enemies said, had the fascination of the devil himself. He remembered something Doña Magdalena had said at Abrojo : " Only a king can wed a princess, so, in the meantime you must wed war and plight your troth with the glamour of glory." He had no intention of wooing with empty hands as well as chronically empty pockets. It would be a different matter if the Tunis campaign materialized next year and proved the first step to his African empire.

He prepared to go down to his cabin. It was time to get ready for ceremony and shouting. The white houses of Sorrento caught his eye and struck a chord of memory. It was the home of the sirens, of whom old Honorato had prosed at Alcalá, those same sirens who, tempting Ulysses, formed part of the decoration of the *Real*. There was no need for him to stop his ears with wax. The liquid Castilian charmed him more than the staccato Italian. Nor did he mean to be chained to the mast. As de Soto had said, he needed some recreation and idleness. Yet, as he put on the gilded armour, some words of Doña Magdalena came back to him. "Idleness will always be bad for you, you need danger and action as an outlet for the wild fire of your heart."

"Recreation and idleness!" he often thought bitterly in the days that followed. They were crammed with business and work, receptions, banquets, papers, despatches to read, sign, answer and discuss. The Cardinal was always lecturing on foreign politics. Very foreign they were too, thought Don John, whose thoughts and ambitions, as well as his exploits, had so far been bounded by the Mediterranean coasts, except for that vague dream of some day rescuing the Scottish Queen. De Granvelle would persist in talking of Flanders, that flat, northern country of grey skies and yellow mud which he himself had always hated, where dwelt the frivolous and extravagant mother whose existence he would like to forget.

The Cardinal's suavely superior manner was irritating. Victory, the sonorous voice declared, was barren unless fertilized by the arts of diplomacy ; and diplomacy did not come naturally to the Prince. The stream of information continued. It was six years since the Duke of Alba had succeeded Margaret of Parma as Governor of the Netherland.

" Mercy is a divine attribute," she had written to Philip before she left Brussels. " Any other course will cause the good to perish with the bad and bring unimaginable disasters on the country." She had been a true prophet. Egmont and Horne had died on the scaffold (1568), victims like thousands of others of the infamous " Council of Blood." They were the first Protestant martyrs. Their blood and Alba's preposterous tax of one tenth on all commerce, which had touched the country in its most vulnerable spot, gave an impetus to the revolt not to be restrained by stern measures nor by wholesale butchery. Finance and trade had been killed by the tax and by the boycott on English goods since Elizabeth had annexed the ships laden with pay for Alba's troops (December, 1568). Merchants and artisans were pouring out of the country into France and England. " There are ten thousand more about to leave if the Duke goes on as he is doing " was the report to the Spanish ambassador to Paris early this year (1572). There was too a general strike owing to the tithe. " Brewers refused to brew, bakers to bake, tapsters to tap." Alba's only idea of cutting the Gordian knot, said the Cardinal with a veiled sneer, was to order an extra supply of halters and gallows. William of Orange, he continued with a sharper edge to his tongue, was hampered by want of money and unable to control the " Beggars of the Sea," corsairs under William de Marck who had sworn never to cut hair or beard till he had revenged the murder of his kinsman Egmont.

Elizabeth of England, ah, *there* was a rare genius in diplomacy. Wiser than her ministers who urged her to come out as the champion of Protestantism, she was now enjoying herself in such a tangle of intrigue as she alone could handle successfully. She had gained all the advantages of war against Philip, with none of its cost, by allowing English volunteers to fight under William of Orange and by encouraging Drake's and Hawkins's piratical expeditions in the Spanish Main in such a way that she could disown them if they failed and claim a heavy percentage of their loot if they were in luck. She had inherited the clear monetary foresight of her Welsh grandfather, Henry VII. It was to her petty, bourgeois parsimony (in everything but her own wardrobe) that England was to owe its financial salvation and to escape the morass of debt which was rapidly engulfing Spain. After concluding an alliance with Charles IX of France, which survived the massacre of St. Bartholomew, Elizabeth was now coquetting with Alba.

These interminable complications, which the Cardinal enjoyed as a chess player enjoys an involved game, usually had a soporific effect on Don John. The mention of Mary

Stuart, however, would bring back his wandering attention as the tale of the friar of Tablate had done in the Alhambra. The Ridolfi plot to assassinate Elizabeth had ended in the execution of the Duke of Norfolk (June, 1572), aspirant to Mary's hand. Elizabeth had turned a deaf ear to Parliament's petition that her prisoner should be attainted and " suffer pains of death," but the life of the Scottish Queen hung by the thread of a vacillating and jealous woman's will. " The release and marriage of the Queen of Scots carries with it peace in Flanders and the restoration of religion in this country," Philip's ambassador had written before his indiscretion caused his banishment from England. Norfolk was dead. The Queen's marriage with Bothwell had not been valid. What more splendid mission could be thought of than her release and England united once more in the true fold ?

Don John said nothing. Next year, please God, the foundation at least of the African empire would be laid. When it was built and consolidated, time enough to think about this new knight-errantry. Then he would have something to offer in exchange for the Scotch and English crowns. Thank heaven, tomorrow was the bull-fight in the Piazza Incoronata. Through the narrow window he could see some stars shining between the clouds. It might be fine, though everyone knew that this was the wettest month of the year.

The Cardinal was saying something about " Your Excellency," " exploits in the field of Mars, a novice in the garden of Venus." " Excellency." The viceregal use of the word was like the flick of a whip to a nervous thoroughbred. It brought back the memory of the slight at Barcelona.

The wind was whimpering round the high tower of the Castel Nuovo as if the ghosts of all who had been murdered in the old Angevin castle were seeking their mouldering bones in the dungeons. It was the *libeccho*, that devilish wind from the African desert which frays nerves and ruffles tempers. Don John felt that he was sick of everyone and everything. He disliked the Cardinal, the curled grey hair under the scarlet skullcap, the neat beard, the plump, well-cared-for hands, the patronizing manner. " A novice in the garden of Venus ! " Don John told himself that he was no more afraid of the Neapolitan beauties than he had been of those in Madrid, Granada, Genoa, Messina, Palermo. He disapproved of their free speech and easy manners, their bare expanse of throats, breasts, arms, so great a contrast to the high ruffs and long sleeves of Spanish women. He pulled his chair nearer the glowing copper brazier. It was cold up here, though the stone walls were covered with Flemish tapestries and Eastern silks. The fur-trimmed gown he wore now had come from a Turkish ship. As he fed the little monkey with marzipan sweets he thought of Ali Pasha's boys. The elder, that fierce, proud youth whom even his charm had been unable to tame, had died at Naples, like a wild animal which cannot survive the loss of liberty. The younger, who had been so devoted to his generous captor, was now in the Castle of Sant' Angelo, prisoner of the Pope. Don John had liked them both. These last years had begun to teach him the strange paradox of human nature, by which a man hates a nation yet likes the individuals composing it. Anyhow men were better company than women. The average woman wanted only to talk personalities and to make love when it was so much more interesting to talk of troops, guns, forts and ships.

The Piazza Incoronata was packed for the bull-fight on Sunday afternoon. The nobility had reserved seats under gaily striped awnings near the däis on which sat the Viceroy and Don John. The people were packed at the far end in the blazing sun, sweating, dusty, reeking of garlic, fish and oranges. They were noisy and good-humoured but merciless to those who failed to get their bull and were dragged out, broken and bleeding. Suddenly the gold chair on the Cardinal's right was empty. There was a roar of excitement and pleasure as Don John leapt the barrier and stood in the arena, alone but for the bull. His red cloak was over his left arm, two ribboned darts were in his right hand. In a few minutes the bull was bristling with darts. There was a fresh roar, of applause this time, as the Toledo blade flashed in the sunshine and the great beast sank dead on his side.

The Prince returned to his seat under the baldacchino. He was hot, dusty, thirsty. The blood was racing in his veins. His Tia was right. Danger and action were his vocation. He gulped down a cupful of snow-cooled *Lagrima di Christo*. He saw a girl leaning eagerly over the balcony of a stand near him. Black hair, black eyes under curling lashes, red lips full as a bent bow, a warm pallor of face and throat and arms which made her pearls look dead and cold—it was all stamped on his memory in a flash. He stooped, hunted feverishly in the pile of darts at his feet for one with yellow and white, the colours of the gown she was wearing. A page took it with a message. She stood up and threw. The old bull gave a bellow of rage as he felt the sting in his neck. Don John was in the arena again. He meant to show them how a Spaniard kills a bull. There was a little gasp as the spectators caught their breath. It looked impossible for that slim figure to escape the furious charge of the maddened beast. The next moment the bull had collapsed onto the red cloak and Don John was kneeling bareheaded before Diana de Falangola. She took the banderola from him, its ribbons unstained by blood or dust, and as she curtsied her thanks she lowered her lashes lest he should see the triumph in her eyes.

The streets of Naples were crowded for the Feast of the Immaculate Conception. Out towards Sorrento, the home of the Falangolas, every rude shrine in orange and lemon grove was garlanded with laurel and bay-leaves and little green oranges. The houses of Sorrento were pearl-white among the deep jade of pines, the chrysoprase of lemons. The sand gleamed silver through the sapphire sea in the bay where the first Greek colonists had landed. Capri and Ischia were opalescent. Golden particles of dust veiled everything with a shimmering spell. Night, too, fell golden and the spell remained unbroken.

The darkness was full of the strange barbaric music of the flutes and bagpipes played by the Zampognari, wild, long-haired Calabrian mountaineers, with gold earrings, crimson waistcoats, sandalled feet and goatskin breeches, who came down to Naples every year from December 8 till Christmas.

That wild, fierce music echoed in Don John's ears. The blood was hammering at his temples and throat. Heart and pulse beat with the deafening throb of drums, like the day he had ridden into Frasno delirious with fever. He was in a fever now. His throat was parched, though he had drunk many cupfuls of strong Ischian wine. His hands were shaking. His voice shook too, hoarse and broken, like that of a stranger. No one could have mistaken the message in Diana's eyes.

Fray Miguel Servia, the simple Mallorcan friar, kept a diary, an unadorned record of facts which began the day the fleet left Messina for Lepanto and ended when he left Don John a little before dying in Palermo in 1574. He notes at Christmas, 1572 :

" His Highness withdrew the Monday before to a monastery of Canons Regular outside Naples, called the *Pie de Grutta*. At the hour of Matins his Highness summoned us and I heard his confession. . . . He made his Communion at the first sung Mass [of Christmas Day] as did all the other nobles who had made their confessions."

XXIV

BARBARY COAST

(FEBRUARY 17, 1573—WINTER, 1573-4)

Don John, fifty yards ahead of his tired and grumbling
followers, was muffled to the chin in his big cloak, the hood
pulled forward over his face. He was enjoying the sting
of sleet and snow, the lash of the north wind, the need for
alertness to keep his black horse on its feet on the steep
slippery slope. That half of him which loved danger and
action and hardness was uppermost. He was happy to
escape from the softness and languor of Naples, its intrigues
and love-making. The " wild fire " which had scorched
him had soon burnt itself out. It had been far worse than the
affair with Maria. That had been a boy's romantic calf-love.
This had been the blinding, devastating passion of a man,
the sudden snapping of a long restraint by physical desire,
strengthened by disillusion and bitter disappointments.

He pulled up his horse. He was at the summit of the
long climb. There was a gleam of blue between the clouds
which the wind sent racing past the snow-peaks of Monte
Vellino. To the north the Aterno gleamed a dull pewter
in the wide valley and on its further banks rose the walls
of Aquila, the long white line of the Apennines behind it.
He could see the square bulk of the castle with its four
towers, tucked into a corner of the town, the home of
Margaret of Austria, his sister and Alessandro's mother.

A fortnight was not long when the journey each way was over a hundred and fifty miles, through vile weather and over viler roads, but it was all he could spare. Most days it was possible to hunt. Don John fancied himself as a horseman but he found it impossible to outride this stout, square-built, elderly woman twenty-five years his senior. Her horses were good, her hawks too, she herself the best of companions. There was an atmosphere of home here as there was at Villagarcia, though he could not imagine anyone less like his Tia than this Amazon, with her moustache, her double chin, her deep man's voice. Nor could anyone be less like the slim, dark, handsome, elegant, sophisticated Alessandro.

She talked of politics with a trenchant commonsense and a tolerant knowledge of the world. She had learnt diplomacy from her aunt, Mary of Hungary, Governor of the Netherlands and an Amazon like herself, from the Medicis and from Pope Paul III, her husband's grandfather. She startled her half brother by a sudden blunt question. Had he any children ? He hesitated before shaking his head. Ana's existence was a secret which was not only his. " If you ever have one, let me have it."

The small, keen grey eyes were unwontedly tender as Don John kissed her big hand in farewell. This yellow-haired, blue-eyed brother would have been a son much more in sympathy with her than the Italian Alessandro.

" Yesterday after dinner I arrived from Aquila, having seen and made the acquaintance of the wisest and bravest woman in the world today," wrote Don John from Naples,

s 2

March 3, 1572. " I should not say it were it not the truth
and there is much more on which I must keep silence."
(Coloma.)

Back to Naples after that short holiday in the bracing,
windy Abruzzi, back to work and the organization of the
summer campaign, to chronic appeals to Philip for money,
to hopes of the capture of Tunis and always in the background, like the mutter of a distant storm, the possibility
of Venetian treachery. Holy Week and Easter were spent
in retreat at the Carthusian monastery of San Martino,
behind the Castle of Sant' Elmo, where he had rooms
assigned permanently to him. From its wide terrace was a
view south across the bay to Capri and Sorrento, with Ischia
on the right, jewel-like in the silver sea and Vesuvius with
its black plume of smoke on the left. The cure which had
begun at Aquila was completed here, amid the peace and
silence of the white monks. The side of Don John which
turned instinctively to austerity, to seclusion and to contemplation, which had been at home at Abrojo and at
Montserrat, was happy here too. The balance was
readjusted.

On March 7—anniversary of the day when Pius V had
hoped to see the ratification of the Holy League—the
Venetian envoys in Rome swore before Gregory XIII to
continue war against the infidel with all their strength.
The same day their ambassador at Constantinople had
signed peace with the Turks.

Don John had already heard the news from the Venetian
agent in Naples the day before he received the official

intimation from de Zuñiga, the Spanish ambassador in Rome. " Today arrived a courier for the Venetian ambassador who, when he was received by His Holiness, told him that his countrymen had made peace with the Turk. His Holiness returned at once to Rome two hours ago and at midnight sent Cardinal Coma to me with the news." (April 6.) " I have just come from the palace where I found the Pope much annoyed about this peace, but he reproached the Venetians as they deserved with great self-control." (April 7, Rosell.)

According to a less discreet account, the Pope had been so amazed and furious that he had rushed at the ambassador and chased him out of the house !

Don John was less taken by surprise. Six months before he had written to de Sesa saying that he feared what had now taken place. He ordered the blue Standard of the Holy League to be hauled down and the royal standard of Spain to be run up instead. From that moment the famous Standard vanishes. (The one Gaeta claimed to have been presented by the Prince cannot be the League Standard, as it is red, with the figures of SS. Peter and Paul.) De Granvelle, de Sesa and old Garcia de Toledo, hurriedly summoned to a Council, agreed that the dignity of Spain forbade the use of violent reprisals, unjustifiable and treacherous as the Venetian conduct had been. De Zuñiga was to be instructed to make a strong protest and to use every effort to secure a continuation of combined action by Spain and the Papacy.

Don John's indignation was as outspoken as might have been expected in his letter to de Zuñiga (April 9). The

Pope's displeasure was lasting and he refused even to see the Venetian ambassador till a special envoy arrived to reopen diplomatic relations. Philip's calm remained unbroken. He replied with cold courtesy to the ambassador who gave him the news that no doubt the Republic had done what it considered best for its own interests. The rejoicings of Catherine de Medici and the French court were all the greater because the treaty had been largely engineered by their own able diplomat, the Bishop of Dax. " The Venetians and the Pasha have sat on it in secret for three months, I have hatched it in three days," he wrote triumphantly to the Duc d'Anjou, for whom, however, he had not succeeded in winning a kingdom from Selim.

The terms of the peace were kept secret as long as possible by the Doge and the Council of Ten. Venice by them regained none of her conquered territories. The humiliating conditions to which she submitted were those imposed by a victor on a crushed and broken foe. The Porte, naturally, was delighted. Aluch Ali put to sea in mid-June and celebrated the obsequies of the Holy League by sacking the Apulian coast and burning Philip's town of Castro.

Naples was busy during the early summer discussing the future of Don John and his fleet. Some armchair strategists supported de Sesa who wished to sail east and repeat the glory of Lepanto. Others agreed with Santa Cruz that Aluch's viceroyalty of Algiers should be the point of attack. Don John himself was in no doubt.

All might be for the best. Freed from the quarrels and insubordinations of the Venetians he was now free to make Tunis the objective of the Spanish-Papal-Maltese fleet. This determination was strengthened by a secret message from the Pope, who ratified Pius V's promise of the crown of a Christian empire in North Africa. Nor had His Holiness stinted his praise of the victor of Lepanto in full conclave. " A Scipio in valour, a Pompey in heroism, an Augustus in good fortune, a new Moses, Gideon, Samson, Saul and David, without any of their faults. Please God I shall live long enough to reward him with a royal crown."

While waiting for orders to sail from Philip, Don John, in addition to the usual inspections and reviews of ships and troops, was busy with arrangements with the Viceroys of Naples and Sicily for a regular supply of stores and provisions for the expedition to North Africa. During the four months between the news of Venetian treachery and the departure of the fleet (August 5, 1573) several events of personal interest had taken place. A Turkish ship entered the Bay of Naples about Easter with the tutor of Ali Pasha's sons whom Don John had released at Corfu. He brought a letter for the Prince from Fatima, the boys' sister and niece of the Sultan, as well as a collection of magnificent presents from her. These included furs, Persian tapestries and carpets, jewelled swords and daggers from Damascus, brocades, embroideries, spices and a golden enamelled bow, quiver and belt which had belonged to Suleyman the Magnificent. Fatima, ignorant of her elder brother's death at Naples a year and a half ago, wrote a humble and pathetic plea for the freedom of " these poor orphans, who have no mother, while their father was slain in battle with your Highness. They depend solely on your pity and protection. I beg your Highness, as the courteous gentleman that all deem you, as a generous and religious Prince, to have pity on my ceaseless tears and to grant me this favour." (Coloma.)

The appeal was not in vain. Mahomet Bey, the younger and surviving brother, arrived from Rome in answer to Don John's request to the Pope and embarked for home at the end of May. He took back with him all his sister's presents as well as a gift to himself by Don John of horses, stores and jewellery. The Prince also sent a letter by him expressing his grief that " the final end of all trouble and labour which is death " had befallen her other brother and explaining his reasons for not accepting her generosity— reasons understandable by the Oriental mind. " My famous ancestors have never been accustomed to take gifts from their suppliants but only to grant their petitions and bestow favours on them."

Even the Bishop of Dax, still in Constantinople when the captive returned, admitted the generosity of a Prince who freely released a prisoner for whom a ransom of fifty thousand crowns would have been paid, though he quickly added a sting to the tail of his compliment by suggesting that some deep and sinister scheme must underlie such seeming virtue.

The letter to Fatima was one of the last written for the Prince by Juan de Soto, who was recalled to Madrid on his appointment as Commissary General of the fleet, a post

given by Philip rather to separate him from his master
than to reward his services. It was a sad parting on both
sides. De Soto had been Don John's secretary ever since
the death of de Quiroga during the Morisco rebellion.
He had been a devoted and faithful servant whom his
master had rewarded with friendship and intimacy as well
as more material gifts. The new secretary, sent to control
the Prince's far-reaching schemes and soaring ambition,
had proved a spur rather than a bridle. Not only did he fall
completely under the fascination which most men and
women found irresistible, but he encouraged the dreams of
a crown and empire to a degree which proved his own
doom.

The death of Ruy Gomez, Prince of Eboli, in the arms
of his old friend and servant, de Soto (July, 1573), proved
an irreparable loss to the Prince. The man whom he had
called old Luis's successor and to whom he had confided
all his hopes and difficulties, sure of sane and balanced
advice, was succeeded by Antonio Perez. His immense
and subtle influence with the King was used, from now on,
against Don John and Escobedo, by hints and suggestions
of overwhelming ambition.

Before news came of Ruy Gomez's death, Don John
had written to remind Margaret of Austria of a promise
she had made to him at Aquila in the spring.

" In about a month's time . . . a child will be born
whose father I am ashamed to be. Indeed I beg you
to forgive me and to be a mother not only to me but also
to the child who is to be born. . . . I entreat you, from
my heart, if you wish to do me a favour, to take this new

burden and trouble off me in as secret and prudent a manner as possible." (Naples, July 18, 1573. Coloma.)

When Diana de Falangola's baby was born Don John was at sea on his way to Tunis (September 11). Margarita, as she was called after her aunt, was sent in November to Aquila with her wet nurse and there she remained under the care of Margaret of Austria till Don John's death. Once more, as his Tia had done five years ago, a motherly and capable woman had stepped in to take the result of his folly and by her inviolable secrecy and discretion avoided scandal and the poisoned chatter of evil tongues.

Bad weather, the invariable companion of Don John's campaigns, delayed the fleet in Sicily and it was not till October 7, the second anniversary of Lepanto, that the storms abated, the wind changed and the hundred and four galleys and hundred and three smaller ships, with over nineteen thousand troops on board, could leave their anchorage near Marsala. Not a single corsair was sighted and, before sunset the next day, the Spanish fleet had passed the site of Carthage and anchored in the bay of Goletta, the fortress guarding the approach to Tunis which the Spaniards had held since its capture by Charles V in 1535.

The last glow of sunset turned the shattered marble columns of Phœnicians and Romans to gold, flooded the three low olive-clad hills to the north which had once been crowned by the richest city in the world. The wings of flamingoes homeward bound for the long shallow lake burned rose-flame. The water was a shining sheet of turquoise.

Don John landed the next morning and entered the
Goletta. The white buildings of Tunis, the most wealthy
and civilized city of Africa, rose tier above tier to the palace
and citadel of the Alcazaba at the end of the lake. The
domes of the great mosque and the golden balls crowning
its towers glittered in the morning sun. Round the city
was the deep green of orange orchards. Hills and valleys
wore the cool silver-grey of olives. Every hill and column,
shore and valley echoed to the sound of great names:
Hannibal, Scipio, Dido and Æneas, St. Augustine, St.
Louis of France, who had died here on his last Crusade,
Barbarossa, cleverest of all the sea-wolves of the Mediterranean, Charles V. The rulers of Tunis claimed descent
from Melchior, one of the three kings who had adored
before the manger at Bethlehem, but, since Charles V had
driven Barbarossa from Tunis, usurpers had continually
disputed the throne. Muley Hamid, dispossessed three years
ago by Aluch Ali, was now in Goletta, where he had been
waiting for the Spanish force to restore him to his throne.

Don John wrote to Philip from the Alcazaba
(October 11) to announce that Tunis had capitulated
without a shot being fired. It had been evacuated on news
of his landing. He scribbled a postscript in his own hand
to the official despatch. " These Turks have shown themselves rotten soldiers. Not one of them even stopped to
have a look at us as they might well have done. They
could also have defended the place better than they imagined
for several days. I must also remind your Majesty that I
am practically penniless and how necessary it is that this
urgent need should be supplied." (Maxwell.)

Mass was celebrated in the Alcazaba and in the mosques as soon as the essential vestments and vessels had arrived from the fleet. The garrison in their hurried flight had left behind provisions and artillery and, in the palace and the houses of rich merchants were large quantities of carpets, silks, spices, leather and other prizes. There was one piece of loot more to the Prince's taste than any other, a young lion cub found in the deserted Alcazaba. "Austria" was adopted by Don John and became his inseparable companion, eating with him, sleeping in his room and going with him whenever possible, as well as figuring with him in several of his portraits. When his master went to Flanders poor "Austria," left behind, was said to have died of a broken heart. He was not the only one to end so.

Philip, in his letter authorizing the Tunis expedition had not ordered the destruction of Goletta as well as the town. Such definiteness was almost unknown with him. In any case, such an order was scarcely likely to have recommended itself to the ambitious young victor who, by his bloodless occupation of the town, thought he had laid the foundation stone of his African empire. The King had merely set out the pros and cons and had left the matter open.

Don John's first care was to plan the erection of a fort half-way along the lake, so as to ensure safe and easy communication between city and port. A site was chosen and the work allotted to Gabriel Serbellone, a tall, stout, competent, elderly Italian engineer, who had designed Alba's wonderful new fortifications in Antwerp. He was to be

left behind as Governor of Tunis, in command of eight
thousand Spanish and Italian infantry as well as sappers
and miners. Poor Muley Hamid, instead of regaining his
throne, was put on board a galley with his son and sent off
to Naples.

Don John acted with his usual speed. Six days after
he had entered Tunis he had finished all arrangements,
received the submission of Biserta, an important town sixty
miles west of Tunis, and ridden back to Goletta to sail for
Sicily (October 17). Even in those few days, though, time
had been found for sport. Lion-hunting in the surround-
ing country had caused more casualties than the taking of
Tunis. One man and horse had been torn to pieces by
lions and a valuable horse had fallen dead with fright at
a lion's charge.

Lack of money and the need to get the fleet into winter
quarters before storms began again, combined to make a
quick departure necessary. Once more the speed with
which the whirlwind campaign had been completed proved
that delays and dilatoriness were never the fault of Don
John and that, left to himself, he would rush things through
with the same passionate haste as had been shown in the
famous ride to Zaragoza.

For all the hurry storms caught the ships on the way to
Sicily. A Neapolitan galley was lost and the fleet driven
out of its course. Don John was met by a courier bearing
news of the death of his sister, the Infanta Juana, who had
been so good to him in his boyhood. He entered Palermo
with yards, masts, oars and bulwarks of his ships painted
black and draped in mourning as deep as that with which

Colonna's fleet had welcomed him to Messina. It was a sad end to an expedition which had realized all his hopes, but there was one great consolation. Philip at last sent permission for a visit to Spain which his brother longed for as he had longed for Madrid when, in the Alpujarras, " every day seemed a year." Spain had not yet welcomed the hero of Lepanto, who so ardently desired to see again not only her and his " affectionate brother, the King," but even more his Doña Magdalena, to whom he had sent Turkish banners captured in his great victory as well as the *Lignum Crucis* he had worn on his breast that day.

XXV

" ELEMENTS SO MIXED "

(WINTER, 1573–4—OCTOBER 29, 1574)

The winter was not only occupied by the usual business
routine and unceasing attempts to keep Tunis and Goletta
supplied with stores, an aim which the Viceroys of Naples
and Sicily seemed determined to prevent. The project
of a marriage with Mary Stuart was again in the forefront
of politics. Catherine de Medici was alarmed by the taking
of Tunis, which she saw would strengthen her hated rival,
Spain. Charles IX was dying of rapid consumption and
the Protestants saw in his blood-soaked bed a judgement for
St. Bartholomew's. The heir, Anjou, was in Poland as
king. Alençon was in prison for conspiracy against his
mother. She therefore thought that a closer alliance with
England was indicated and Alençon, for all his bulbous
nose and pockmarked face, was suggested as a suitable
match for the English queen, old enough to be his mother.

As a counterblast to this, the Spanish ambassador in
London put before Philip a plan for a double marriage.
The Earl of Argyle was to kidnap the seven-year-old
James of Scotland, who would betroth in Spain the Infanta
Isabella Eugenia, his own age. The captive Queen of
Scots had approved this idea and consented to her own
marriage with Don John, after he had rescued her and
restored her to her kingdoms.

These wild plans were scarcely in tune with Philip's cautious and suspicious nature, but they were ably pressed by the learned Jesuit, Dr. Nicolas Sanders, now in Madrid. This ex-Fellow of New College, Oxford, Regius professor of Theology at Louvain and author of numerous controversial works, had been authorized by Mary's most intimate friends and advisers to assure Don John of her affection and to urge on the plot for her release. Philip listened, made marginal notes, told Perez to give encouraging but non-committal answers to the ambassador and the Jesuit. He was always busy. The exchequer was being bled white by the troubles in Flanders, where it was to be hoped that Luis de Requesens, who had succeeded Alba, might sooth some of the hatred created by his predecessor and the Council of Blood. The plans of the new cities among the remote valleys of the Andes had been finished and approved. The English pirates were a perpetual menace to trade with the New World. If one year they caught the treasure fleet on its way home to Cadiz, that would be a death blow to national finance. Tunis and Goletta too were an added expense. He was not sure that it would not have been better to have razed them both to the ground. There was another letter from Don John with the inevitable appeal for more money. Things could be talked over when his " good brother " was in Spain. Meantime Antonio could send him an account of the learned Jesuit's schemes.

Don John's life during this winter was similar to that of the next three years, in Naples, Sicily or in North Italy.

A legend has grown up which pictures him as a luxurious
and effeminate libertine, with floating little-Lord-Fauntleroy
curls, jewels, velvets and silks, spending his time in idle
dalliance with the local sirens. Historians have found it
difficult, if not impossible, to believe that a handsome and
attractive young royal hero of the sixteenth century should
be anything but sexually immoral all the time.

Girolamo Lippomano, Venetian ambassador to Naples,
wrote home a long and detailed report about " Don
Giovanni d'Austria " in 1575. Like most Venetian reports
of the day it is detailed, vivid, shrewd, caustic and cynical.
He describes the Prince's " most beautiful face and
admirable charm," his splendour of dress, his skill at
" riding, jousting, all kinds of military sports and tournaments," his keenness at tennis and other games, " not
sparing himself more than his rivals but playing with all
his might . . . thinking that even in such small things
honour is at stake." " In the morning he rises betimes,
hears Mass, gives audience to those persons of the fleet or
of the court who need something, then retires with his
secretaries to read letters, examine and answer memorials
and discuss public affairs. He next receives the Spanish
and Neapolitan gentlemen who have come to pay their
respects. If there is no Council meeting he listens till
dinner-time to anyone who wishes to speak to him—not in
private nor in public audience, but in the presence of
persons of distinction. After dinner, if there is no Council
of War or State he applies himself to studies . . . but
often he remains till the evening in his library, writing.
Besides Spanish he speaks French extremely well. He

understands Flemish and German and can also speak Italian, but not with great fluency. In short he desires in all things to be considered a Spaniard."

Add to this programme the riding, jousting, hunting, "playing at tennis five or six hours a day" and (surely for one who had been such a keen bather in the icy streams at Valsain) swimming in that sea of blue glass with its silver sand, and the day is scarcely an idle one.

"His Excellency is wise and very prudent, eloquent, wary and adept at business, well able to dissemble and to use courtesy and caresses."

The bitter school of life was teaching one who was by nature direct and straightforward that it was necessary to fight men with their own weapons. He had learnt the wisdom of the Arab proverb : "It is good to speak the truth, but better to know the truth and speak of date-stones."

"He is well versed in fortification and artillery and talks of little beside military enterprises and victories"—a form of conversation rarely popular with women. Then comes the inevitable gossip. "Some say that he is much given to women, which may quite well be true as he is so young, but he has never given any cause for scandal by which unrest or discontent has arisen among the nobility of Naples." The Venetian, anxious as he naturally was to report the worst against the enemy of his city, is driven to base his hypothetical scandal on the insecure basis : "Some say."

"The charms of the city and the ladies were suited to his gallant youth," says Vanderhammer vaguely, and even Stirling Maxwell, not prejudiced in favour of his hero, remarks that the name of only one of "his female favourites" is known, that of Diana de Falangola. There was one other whose very name is unknown, as her existence would have been but for a brief reference to her in a letter of Don John to an intimate friend, Rodrigo de Mendoza, brother of the Duke of Infantado (Marché-en-Famine, February 17, 1577).

"How can I talk of happiness today? It is just a year since I bade farewell to my most beloved friend, whom, for the rest of my miserable life, I shall love more than any other being. Even now I can think of nothing but that parting, which ever deepens my grief. In sober truth, when I remember it my agony now is as great as when I heard of her death, pierced as I was with unbearable pain. May God have her safe in His keeping as I trust she is, for that is the only happiness left me." (Maxwell.)

Carnival, 1574, was celebrated with great festivities, tournaments, bull-fights and musical rides, in all of which the Prince took part. There was a splendid function on Lady Day in the church of Santa Chiara, where the League Banner had been handed over. A special envoy, a Papal Chamberlain, invested the Prince with the Golden Rose as a reward "for so many labours and perils undertaken and endured for the Catholic religion" and "a sign of good will and fatherly love." Besides this signal honour the Pope was urging Don John's interests at Madrid, the increase both of the fleet and of his authority.

"Consider," he wrote to Philip, "if it would not add to his power and influence if he were given the title of King of Tunis. In this way you would show your gratitude to

T 2

God for this conquest as your ancestors were wont to do by founding a new Christian kingdom." Otherwise let him " undertake the expedition to England as the English Catholics have already expressed their desire that he should become their King by marriage with the Queen of Scots."

Probably this Papal interference did Don John more harm than good, as it accentuated the suspicions of the King, which were fostered by Perez, that his brother's ambitions were soaring so high that they might escape his own cautious control.

Meantime the ex-king of Tunis and his son were housed in Don John's own rooms in the Charterhouse of San Martino. There the youth was baptized as Don Carlos of Austria, with the Prince as his godfather. The grief of old Muley Hamid at his son's apostasy was so great that he begged to be allowed to leave Naples for Palermo, where he soon died.

It was to these rooms that Don John himself often withdrew to find a refuge from ceaseless activity of mind and body, from the noise and turmoil of Naples. That side of him which was drawn to silence and solitude, which found happiness here as at Abrojo and Montserrat, was no passing phase of disillusion and disappointment, but a fundamental part of his nature which remained as strong as ever on his deathbed.

" On 14 of April, 1574, to the great delight of all the Spaniards, his Highness ordered his flag to be hoisted " and the next day embarked for Spain. Not only did he long for home ; he needed a change from the heat and languor of Naples. A little while before de Zuñiga had

written an alarming account of the Prince's health, internal
trouble, fever, blood pressure. "I pray he be cured, for
certainly there is great need of him."

It was good to be at sea again, better still to know that
one's goal was Spain. There was a stop at Gaeta, to confer
with de Zuñiga, Colonna and the Pope's nephew, to fête
them on board and be welcomed by the town. A courier
arrived post-haste from Madrid. The orders were to sail
straight to Genoa, where the " Old " and " New " factions
were rapidly plunging the republic into civil war. There
was one bright spot in the misery of hope deferred, a
visit to the monastery of the Santa Trinità, which belonged
to the Benedictine monks of Monte Cassino. The Prince
spent the night there, made his Confession and Communion.
The little round chapel was dim and cool, glowing like a
peacock with mosaic and paintings. Its light was the guide
to shipping entering the bay which, with those leaving,
saluted the shrine.

Fray Miguel's successor, who fancied himself as a scholar,
gives a detailed diary of the voyage to Genoa, plentifully
sprinkled with classical allusions and quotations. The
Prince landed on Elba and inspected the castle which, two
hundred and forty years later, was to house the exiled
Napoleon. Genoa was reached on April 29.

The great mercantile republic, of which Philip was the
official " Protector," had been in a state of disorder for
years from the quarrels of the nobles. The party of St.
Peter—the new and popular one—had denounced Doria
after Lepanto as the betrayer of his country and the puppet
of Spain. Earlier this year (1574) Idiaquez, Philip's agent

in Genoa, had allowed the " Old " nobles of St. Luke to bring bands of armed peasants into the city with the natural result of aggravating unrest. Doria was attacked. Streets were barricaded. Squares were occupied and protected by artillery, couriers stopped and robbed. Only one breath was needed to blow the fire into the full blaze of civil war. Each party appealed to Madrid and Vienna for help. Philip, as " Protector," felt that it was his business, not the Emperor's nor the Pope's ; hence the urgent orders to Don John to leave at once for Genoa and to remain for at least three months in the north to watch events.

Genoa became the centre of international politics. Like vultures descending on a wounded beast, envoys collected from every part. The Pope sent a Bishop and then a Cardinal. The Emperor, Maximilian III, the Grand Duke of Tuscany, Henry III of France, all had agents there too. It was Don John's business to prevent civil war and to counteract French influence. Idiaquez was in favour of leaving the decision on the dispute in the hands of the Pope's legate and those of the Duke of Gandia (son of Francisco Borja), but the latter was delayed by gout, so nothing was done. The Senate, terrorized by the armed mob, gave in to the clamour for " reform," and the " Old " nobles, including Doria, had to leave the city.

The dreary dispute dragged on for another two years, during which Don John was frequently in the north of Italy, engaged in a diplomacy which was not at all to his liking. A final settlement was only made in the winter of 1575–6 and, like most such settlements, left things as they had always been.

The summer of 1574, in spite of the disappointment about Spain, was not at all an unhappy one. Don John spent two months in the high-perched castle of Vigevano, a little town overlooking the fertile plain of the Ticino. The castle had been recently modernized and improved by Ludovico Sforza, and the country abounded with game. The Prince won the hearts of the townsfolk by his friendliness and the keenness with which he joined their *palla* matches. On his way to Milan he was met by Ottavio, Duke of Parma, and a grand masque and ball were arranged by the famous dancing master who had presided over the fifty-two white and crimson beauties at Genoa's welcome to the Prince in 1571. There was a tournament at Piacenza and, as in the Neapolitan bull-fight, Don John, " without forethought or preparation " descended into the lists in black and gold armour, gold and black plumes and " breeches cut sailor-fashion " !

Here he met Maria, Alessandro's wife, the Portuguese princess. The two made instant friends. Directly the tournament was over " he retired with the most Serene Princess to the citadel " and, after breakfast next day, " passed the rest of the day in agreeable talk with her." She sent him away laden with presents, including the useful one of " fifty pairs of the finest gloves."

He had been chafing to get south ever since news had come on July 7, during a visit to Milan, that the Turkish fleet was at sea, sails set for Tunis. Soon after had come an appeal from Gabriel Serbellone, who wrote that not only was Aluch's fleet off the coast but that Goletta, Tunis and the half-finished fort were surrounded by Arab hordes

from the desert. The Prince ordered every available soldier
in Milanese territory to embark, and himself left Genoa at
the beginning of August. A terrible storm delayed the
fleet at Spezia and it was not till August 22 that Naples
was reached. The very next day he left with all the ships
and troops for Messina—as usual short of money, balked
at every turn by de Granvelle and the Viceroy of Sicily,
who were apparently bent on bringing to pass the evil they
had foretold for the Tunis expedition. A letter from the
King made matters worse. A hundred thousand ducats,
raised with the utmost difficulty must, he wrote, be made
to last as long as possible. Discretion and caution were
essential. " I most expressly order and command you on
no account to go on board the fleet while the enemy remains
on those seas, . . . seeing that your courage and zeal in
my service are so great as to make you endanger both your
own person and the fleet, whose safety is so much more
important than the places you wish to relieve or than
anything else."

There is little doubt that, for once, Don John would
have disobeyed orders. The weather saved him from disobedience and smashed the last hope of his African empire.
Detained at Messina by contrary winds, storm bound at
Melazzo and again at Palermo, the troop ships were driven
back again and again. Near the end of September came
news of the loss of Goletta after a five weeks' siege. Another
attempt to sail from Trapani was baffled by continuous
gales which wrecked or dismasted several galleys. A fresh
cry of despair came from Serbellone, whose only hope now
consisted in the speedy arrival of the fleet to force Aluch

to a naval battle. Aluch, determined to retake Tunis, which he himself had conquered for the Sultan, had arrived in the bay with three hundred sail in mid-July. He landed half his forty thousand troops to join with the Arab-Turkish force. The only effort made by the Spanish commander of Goletta was to send to Serbellone an appeal for reinforcements. The result of his lethargy, Aluch's determination and the clever tactics of Mustafa, a renegade Italian engineer, was the fall of Goletta and the massacre of most of the garrison (August 23, 1574). Serbellone, in his unfinished fort half-way between Goletta and Tunis, put up a very different resistance. Practically all the garrison were killed or wounded, walls and fortifications in ruins. Finally, in a third assault, he himself, easily recognizable from his height and stoutness, was taken. The citadel fell and, like Goletta, was destroyed by orders of Aluch. Barely two hundred men escaped.

Aluch had accomplished his purpose and saw no reason to wait for the probable arrival of the redoubtable young admiral of Lepanto. He sailed for Constantinople, taking with him the sturdy old fighter Serbellone, who, a year later, was exchanged for a Turkish Pasha taken at Lepanto.

Don John, still stormbound at Trapani, nearly frantic with the delay, wrote to the King on October 3 news of the disaster. " Your Majesty honours me by your reasons for forbidding me to sail in person against the enemy. All the same I must say that, since I know in what the safety of the fleet consists and my duty to your Majesty, no personal idea nor self interest will ever prevent me from undertaking anything which I believe to be for your

Majesty's best advantage." This outspoken protest against trammelling orders was not well received. The King wrote coolly about the loss of Tunis which : " I regret as much as is reasonable." He also refused his brother permission to visit Spain. " Though I should be very happy to see you here, I have determined to defer my private pleasure for the good and safety of public affairs and you must be content to do the same."

The Pope did not take the misfortune so philosophically. " These unhappy events in Africa," he wrote with his own hand to Philip, " have filled us with grief and confusion. Nor could we believe that the ministers of your Majesty would have been so negligent in giving aids of all kind to these poor people. . . . Your Majesty is very ill served."

But words did not help. Don John returned to Naples with all hopes of the African empire vanished like dust before the wind. Man can conquer much, but the elements are still his masters.

XXVI

SPAIN AT LAST

(November, 1574—March, 1575)

Don John was barely a month in Naples before he went
north to Genoa. Her petty internecine quarrels seemed of
little importance to him, but she was on the way to Spain
and to Spain he was determined to go, orders or no orders.
He had already written to Philip : " The distance between
Italy and Madrid is so great that invaluable time is always
being wasted." If he saw the King he might be able to
persuade him, which could never be done on paper, to
allow a certain initiative to the man on the spot and so
avoid further disasters from that over-centralization which
was the curse of Philip's government.

Of course the weather was against him. An overland
journey through France was inadvisable, for one of the
new king's first acts on reaching Paris from Poland in
September had been a declaration that he would make no
concessions to the Huguenots. They had at once begun
to make preparations for a fresh insurrection under Condé
and civil war was expected at any moment. However, in
spite of adverse winds and French politics the Prince
landed at Palamos (a hundred miles north of Barcelona)
just after Christmas, 1574, blissfully unconscious that
he had missed a long and complicated letter from
Philip telling him to spend the winter in Italy and

retailing an interminable programme for the next few months.

Don John, though he had not had this order, was doubtful about his welcome, as is obvious from the letter he wrote Perez from Barcelona.

" God is my witness . . . that up to now no one has understood how dangerous is the state of his Majesty's affairs in Italy. . . . I have left my post and incurred the guilt of disobedience rather than the certainty of dishonour. . . . Welcome I do not expect to be, however much my zeal may deserve it."

Eager as he was to reach Madrid he spent two days at Montserrat, days of peace to strengthen him for the ordeal before him, to heal the wounds of disappointed ambition and injured feelings. After all Philip showed no displeasure. He greeted his brother affectionately, allowed the justice of his complaints against the two Viceroys and appointed him Lieutenant General in Italy, with precedence and authority over all Viceroys and Governors in Spanish states of Italy. The appointment, however, was to be kept secret for the present and, to the request that he would authorize the rank and titles of Infante, already used by most people, Philip made his pet answer. The time was not yet.

There were endless talks about Italian affairs, consultations about future plans. " Always Councils," Don John wrote on February 15, 1575, to Margaret at Aquila. " Every day I have two, to say nothing of a thousand other things which leave me no time to call my own. . . . The spring is already so far advanced, and it makes me miserable to see nothing done." (Coloma.)

The chief subject of discussion besides Italy was the Papal scheme for the liberation of Mary Stuart and her marriage to Don John, which had been in the air for so long. When the Legate had urged it on him the King had replied that all his forces in the Mediterranean were needed against the Turk, all those in the Low Countries against the rebels. As Elizabeth was helping the rebels with men, money and influence, retorted the Legate, the best way of stamping out the revolt was to dethrone her. Not one man could be spared from Flanders to do it, was the answer. The same arguments and counter arguments were repeated now. The most Philip would promise (" and with no intention of fulfilling it," wrote Perez later) was that he would favour the English project if there were no recrudescence of the war with the Turk this summer.

There was perhaps a touch of the cat in the way the King brought up the unpleasant subject of Don John's mother and showed a letter from Alba, that veteran capable of drenching the Netherlands with Protestant blood but helpless before the virago. " A terrible woman, with a head hard as a block of wood so that the only thing I can suggest is to kidnap her and to pop her into a convent without a by-your-leave." Philip's idea was that she should be brought to Spain and placed in charge of poor Doña Magdalena !

In early March Don John rode out of Madrid on a bright, still morning. Halfway to the Escorial, in the Guadarramas, the wind suddenly got up and rose to hurricane force. Lightning split trees and sent rocks

crashing down the slopes. Some of the suite were flung
down with their horses. Others were forced to take
shelter. Don John, on his big horse, galloped on through
the storm and arrived at the monastery gates alone. The
Prior and friars hurried to greet him but he would not
allow them to come out, saying with a laugh that the
weather was only fit for soldiers like him. He was shown
all the sights of the half finished " Eighth Wonder of the
World " ; visited three old and sick friars ; and the next
morning set out again.

He did not go to Villagarcia (" so as not to enter Valladolid, I do not know why," says Vanderhammer) but to
Abrojo. There he was joined by Doña Magdalena, with
a supply of new shirts and fresh linen. There were the
doings of four years to talk over during the four short
days they were together. They were happier days than
any since the week at Aquila two years ago. How different
was his Tia, in her nunlike white wimple, black veil and
sweeping skirts, her slender white hands and soft voice,
from his burly, moustached, masculine sister. Yet with
both of them he could be absolutely happy, frank and
natural, sure of unfailing sympathy and unbroken discretion.

There was Fray Juan de Calahorra too, more anxious
to hear of San Martino, Santa Trinità, Monte Cassino (on
the way from Naples to Aquila) and Montserrat, than of
Lepanto and Tunis. He had aged and was very frail,
but the eyes of the spirit were clear, though bodily ones
might be dim.

The hour of farewell came with terrible swiftness.

Every time it might be the last. Don John held his Tia
for a moment tight as he had done at Caniles before they
had closed Luis's eyes for ever, flung himself into the saddle
and was gone, galloping furiously down the wide valley
along the road to Madrid.

XXVII

"THEIR EXITS AND THEIR ENTRANCES"

(SPRING, 1575—LATE OCTOBER, 1576)

All that summer of 1575 and the following winter Genoese affairs, which were ostensibly the reason for Don John's stay in Italy, were really only a camouflage for the northern adventure. Gregory XIII's ambition was to make the restoration of England to the Catholic Church the great glory of his Pontificate as the formation of the Holy League and the consequent victory of Lepanto had been that of Pius V. The English College at Douai had already begun to pour into England the stream of priests ordained abroad of whom Cuthbert Mayne was to be the proto-martyr (1577).

English and Irish exiles haunted the courts of Rome and Madrid with eagerly enthusiastic and pathetically inaccurate promises of help from English Catholics for an invading force. The English have generally shown that they prefer to wait for its success before supporting an invasion or revolution, foreign or British. The mentalities of Rome and Spain were incapable of understanding the English character or the situation in England, though here, for once, Philip's caution and delays were favourable to him. Dr. Sanders in Madrid was still working indefatigably to extract from Philip a definite pledge of support for the rescue and marriage of Mary Stuart. It was not likely that even the most learned Jesuit controversialist would succeed where Don John, with all his personal fascination, had failed. Philip's confessor had been bold enough to write to him that his incapacity for quick action made him liable " to eternal condemnation," but even the threat of hell did not work a miracle.

A new actor now appeared on the stage, an Irish friar, Patrick O'Hely, who arrived in Rome in early June of this year. He stated that he had come commissioned by the King of Spain to tell the Pope that numerous influential Irish Catholics were only waiting the word to rise against Elizabeth, who would be dethroned in a few days and that the crown of Ireland was waiting for Don John of Austria. De Zuñiga was cautious, as well he might be, before this roseate vision of a hundred Irish chieftains uniting to welcome a new foreign ruler after freeing themselves in the flash of an eye from a foreign tyranny under which they had groaned for four centuries. The King's reply to de Zuñiga's letter was that he " had not had time to attend to Father O'Hely's business."

Another exile was also in Rome, a rather shabby soldier of fortune from Devon, Thomas Stukeley. He had been in Spain five years ago and had had a bitter taste of Spanish delay in supplying cash for wild adventures. He now (October, 1575) appeared in Naples, where he fancied that the ardent young Prince would easily catch fire from his own will-o'-the-wisp. He laid before him a plan for the invasion of England by a force of fifteen hundred Italian troops under his own command and the Papal Standard. The English Catholics would rise and the captive

Queen be rescued. This wild-cat scheme was received coolly. The Prince pointed out the insuperable difficulties : the smallness of the invading force, the impossibility of secrecy, the improbability that the Queen of Scots would be left by her gaolers near enough the sea to be easily and conveniently rescued. Stukeley returned crestfallen to Rome " to continue the negotiations." He was probably fatter in person and pocket than when he arrived for, as Lippomano had pointed out, the Prince " is of a very liberal nature, thinks that it is commercial to save money, praiseworthy to spend it, and that the more he has the more he should give away."

The King, however, seemed to think that an invasion of England under Papal auspices might be a good way of getting his own chestnuts pulled out of the fire. In fact, like Elizabeth, he would get the advantages of war without the disadvantages.

All the winter Escobedo was to and fro between Rome and the Prince. The Pope sent a verbal message that he took a deeper interest in Don John's throne and marriage than he could express in letters to Madrid.

The civil war in Genoa was ended at last, but there was plenty to do in Naples. Selim was dead, but not his ambition, and rumour said that his son was preparing to attack Southern Italy. The work of strengthening its ports and those of Sicily was made no easier by de Granvelle being succeeded as Viceroy of Naples by Don John's former opponent, the Marquis of Mondejar. Now over seventy the old man was slower, more pompous and crotchety than ever. A flippant Neapolitan said after an interview with him that he had gone to see the Viceroy of Naples but had found the King of Spain ! The Marquis, compelled to yield precedence to the Lieutenant General, retaliated by wilful delays and opposition. Relations between the two were always on the point of becoming impossible. Escobedo was distracted trying to keep the peace, in letters and by verbal messages begging the King to remove his brother from continual slights and obstructions. The early autumn and winter months, in fact, produced a perfect torrent of letters from the Prince and his secretary, to Madrid, Genoa and Rome : exasperated outbursts against Mondejar, despairing appeals for money ("I assure your Majesty things could not be worse here, for I cannot get credit for a single real"), comments to Idiaquez on Genoese affairs, to Rome about English, French and Genoese politics.

On September 2, 1575, Don John wrote to Philip with a scheme for visiting the Pope incognito on his way to Loreto, to which he had vowed a pilgrimage. He suggested riding to Rome, entering it after dark in disguise, then to spend a day sightseeing and end with a secret interview with His Holiness. Behind the lure of the wild ride and the disguise was the knowledge that in one personal interview he would gain more than in a thousand letters. There is no command to bury the talent of personal fascination in a napkin. Strange to say, on the margin of this letter there are none of the usual comments by Perez and the King : "This seems inadvisable and should on no account be done," or "This is a bad business and worries me very much, I must see what is to be done about it."

The visit to Rome did not come off. The pilgrimage to Loreto did, and it was indeed a pilgrimage. The weather, as usual, was appalling, bitterly cold, with torrents of rain, roads morasses and rivers flooded. The way lay past Aquila—which Don John would hardly have left unvisited —more than two hundred miles through the Abruzzi and over the snowbound Apennines to the shores of the Adriatic. The rain was coming down in sheets at Porto Recanati, but as soon as he caught sight of the great dome over the Holy House he snatched off hat and cloak and rode on, bareheaded and drenched, " as if he wished to make a sacrifice of himself to the Blessed Virgin to whose protection he owed his life." It was the last of her shrines which he had longed as a boy to visit : Guadelupe, Zaragoza, Montserrat, and now Loreto. It was her blue Banner which had led to victory at Lepanto. Her name, with that of her Divine Son, was to be the last word his dying lips would murmur. Lippomano had reported some laughing words of his : " I would throw myself out of the window in despair if I thought there was a man in the whole world greedier of honour and glory than I am." The desire for glory was true, but that for " the greater glory of God " came first and after it the service of the King.

The winter crawled by, marked only by perpetual bickering with Mondejar. It was enough for the young Lieutenant General to propose anything for the old Viceroy to oppose it to the limit of his power. " His Highness is youthful and hot-tempered," wrote Escobedo in cipher to the King : " but truly noble and easy to persuade to justice. . . . The Marquis of Mondejar is a fire and, as I have told your Majesty, has the vice of vanity to the last degree." (November 30, 1575.)

The Grand Commander, Luis de Requesens, died suddenly in Brussels at the beginning of March, 1576, and such was the critical state in which things were left in the Netherlands that Philip's decision as to the new Governor was made in the incredibly short time of a fortnight. His letter reached Don John on May 3. The first necessity for the pacification of the Low Countries and the maintenance of religion, wrote Philip and Perez, was the governorship of a Prince of the royal blood. Philip wished his letter had wings that it might reach his brother the sooner, that his brother had wings to reach Flanders the sooner. He was to ride north at once with only a dozen attendants, on no account to visit Spain. De Sesa was to be in command of the fleet during the " temporary " absence of its commander. Fifteen or twenty thousand ducats for the expenses of the journey were to be deducted from the money sent to pay the sailors ! Utmost secrecy must be observed and none but Escobedo must know the real goal of the journey.

Don John was far from accepting eagerly an appointment which might have seemed to bring him nearer to the realization of the English plan. Over three weeks elapsed before he answered Philip's letter. Then it was only to point out the hopeless state of affairs in the Netherlands, the country ravaged by troops whom the King could neither pay nor dismiss, the very name of Spain execrated, heresy increasing, an invasion both from France and

England more than likely. If he were forced to go he begged to be left free to use his own judgement and not be tied by orders from a distance. " I do not believe myself fitted for that nor for anything else, unless it is your Majesty's pleasure. But the world considers it my duty. It is of greater value in my eyes because it agrees with my own immovable resolution to ask nothing from your Crown, even should your Majesty offer it." (Naples, May 27, 1576. Gachard.)

Escobedo, the bearer of this letter, reached Madrid in July only to be sent straight back to Naples with orders to his master to start within twenty-four hours, via Savoy and Burgundy. " In no wise and for no reason whatsoever are you to think of coming here," wrote Philip. " Though when such a visit is possible no one can long for it more than I do, such is my pleasure in seeing you." He need not have bothered to sugar the pill. It was not taken. For the first and last time Don John flatly disobeyed orders, sailed from Genoa with three galleys and landed in Barcelona on August 22.

He was welcomed at Guadalajara by his friends, the Duke of Infantado and his brothers, Rodrigo de Mendoza and the Count of Orgaz, as well as by Antonio Perez, who brought him to his own house in Madrid, la Casilla. This was of more than Oriental magnificence. Gossip declared that visitors were requested to take off their shoes before entering as if it had been a mosque. When Don John lay in the huge silver bed guarded by angels, in the room whose furniture was all of silver, its hangings of gold and green damask, he was grateful to the friend who had given him the use of all this wealth. He did not remember Doña Magdalena's warning nor the Italian proverb she had quoted about false friendship.

The Court was at the Escorial, and Philip, in spite of disobeyed orders, received his brother graciously. After kissing the Queen's hand, Don John was just turning to greet the five-year-old Prince Ferdinand when the scabbard of his sword swung out, knocking the child to the ground. There was a scene of confusion, the Infante howling, the Queen terrified, Don John miserable and confused. The King, philosophic as ever, seeing the injury was nothing worse than a bruise, reassured his brother. The omen cast a deeper shadow on the already gloomy court, though opinions varied as to which of the Princes it foreboded evil.

During the next month affairs in the Netherlands were discussed in detail and Philip definitely approved the scheme for the invasion of England and the marriage with the Queen of Scots. It would keep Don John busy, absorb his energies and ambitions, provide him with a wife, a crown and a kingdom at no cost to Spain. Also it would have the double advantage of restoring England to the Faith and bringing her under Spanish influence.

The invasion-marriage plan had everything to recommend it from the Spanish point of view. Unluckily it was not practical politics. Fifteen of the seventeen Provinces were in revolt. Spanish troops were unpaid and mutinous. The " Beggars of the Sea," surreptitiously supported by Elizabeth, commanded most of the coasts and ports. The only government with any pretence of authority was that of the National Committee, led by the Prince of Orange.

The letter of " congratulation " to the new Governor from the Belgian Council of State (received early in September) was hardly cheering. It expressed the hope that he would soon arrive and rescue the country " from the dangerous state and tangle " in which his predecessors had left it, that he would bring no troops with him, " the country already groaning under the burden of fifty or sixty thousand . . . living in the towns and devouring the people," that he would immediately send at least a hundred thousand crowns or " all would go to ruin," and more in the same strain.

Don John could do no more than write (September 11) promising to reach the Low Countries as soon as possible and to lay the petition before the King. Long and bitter financial experience had taught him the impossibility of extracting blood from a stone. Philip could not give what he had not got, though Don John had somehow achieved that feat more than once. Money, he knew, was the crux of the matter, now as for the past seven years. It had been Alba's ill-omened tax of a tenth which had set ablaze the smoulder of revolt, lack of money which had caused the troops to sack, loot and mutiny. There were endless discussions of ways and means, both at the Escorial and in Madrid, whither Philip returned with his brother.

Perez was prodigal not only of promises of help but also of entertainment. La Casilla was always open and always full. *La Tuarte* was to be found there. After her husband's death she had had a violent attack of religious fever and had even gone so far as to buy herself an expensive habit in which to enter the Carmelite convent founded from Avila by Teresa of Jesus at the Prince of Eboli's country seat, Pastrana. Strangely enough the Prioress did not consider that the Princess had a vocation and certainly there were no signs of it now. Violent out-of-door activities were the order of the day, in honour of Don John. The old game of tilting at a figure which, if not struck squarely, swung round and swept the tilter from his horse, was brought up to date by a large ticket " *El Taciturno* " being affixed to the dummy. On one occasion it was hit with such energy that the sandbag knocked Perez, who was a spectator, so violently that he fell stunned and had to be carried into the house. A little later Don John went in to enquire. A duenna in the anteroom of the famous green and silver bedroom rose hurriedly, murmuring that the secretary was asleep and must not be disturbed. At that moment there was a burst of laughter, a man's and a woman's voice. They were those of Antonio Perez and the Princess of Eboli.

Don John had begun to see the truth of the Provençal troubadour's bitter saying: " Who drinks of life tastes poison." His letter to his old friend Garcia de Toledo (October 17, 1576) shows him under no illusions about the future, its labours and perils which would need a miracle to bring them to a successful end. " God must take the matter into His own hands and help me, if He so will, by a miracle."

Philip broadcast the fact that the new Governor was about to sail for Genoa on his way to Flanders. Prayers

were offered for his safe voyage and journey through Savoy
and Burgundy. Meanwhile Don John mounted and rode
north, the way he had travelled over twenty-two years ago
with the stout Charles Prevost in " the house on wheels."
The Escorial, its great grey bulk as enduring as the granite
hills from which it sprang; the snow-streaked Guadarramas, with their grey scrub, grey olives and little quicksilver streams; Avila, within its mighty yellow walls and
towers, a spiritual powerhouse whose force was to be felt
throughout the world; Medina del Campo and its square
castle, then at last the familiar outlines of the ash-grey,
rust-red hills towards Valladolid and the wide valley where
the vineyards were ravaged and the dun stubble was being
broken by the plough.

He lay in his narrow cell at Abrojo, with no sound save
the shuffling of feet on stone and the distant chanting of
Matins and Lauds, and always the mournful cry of the
autumn wind, blowing north from the Alpujarras, over the
bare plains of Castile, through the pines of the Landes to
the flat plains of the Netherlands, grey under a low grey
sky, grave of so many hopes and reputations.

It was not of the Netherlands that he talked to Doña
Magdalena, but of foolish things, the tricks of Monecilla,
" Austria's " rough mane and adoring yellow eyes. He
had the old Crucifix with him as he would always have it.
She had fresh shirts for him. When would he need more ?
Fray Juan would keep them company, saying little, but
with a smile that said all. The thread that bound him now
to earth seemed frailer than gossamer.

Don John had made his confession to the old man the

day of his arrival. The next morning he knelt beside his Tia at the altar of the Prior's chapel as he had done twenty years ago at his first Communion at Villagarcia. He had obtained from the Pope various privileges and indulgences for the Jesuit church and college she was building there. Old Luis already lay beside its altar. The Turkish banners from Lepanto hung on the walls and the *Lignum Crucis* he had worn in battle was there too.

He was to ride through France disguised as the Moorish slave of Ottavio Gonzaga, son of Ferrante, the famous Viceroy of Sicily. No one but his Tia must dye his hair and stain his face. He knelt in front of her and laid his head on her lap, laughing. She was nearer crying as she frizzed the thick waves and hid the lovely yellow with black. The fairness of cheeks and throat and hands had to be darkened too before he put on the coarse brown tunic and big felt hat, the heavy black riding boots. Yet even then she could not believe that any but a fool would be deceived. No stain could hide those brilliant blue eyes nor that proud, easy grace of bearing. The Prince still showed through the peasant's smock.

The horses were impatient. There was no more to be said. The love which, as he had written to her, " has never been nor ever will be equalled in this life," had no need of words. Each parting they had feared would be the last. This one they both knew *was* the last.

There was nothing left for her but to pray. From now on she had Mass said every day for her beloved " son."

XXVIII

THE LOW COUNTRIES

(October 24, 1576—May 1, 1577)

Don John covered the two hundred and fifty miles with his usual furious haste. "I have just arrived at Irun. Never in my life have I endured such fatigue. . . . Horses being few we have often been obliged to ride the same ones for more than forty or fifty miles. . . . Your Majesty may believe that we have suffered much from exhaustion and lack of sleep. Though we have got on slowly I have been troubled by a return of my old complaint. God willing, that shall not stop me, since it is of such importance to the service of God and your Majesty that I should overcome all weakness and difficulties. . . . Circumstances may arise when you would be willing to help me with your own blood, if it would be of service. Therefore once again I entreat you to supply my most urgent need, money, money and more money. Without it it would have been better not to have gambled for such high stakes." Paris was reached in a week, in spite of continuous rain, terrible roads and a delay in Bordeaux. "We fell in with a Frenchman with whom I travelled for three days as his servant, carrying his portmanteau for three days."

The old gossip Brantôme has a spicy tale of the Prince having attended a masked ball at the Louvre, where he met Margot of Navarre and fell in love with her ! Don John arrived in Paris late one night, was up at six next morning writing to Philip that he had been recognized by a servant at the Spanish embassy, so must push on at once, and left that morning. He had an interview at Joinville with the Duc de Guise, leader of the Catholic party and cousin of the Queen of Scots, whom he captivated. It was November 3, 1576, when the weary, mud-caked little party dismounted stiffly at the gates of Luxemburg fortress, where Don John was thankful to wash and comb his frizzed hair and to clean the stain from face and hands. He had come as fast as human endurance would allow, but he was too late to avert the worst catastrophe that had yet befallen the Spanish cause in the Low Countries. Only the day before the mutinous, unpaid soldiers had sacked and burned Antwerp and other towns. The " Spanish Fury," as the looting and massacre of Antwerp was called, roused the people to such a fierce thirst for vengeance that even the nominally Catholic states now flung in their lot with the Protestant ones in open revolt. The Pacification of Ghent, signed November 8, 1576, bound Brabant, Hainault, Flanders, Namur and other Catholic states and cities to support Protestant Holland and Zeeland against Spain till all Spanish troops were withdrawn, the States General convoked and all the late tyrannical edicts withdrew. Soon only Luxemburg and Limburg remained loyal.

Philip's public and official instructions bade the new Governor bring about " a true, stable and lasting peace " by " love, gentleness and benevolence." (Those who had experienced Alba's interpretation of those virtues might be pardoned for remaining sceptical.) Old privileges were to be restored, the Council of Blood abolished and a general pardon proclaimed for all but the Prince of Orange. The secret instructions arrived later. As good a bargain as possible was to be driven. If it was found necessary to withdraw the troops the States General must provide their pay. On no account must it be known that the King was in correspondence with " Messire Jean D'Autriche " as he was now to be called, to avoid the Spanish title and name.

A deputation from the Estates came to Luxemburg to place their terms before the new " Lieutenant-Governor and Captain-General of the Low Countries and the County of Burgundy." Cold and distrustful at first they soon thawed under his courtesy and charm. The paper, inspired by Orange, was laid before the Governor on December 6, just before the welcome arrival of Escobedo. It demanded the instant departure of troops, release of prisoners, acceptance of the Treaty of Ghent, a general pardon, con-vocation of the States General and an oath from the Governor to maintain all the privileges and customs of the country. The terms were those of a conqueror to a defeated foe. Orange never had any intention of their being accepted. In spite of heroic self-control on Don John's part the discussions which followed were hardly carried on in a conciliatory spirit. As he wrote to the King, obedience to him " is lost as soon as Orange gains not only pardon but thanks, honour and employment, he who is so great a traitor and a greater heretic." (December 6, 1576.)

Don John already realized that William of Orange was the guiding spirit and inspiration of the whole revolt.

Orange, as Don John wrote bluntly to Philip a little later, " is loved and feared as much as Your Majesty is hated and despised . . . the pilot who guides the bark, who can save or destroy it." The Prince was unlucky in having for his opponent a man whose genius was for diplomacy, which is only a polite name for deceit, while his own genius for war was now a weapon to cut the hand which wielded it. The dash, the reckless courage, the quick and decisive action which had won his laurels in the Alpujarras and at Lepanto, now told against him in a struggle only to be won by waiting, dissembling and treachery. He was conscious of this. Again and again the note is struck in his letters to the King, begging to be allowed to return to his own job, to be freed from this tortuous negotiating which he hated. " Everything in the world is unimportant to me except naval affairs and the sea." " Arms, not government, are my true vocation." " I must now prepare for the worst labour and misery of body and spirit possible to an honourable man, that is to do vile and dishonourable things knowing that they are so." On hearing the Turkish fleet was likely to attack Italy : " I beg Your Majesty not to spend time arguing with doctors, which is not to my taste, but to give me permission to sail."

Orange, indeed, had every advantage in the duel which ended only in his opponent's death. To his genius for intrigue and diplomacy he added endurance, patience and a cold detachment of intellect which left his judgement unbiassed and his decisions unobscured by anger or personal interest. Brought up as a nominal Catholic he was without real religion, till, later in life, he declared himself a Calvinist. He was the only one far-sighted enough to stand for religious toleration because his goal was not primarily religion but the liberation of his country from the tyranny which had drenched it in blood for the last ten years. For its freedom he was content to stand aside and let an Austrian or French puppet be set up as nominal ruler. He was not to be diverted by scruples or side issues. To serve his country he was ready to use, and did use, any weapon that came to hand. He was answerable to no authority and had the devotion of a whole people behind him, while Don John was crippled and bound by orders from the King and by the opposing pull of two forces : his loyalty to the King and his own honour. Walsingham, a shrewd observer, perceived this internal struggle in Don John. " In conference with him I might easily discern a great conflict in himself between honour and necessity. Surely I never saw a gentleman for personage, speech, wit and entertainment comparable to him."

As if there were not already enough miseries and worries, yet another unpleasant task was laid on Don John, an interview with his mother, the first and last. He had been making her a liberal allowance in addition to that granted by Philip. She showed her gratitude by telling the world that he was not the Emperor's son. Nothing is known of this first and last interview. It was successful in one thing, the consent of the lady to leave Flanders for Spain, where she died two years later. The position was an impossible one while she remained in the Low Countries.

Negotiations still dragged on into the new year. The envoys, inspired by William, stiffened their demands.

The troops must be marched away overland, not sent by
sea. This did not suit Don John at all. He had planned
to embark them on Medina Celi's ships as a preliminary to
the invasion of England. By the end of January, 1577,
the thing was boiled down to two points. Would Don
John send away the Spanish troops at once and by land?
Would he approve the Treaty of Ghent? His answer was
worthy of Philip and contained twenty-seven clauses and
arguments. At ten o'clock the next night the Commissioners returned with a lengthy document, throwing all
responsibility for future bloodshed on Don John. His
temper snapped as it had done when he had seen the four
Spaniards dangling from Veniero's yard-arm. He called
the Commissioners rebels and traitors. He would bear no
more. He was ready to draw his sword in the King's
name, as they were forcing him to do. The new war they
were starting would be the bloodiest the country had ever
known. An end was put to the scene before personal
violence had actually taken place.

The envoys were roused from their beds at midnight
by a Jesuit who brought a note from Don John agreeing
to ratify the Peace of Ghent. The next day he also agreed
to the departure of the troops by land. He had been made
to see that he had only played into William's hands by his
loss of temper.

Meanwhile the Prince of Orange had been fomenting
Elizabeth's fears of an invasion of England, at the time
when he was making it impossible. Her envoy taxed Don
John with the plan. He replied evasively that the ultimate
destination of his soldiers was Turkey, whatever route

they took to get there. He begged for the English Queen's portrait and said he hoped soon to make a private visit to kiss her hands. No doubt if this pious aspiration had been realized Elizabeth would have been delighted to add him to her collection of handsome young men and would have bestowed an affectionate nickname on him. Philip's marginal note on his brother's letter regaling him with this amusing conversation was unwontedly terse. " That was saying rather too much."

Rudolf, the young Archduke who had been educated in Spain with his brother, had just succeeded his father as the Emperor Rudolf II. He also sent a special envoy to his uncle begging him to do all in his power to bring about peace in the Netherlands. Finally, a long document was drawn up and signed by both sides at Marché-en-Famine, February 12, 1577. The worst clause in " The Perpetual Edict," from Don John's point of view, was that which stipulated the evacuation of the Spanish troops by land within forty days. " If the conditions are neither such as I desired and worked for, we have arrived at something possible. . . . The Spaniards are leaving. They take my heart and soul with them. I would rather be bewitched than see this. . . . I have kept my temper with these men [Commissioners] but they have so often driven me to the limit of endurance that, though I have generally succeeded in keeping my temper, there have been occasions when I have lost it. . . . They are afraid of me and think me very hot-headed. I abhor them and consider them to be the greatest villains. So it is most necessary that I leave here and another come to take my place. I have therefore written home very urgently (keep this secret) that I neither can nor will remain here longer, since I have, with God's help, done that for which I came, put an end to the war." (To Rodrigo de Mendoza, February 17, 1577. Maxwell.)

As always, the chief difficulty about the soldiers leaving was the lack of money. The sum guaranteed by the States was not forthcoming, and Don John had to advance a considerable sum out of his own pocket. Difficulties arose too about evacuating garrisons and appointing officers. As a friendly gesture Don John appointed a Fleming to command on the march to Italy. The Spanish officers nearly revolted. By the end of April thirty thousand men, women and followers were on the march, the men deeply insulted at not having been reviewed by the Governor nor complimented for their long services. All he could do for them was to urge the King to reward them on their arrival in Italy.

During the spring he was in constant and friendly communication with Elizabeth. It was a game as stately and complicated as the movements of the pavane and neither player was deceived. Elizabeth would not have been flattered if she could have seen the terms in which " my cousin, Señor don Jehan d'Austrice " wrote to his brother about the marriage possibility hinted at by the English envoys. " Though I see that by this means a queen and a kingdom would be restored to religion and to Your Majesty's service, nothing in the world would make me do anything dishonourable. Believe me, at the moment of writing this, I am scarlet with shame at the very thought of marriage negotiations with a woman of such scandalous life and manners." (February 2, 1577.)

Plots and counterplots, poverty, unpopularity, overwork and depression, the long, wet months of a northern winter and spring were fast breaking a body which had always lived up to, if not beyond, its slender reserve of strength. Don John had been down with fever three times within two months of his arrival at Luxemburg. He grew pale and thin. Nothing seemed left but " death and disgust," wrote Escobedo to Perez, worried about his beloved master and anxious for the King to be persuaded to release him. " Otherwise we shall see the destruction of our dearest friend. He will fall seriously ill and such is his bodily delicacy that I fear in that case he would bid us all good-night."

Then, at their darkest, things suddenly began to brighten. During a stay at Louvain, where he perfected his French, Don John won all hearts. He was publicly entertained at the Town Hall, supped at home with burgesses and their wives, proved his mastery of the bow, which he had learnt in childhood at Leganes and Villagarcia, brought down the bird at the trial of skill on the Archers' Feast (April 14) and was crowned their king. " He surpasses Circe," wrote a patriot sourly. " All are changed to worshippers, the lords drunk with his favours."

The Governor at last was able to make his state entry into Brussels on May 1. Dressed in a green cloak instead of his favourite crimson, he rode between the Papal Nuncio and the Bishop of Liège. There were all the familiar accessories ; triumphal arches spanning the streets, flags and draperies, crowds at windows and on roofs, flowers showered on him and under his charger's hoofs. Bells pealed. Trumpets shrilled. The Mass of the Holy Ghost was celebrated in the Chapel Royal. Clouds of incense dimmed the blood red of the vestments. Wine, beer, and oratory flowed outside the Town Hall and St. Gudule. On Sunday the Governor carried his light in the torchlight procession of the Blessed Sacrament. The next day came Philip's ratification of the peace and, quite as welcome, four hundred thousand crowns and the promise of more to come.

All seemed sunshine. It was no more than " the uncertain glory of an April day."

XXIX

"MORTAL MIXTURE"

(MAY, 1577—JULY, 1577)

This summer, on his way home from offering Eliza-beth's congratulations to the new Emperor, Philip Sidney had an interview with Don John. "That gallant Prince," says Sidney's biographer, "found himself so stricken with this extraordinary planet that he gave more honour and respect . . . to this hopeful young gentleman than to the ambassadors of mighty princes."

This meeting with one seven years younger than him-self, but so like himself in charm, courage, chivalry and love of adventure, must have been to the Prince a welcome oasis in a desert of traitors and time-servers, of plotters against his life and liberty. As long ago as March, 1577, he had been warned by the French king's agent in the Low Countries of a Frenchman who had come there commis-sioned, it was said by the Duke of Alençon, to assassinate him. "This is spoken of in Brussels as an act of great merit and glory," he had written to the King. "I therefore beg your Majesty's permission to offer my person to Alençon by other methods than a treasonable one, so that he can do what he so much wishes to." (March 24.)

The last suggestion is typical of Don John, both in its recklessness and its lack of statesmanship. The attempts, first to capture him, then, as Orange saw in him an opponent more dangerous than he had thought at first, to murder him, continued during the rest of his life. " The only difference between the new Governor and Alba or de Requesens," Orange had written soon after Don John's arrival, " is that he is younger and more foolish, less capable of concealing his venom, more impatient to dip his hands in blood." This opinion he afterwards had reason to modify. Indeed, considering Don John's natural dislike of pretence and his extremely hot temper, he was with few exceptions surprisingly courteous and self-controlled with his opponents. His real feelings towards them are expressed in no uncertain fashion in his letters to his brother. " Everyone and everything here are full of the devil. May he fly away with them ! If one who suffers so much from them may say so." " Their rudeness and insolence make me long to declare war, to smash, destroy and bathe them in blood." Hardly Christian sentiments but natural enough for a passionate young man who knows he is tied to work which, as he often writes, would need for success a miracle worked by God Himself. All the time, too, that he is imprisoned in this hell, his thoughts and desires are away south with the Mediterranean fleet. He is continually making suggestions about it, enquiring for details of its movements, angry when changes in organization are made without consulting him who is still Admiral in command.

He was now to lose the friend and secretary who was even more necessary than " money, money and more money." Escobedo left on July 10 for Madrid to put before the King the whole state of things in the Netherlands " and specially in financial matters, which at this

moment are of the first importance in this poor country
. . . that provision may be made as quickly as possible."
The secretary also hoped that he might induce Philip to
release his brother from the hell of which he had written
tragically to Perez : " My life, honour and soul are at
stake, the first two certainly lost, the last in grave danger
from my state of absolute despair."

There was of course truth in Perez's oft-repeated assertion of the necessity of the Prince remaining in Flanders,
and in this he was steadily supported by the King, who was
kept busy soothing his brother's angry despair, hurt pride
and fierce desire to get back to his own proper work on the
sea. He assures him that his hot temper and irritation
with the rebels have not created such a bad impression as
he thinks, that he has already done work which no one
else could have done and that it is as yet impossible to
release and replace him. " You are even more necessary
for what still remains to do than you have been for what
has been done." Certainly if anyone or anything short of
a miracle could have rescued the country from the morass
of blood and ruin into which Spanish misrule had plunged
it, it would have been Don John, had it not been too late,
had he been sent years before, with money enough and a
free hand. As it was, no miracle was worked for the
Spanish cause, though the Protestants claimed Don John's
death as one conveniently supplied by a Calvinist Providence. " God dealeth most lovingly with her Majesty in
taking away her enemies," Walsingham wrote jubilantly
when news came of the Prince's death.

It was inevitable, Philip's character being what it was,

that he should be ready to sacrifice his brother, in spite of his genuine affection for him, on the altar of what he believed to be God's and Spain's interest. But there was behind him the sinister influence of Perez, twisting the most innocent phrases of Don John's impatience and depression and Escobedo's indiscreet enthusiasms into something dark and treacherous. As he decoded the cipher letters he had every chance of putting his own interpretations on them. Indeed on more than one occasion Escobedo begs him to tone down the violence of some of Don John's expressions before putting the deciphered letter into the King's hands. Perez's reasons for plotting the Prince's ruin and Escobedo's death are difficult to fathom. No doubt he was forced to the murder of the latter by the fury and jealousy of the Princess of Eboli, but it would rather have seemed to his interest to be friends with Don John, who, in the event of the King's death, would almost certainly have been regent. The whole affair is discussed at length by Bertrand under the appropriate title of " A Dark Affair."

The stage was now ready for the last act of the tragedy, and Escobedo walked into the trap set by the villain of the piece, while the hero, alone and exiled, was eating out his heart. It is a terrible sight to be compelled to witness a long drawn out agony of mind and spirit, to see a man slowly bleeding to death. That is the story of the next fourteen months.

In an atmosphere of hatred, failure, treachery and desertion, it was natural that the side of Don John which had always been drawn to solitude and contemplation, should again show itself. From the moment he had arrived in Luxemburg, if not in Naples, when he got Philip's letter appointing him Governor of the Low Countries, the Prince had felt that this was the end of glory and success, more than that, it was a death sentence. By mid-February, 1577, he wrote to Perez that he saw nothing for it but to withdraw to a hermitage. It was no mere passing whim, the result of depression, but a resolution which grew stronger with the passing of the months. " All my thoughts are of a hermit's cell, where a man does not labour in vain because his goal is a spiritual one," he wrote. And again, in July, 1578 : " I am resolved to retire to a hermitage rather than ever return here, if I escape this danger as well as the many others from which God has delivered me." On his deathbed he confided to the Jesuit Father, Juan Fernandez, the determination he had taken months before to retire, when his work in the Low Countries was done, to one of the cells in the rocks above Montserrat, below the " Stone Watchmen."

Meantime work was still to be done, the work which he hated and which came so unnaturally to him but which he did " for the service of God and your Majesty." Negotiations had been reopened with Orange, " the pilot who guides and governs all." Don John still retained his humour ; there is plenty of it in his long and intimate letters to Rodrigo Mendoza, but it had a bitter flavour now. There seems to be more than a suspicion of irony in the way he points out to William the chance offered him " of living from now on in peace, riches and honour. . . . Let your lordship consider that the discretion and prudence of

honourable men consists chiefly in recognizing their
obligations and fulfilling them. . . . I assure you that it is
impossible for me to break my word, nor have I ever done
so." (May 15, 1577.)

Both Don John and William knew that war must be the
ultimate issue, but William saw that delay and diplomacy
were all in his favour. He had no wish to be the first to
draw the sword, while the Prince asked nothing better
than to be done with temporizing and intrigue. The
second mission to Orange at Middelburg ended, as might
have been anticipated, in a deadlock. The Prince wrote a
little later (at the end of July) to the King that there was
nothing in the world more loathed by Orange than the
King, whose blood he would like to drink !

Before then, however, Elizabeth's portrait and Margot
of Valois had both arrived. Don John studied the portrait
for some time in silence. His only comment was a question
as to whether the Queen ever wore Spanish dress. This
was hardly the admiration expected by Gloriana's envoy.
He would probably have been more surprised still if he
had been a thought reader. Henry of Navarre's wife was
officially on her way to take the waters at Spa. Really
she came to prepare the way by her intrigues with the
States for her favourite brother, Alençon, whom she
hoped to get appointed Governor after Don John's death,
which was hardly to be expected in the course of nature.
She brought all her batteries of beauty and wit to bear on
the Prince. Namur was in a whirl of gaiety for four days
in July : open-air fêtes, dances and banquets. Her would-be
victim admired but was not deceived. " Her beauty is

more diabolical than human," was his verdict, " made rather to damage and destroy men's souls than to save them."

His mind was occupied with a more interesting plan than the amusement of a loose woman. He bade her a ceremonious farewell on her barge early on the morning of her departure, mounted and galloped off, ostensibly to hunt. He had other game in view than that which swarmed in the woods round Namur. All the time he had been in Namur the citadel had been commanded by an officer who refused to acknowledge his or the King's authority. Now, with the Count of Barlaymont and his four sons, Don John rode up to the citadel and was soon seated at breakfast with the commanding officer, who could not well refuse hospitality.

At a given signal Don John suddenly rose from table, drew his sword and demanded the surrender of the citadel in the King's name. Faced with a drawn sword, covered by five de Barlaymont pistols, the gates and towers of the citadel in the hands of German soldiers who had been hidden in the wood by the Prince's orders, the officer had no alternative but to surrender.

Everyone was pleased. Don John was delighted to have a sword in his hand again instead of uselessly at his side, to have regained an important post by military strategy and at the point of the sword, though without bloodshed. Orange congratulated himself because he could now truthfully call high heaven to witness that the treacherous and bloodthirsty Spaniard, not he, had first infringed the Peace of Ghent, which had always irked him.

The clouds seemed to be lifting a little. It was time.

The climate, ceaseless work and worry had undermined the Prince's health, not strong at the best of times. The atmosphere of fear, hatred and distrust in which he lived was poison to one who had always been a popular hero, whose charm had seldom failed to win over his opponents, whose feelings were sensitive to the smallest slight or hurt to his pride and honour. There was the continual nightmare, want of money (a mean and degrading trial), as well as the secret menace of assassination which shakes the most iron nerves. The note of failure and despair running through his letters is not to be wondered at. " I am broken-hearted to be in this hell and to be forced to remain in it." " Up till now I have been nothing but a voice crying in the wilderness." " God knows how much I wish to avoid pushing things to extremes but I do not know what else to do." " I never desired anything more than to win the crown of peace for these poor States, but we must take up arms lest our throats be cut." " I thank our Lord Who has given me a heart strong enough to bear all, so that I am resolved not to drown in this flood till it turns to pure blood. . . . It is with such labours and perils that I guard Christianity for God, the States for the King and for myself my honour, which is still within my grasp, though hanging by such a frail thread."

XXX

THE SWORD

(Summer, 1577—July, 1578)

Far from fulfilling Don John's pious aspiration and flying away with the Netherlands, the devil amused himself by making confusion worse confounded. Some of the patriotic Catholic nobles founded a " Centre " party equally opposed to the Governor and the Spaniards and William and the Protestants. They invited the Archduke Mathias, younger brother of the Emperor, to be their leader. William would not have chosen a young Catholic of twenty, weak, amiable and ambitious, as sovereign of his country, but the thing was done and it would prove another thorn in Don John's fevered flesh. The latter was indeed in a difficult position. He wrote to Alessandro that it was useless to decide on a course of action till the Archduke arrived, but that, if he joined the rebels, he must expect to be treated as one. Elizabeth and her ministers were not pleased either by this new turn of events. They wrote to William that no more support would be forthcoming unless he himself was appointed Lieutenant General in order to control the Catholic sympathies of the new party.

Things were rapidly coming to a head. The capture of the Namur citadel by Don John and the rising in Antwerp which resulted in all foreign troops having to leave the city, showed that open war was only a question of time.

Don John, thankful that the sword had at last outworn its sheath, wrote to the King that the aggressive attitude of the States and rebellion in several towns, rendered the recall of the troops from Italy an absolute necessity. The King acted promptly. He wrote endless letters : to Italy ordering every available man to be marched at once to Flanders ; to de Granvelle in Rome telling him to hurry to Aquila and persuade Margaret to resume her governorship of the Netherlands ; to Alessandro asking him to set out at once for Flanders.

Alessandro was on a visit to his mother when the Cardinal arrived at Aquila. Margaret, like a wise woman, declined with thanks and stayed in the peace of her mountain home. Alessandro, equally delighted at the prospect of reunion with his friend and the chance of active service, rode off at once and, imitating Don John's method of travel, arrived in the Low Countries on December 18, 1577.

Eleven days before that the Estates had ended futile negotiations by declaring the deposition of Don John from all his offices, as a breaker of the peace he had sworn to observe and as an enemy of the Commonweal. An Act of Union was signed by all ranks of the people, even by the Catholic nobles, recognizing the right of every man to his religious beliefs and the duty of toleration. It was the voice of Orange speaking through the Estates.

Poor Mathias had made a dramatic flight from the palace at Vienna in his night attire and had then ridden through Germany in disguise, in the best Don John romantic style. He had now been waiting for recognition by the Estates

for two months and when it came he found himself a
puppet in the clever subtle hands of " The Silent." However he was installed at Brussels with much pomp and
eloquence on January 18, 1578.

The French Catholic party under Guise, whom Don John
had met and won on his way to Luxemburg, was whole-
heartedly in his favour.   Henry III, though he had not
supported the intrigues of his brother and sister for Alençon
to succeed Don John " when dead," was all the same
suspected of being hostile.   Elizabeth had a new matri-
monial fit and sent a special envoy who assured Don John
that the Queen had no intention of marrying her " Frog "
(as she had lovingly nicknamed Alençon) but would prefer
an Austrian husband.   If the Prince could obtain from the
States General his nomination as Perpetual Governor of
the Netherlands he might hope to share the English throne.
The Pope, as great a dreamer as Don John had once been,
and as incapable as most Italian ecclesiastics of understanding the English character or English politics, was fired by a
vision of the withered middle-aged spinster transformed
into a Catholic wife and mother, the " Dowry of our Lady "
restored again to the bosom of the Church.   Don John,
with only a few miles of grey stormy sea between him and
the white cliffs of Kent, knew better.   Also he was sick
to death of these ridiculous pretences.   He replied to the
envoy bluntly that he was just about to obey, with all his
heart, the commands of his sovereign to make war on the
rebels, that he was a soldier, not a diplomat, and knew
nothing of foreign policy, English, French or Imperial.

Elizabeth flew into one of her Tudor rages when she

heard of the coldness with which her advances had been received and cursed Spaniards and the " Bastard " with gusto. As she knew that her Catholic subjects considered her one the retort was merely the childish one of " *Tu quoque.*"

Spanish and Italian troops were massing on the frontiers of Savoy. Alessandro had arrived. Don John was not worried about the English Queen's rather shop-soiled offers of marriage. Soon he would be in the field, his proper place, away from endless arguments and intrigues.

A huge three-tailed comet appeared about the same time as Alessandro and blazed across the murky Flemish skies for two months. An omen of evil, muttered men whose nerves were strung to the last pitch of fear and expectancy. For once the omen was to be fulfilled.

After fourteen months of hell Don John was happy. He was in the saddle and in his element again, collecting troops and organizing in preparation to taking the field. For the first time since Escobedo left he had a friend to whom he could confide everything. Nearly a year ago he had begged Philip to send him the Prince of Parma. Now Alessandro was there and could be shown all the plans of the campaign as well as seeing all Philip's and Perez's letters and hearing all the difficulties and intricacies of the position. Alessandro was delighted, too, to be on active service again—his talents had been rusting since the year after Lepanto—and to be with his uncle again. But he was shocked at Don John's appearance. The Prince was thin and pale as a ghost, wasted with fever of mind and body, had lost all the old charming gaiety and splendour of manner and bearing. Though barely thirty-one he now looked more.

The scheme which had cheered him on his arrival in the Low Countries was now impracticable. He had to send an envoy to Guise to tell him that there was neither money nor men to spare for any undertaking but the suppression of the revolt, though he still hoped later to be able to restore Mary Stuart to her throne and England to the Church. In his heart he knew that a dream, once shattered, can never be recaptured.

He was at Namur by the end of January, 1578, with twenty thousand foot and two thousand horse, under experienced officers and old friends. The army of the States at Gemblours (nine miles north-west of Namur) was slightly superior in numbers, much inferior in quality. It was commanded by de Goignies, a veteran who had served under Charles V and had been in the famous cavalry charge which had won the battle of St. Quentin for Philip. He began to advance on Namur, then courage or resolution failed. He withdrew again to Gemblours and most of his officers returned to Brussels for a fashionable wedding.

Don John and the Prince of Parma spent January 30 on horseback, exploring the country round the enemy's position. Their army advanced at dawn next day, Don John with Alessandro in the centre, beside his Standard, embroidered, as that of the League had been, with a Crucifix, but with the motto: " *In hoc signo vici Turcos, in hoc signo vincam haereticos.*"

The road from Namur to Gemblours runs along a wind-

ing valley watered by a stream. The heavy winter rains
had flooded the stream so that the whole valley was a
marsh, the road deep in water. Alessandro had joined
the cavalry in the van. He saw the enemy retreating along
the higher ground to avoid the wet, saw too from the broken
lines of their lances that their progress was slow as well as
disordered. He had one of those flashes of inspiration
typical of his military genius. If he and some of the horse
could get through the flood they would be able to take the
enemy in rear and flank and turn a retreat into a rout.
He sent back a message to Don John. " I am about to
plunge into the gulf like the ancient Roman. By God's
help and under the star of Austria I hope to win a great
victory." He snatched a lance from a pikeman, borrowed
a horse bigger and fresher than his own, set spurs to it and
dashed into the deep, muddy water, followed by the cavalry.
All depended on the depth of the floods and the ground
underfoot. Horses and men might go deep into water and
mud and, weighed down by armour, sink to an unpleasant
and ignominious death. " The star of Austria," however,
and the genius of Parma were in the ascendant. Alessandro
reached dry land and waving the borrowed lance led his
men in a furious charge against that part of the enemy's
line which had considered itself safe from attack. It fled.
All the efforts of de Goignies and young Egmont failed to
restore the broken morale. Fleeing cavalry galloped over
and through running infantry, who threw away their arms
and ammunition to join the race for safety. Thirty-four
standards, artillery, ammunition and baggage were taken.
De Goignies and the few officers who were not safely at

the rear or in Brussels for the wedding were also captured. Thousands were killed, while the Spanish loss was practically nil. The army of the Estates had ceased to exist.

Gemblours was spared from pillage and massacre by Don John's orders. Few of the four hundred common soldiers taken prisoner escaped hanging or drowning.

The Archduke and his Council at Brussels were busy discussing the best use to make of the army when news came that it had been annihilated. William arranged for the defence of the capital and withdrew with his puppet and counsellors to Antwerp.

An immediate advance on Brussels was urged at the council of war held after the battle. Don John, cautious for once, probably under Parma's advice, decided that his resources in men and money did not justify a step whose failure would more than undo the advantages of his late victory.

Most of the towns in the southern provinces fell to the Spanish army. A mutiny of German troops before Nivelle was crushed by Don John sharply and sternly, though only one ringleader was executed. These successes, however, were balanced by the loss of control in Antwerp, where the townsfolk had driven out not only the Spanish garrison but also all the Catholics, lay and clerical.

Still, Don John felt that, as far as his part was concerned, the tide of war had set definitely in his favour when, at the end of February, came an envoy from Madrid with amazing instructions. There were letters and messages to the Estates, expressing the King's ardent desire for peace and his intention of appointing as successor to his brother

either the Prince of Parma or (if he would make his submission) the Archduke Mathias. The Catholic nobles,
tired of the young fool, had reopened intrigues with France
and invited Alençon to be their sovereign. Elizabeth,
now flirting again with her " Frog," promised the unusually
large subsidy of a hundred thousand pounds. Orange, on
the strength of this, arranged with John Casimir, Count
Palatine, to lead twelve thousand German troops across the
Rhine. New taxes and subsidies were gladly raised through
all the revolting provinces. Recruits were pouring in to
the patriot army.

The appointment of a successor and his own departure
had long been Don John's keenest wish but this move of
Philip's was like a stab in the back just when things had
begun to improve. Still, nearly two million crowns from
the King and the promise of two hundred thousand more
every month, were cheering, and the camp in Hainault
excited the admiration even of the English agent. Discipline
was strict, pillage forbidden, all goods had to be paid for.
The country folk found the enemy good customers, as the
Irish found the English garrisons in old days. The Spanish
devil was not so black as he was painted when properly
paid and disciplined. The Governor himself began to be
popular. " By these humanities he maketh deep impression in the hearts of the people and so changeth the course
of the war that he beginneth to make less in the popular
sort the hatred universally borne to the nature of the
Spaniards." Such was the report sent home to Walsingham.

But Fate had a worse blow in store than any she had yet
dealt. News came at the end of April that Escobedo had

been assassinated in Madrid. The crisis had been brought about by his discovery of the adultery of Antonio Perez and the Princess of Eboli. It was necessary to strike at once to prevent him, with his usual fervent indiscretion, rushing off to tell the King. It was not long before the Madrileños fixed the guilt on the right culprits. Why they were not brought to immediate and summary justice is a long and tangled story.

Don John was plunged in despair. It was bad enough to lose his faithful friend and invaluable secretary, through whose hands all letters and business passed. To know him murdered and to guess his murderers was the worst of all. The daggers of Perez's hired assassins struck a mortal blow at the master as well as the servant.

This was the last straw. The body whose strength had long been undermined by work, worry, misery and an unhealthy climate refused any longer to answer to the spur of mind and will. The Prince broke down completely in the early summer and had to be taken to Namur for treatment. Luckily Alessandro was there and could be left in command. He brought the siege of Limbourg to a successful end after a few hours.

XXXI

FLIGHT

(July—October 1, 1578)

Convalescence was a slow business. It is difficult to pick up strength when there is none to pick up. As long ago as the previous October Don John had written of " the ill-health I drag about with me as a fitting companion to my other misfortunes," of the drastic purgings and bleedings which were the doctors' only idea of a cure for dysentery and fever, of his tired and overworked body as well as of his mental and spiritual sufferings.

These weeks of forced inactivity, with his responsibilities delegated to Alessandro, seemed almost a foretaste of the solitude and silence of the cloister to which he had turned with such longing. The resolve which had long been forming itself now took definite shape. He dreamed of ending his days in one of the hermitages tucked into the strange enchanted mountains above Montserrat. It was there rather than to Abrojo or San Martino that his sick thoughts turned. It was the peace of the Benedictines, whose Order has been called the heart of the Church, for which his broken heart craved.

These twenty-three months in the Netherlands, though he had called them hell, had in truth been Purgatory. During that time the old arrogance, impatience, ambition, self-glorification were purged away till only the pure gold was left. His confessor, the Franciscan friar Francisco de Orantes, tells us that during these two years the Prince never frequented the Sacraments less than twice a month, often three times, as well as making a general confession on such occasions as the eves of the battles of Gemblours and Mechlin. He had another priestly friend and confidant as well as the friar, a wise and saintly Jesuit, Father Juan de Fernandez. In him the Prince found the same help and holiness as he had found with Fray Juan at Abrojo and the Jesuit Cristobal Rodriguez on the *Real* before and after Lepanto.

Don John proved himself too a father to his soldiers. He took endless care for their spiritual as well as for their physical well-being. He visited sick and wounded in camp as well as in hospital or billets and saw that they were not neglected nor forgotten by those told off to attend to their bodily needs nor by the priests charged to give them the Sacraments. No doubt the good friar is exaggerating slightly when he assures us that the camp was like a great monastery, but it is true that Don John, not content with delegating duties, himself saw to it that they were performed. No wonder that the soldiers declared after his death " that he had not died like a man but had flown straight to heaven like an angel."

He was up and about again by the end of July, 1578. The weather had been miserable. He ends the last letter he was to write to Rodrigo (July 20) " and without sun for more than a month." He was then at Tirlemont, whither he had advanced with every available man against the new patriot army, now twenty thousand strong, near Mechlin.

A large proportion of his own men was needed for garrison duty and to watch Alençon on the French frontier. He had with him twelve thousand foot and five thousand horse. The entire Council of War, except Parma and Serbellone, supported his suggestion of attacking the enemy. Parma gave as his reasons for dissent the superiority of the enemy both in numbers and position and his belief that a defeat would mean the final destruction of the royal cause. He was supported by Gabriel Serbellone, the stout old defender of the Tunis fort, who, released from his Turkish prison, had hurried to Flanders to serve again under Don John. The two were overruled. Attack was decided on. The Spanish troops deployed in order of battle, flags flying, drums beating, trumpets blowing. It was the last time Don John was to see the " beauty of an army with banners." The weather, after all these sunless weeks, had changed suddenly to oppressive heat, all the more unbearable because so unusual. The sun blazed mercilessly down from the colourless sky of northern heat.

Bossu, now in command of the rebel army, remained within his strong entrenchments and refused to be drawn even by the feinted attack and retreat of a company of musketeers. Alessandro jumped from his horse, snatched a pike and placed himself at the head of the advancing infantry. A messenger galloped back with news that the enemy was in full flight. Both Don John and Parma refused to swallow the bait and an order was sent to the vanguard to halt. It was too late. They were in the trap.

The Scots company in Bossu's army discarded their plaids to be cooler for their psalm-singing. The psalms finished, they came to the conclusion that kilts also were unnecessarily hot, tore them off too and, practically naked, charged and broke the startled Spaniards. Parma, sent to the rescue, found a narrow path through the wood and gardens, led his infantry along it, attacked the enemy cavalry by surprise and enabled the remnant of the vanguard to withdraw to safety.

As at Sheriffmuir in 1715 each side claimed a victory. This meant that it was barren for both. The Spanish losses were heavy, but the genius of Alessandro, the courage of officers and men, were some consolation to Don John. At Tirlemont, where he withdrew after the battle, he recognized in a man at his public audience an Englishman, Ratcliff, who, the ambassador had warned him, had come to assassinate him. The Prince received the suppliant coolly, listened to his pathetic tale of a Catholic exile, wife and children, no money, etc., and then dismissed him. Ratcliff and his companion were caught, admitted under torture (never a test of truth) that they had been released from prison by Walsingham to murder the Spanish Prince. He did not even have them executed, though, after his death, they received swift justice from Parma.

He was soon to meet the reputed sender of assassins. Once more negotiations were on foot. Soldiers were pushed into the wings while diplomats filled the stage. Racked with fever, Don John rode out to a huge oak-tree on the plain outside Namur which had been chosen as the meeting place for him, the commissioners of the Estates and the English and imperial ambassadors. He read the proposals and returned them with the brief assertion that they were impossible. Walsingham's explanation that the Queen's help to William had only been to guard against a French invasion was received with the silence such a ridiculous lie deserved. Presently the Prince asked Walsingham, in that odd mixture of Spanish, Italian and French in which the conversation was carried on, what he thought of the proposed terms. " Indeed they are hard but it is only by pure menace that we have extorted them from the Estates." " Then you may tell them to keep their offers to themselves. They will not do for me." The soldier cornered the diplomat by asking for his advice. After a long pause Walsingham evaded the issue. He was " the physician who declined to prescribe medicine until he was quite sure that the patient would swallow it. 'Tis no use wasting counsel nor drugs." It was after this interview that the English minister wrote his appreciation of " the incomparable gentleman for personage, speech, wit and entertainment."

By the beginning of September Alençon had signed the bond in which the States granted him an empty title and nothing more. John Casimir, with his twelve thousand Germans, had joined Bossu near Mechlin. Protestant volunteers were still hurrying to the national standard. Henry of France was prepared to invade Spanish Burgundy if his brother was successful in Hainault.

Don John, hopelessly outnumbered, his army unpaid and decimated by plague, could do no more than hold Namur and keep open the way for reinforcements, of whose arrival he had little hope. With Gabriel Serbellone he drew up and began to put in execution the plans for a large

fortified camp on the heights of Bouges, a couple of miles
from Namur and commanding both the Meuse and the
Sambre. The camp had a sanitary as well as a military
reason. It was absolutely necessary to get the troops
away from the town, where the plague was rapidly spreading
in the old houses crowded round the castle. The ramparts
were finished and part of the army moved into the camp by
mid-September. Don John, who had been daily visiting
the hospital as well as the sick in billets, went down on
September 16 with alternate fits of shivering and burning
heat, and pains all over him. He dragged himself from bed
the next morning to hear Mass and attend to business. He
knew himself that it was the beginning of the end, though
the doctors were worried about seventy-year-old Serbellone but not about the young Prince.

Though he collapsed he was determined to move into
camp as he had intended. Too weak to sit a horse or
endure a litter he was carried in his camp bed on men's
shoulders, up through the stubble fields, bare vineyards and
woods in their autumn glory. His arrival at the camp was
unexpected. Nothing had been prepared. He refused to
allow any of the officers to turn out of such quarters as
they had managed to secure. One of his captains was
camping in a barn. A half-ruined pigeon-house attached
to it was hurriedly cleaned, the pigeons chased from their
home. The leaking roof was patched up and a skylight
covered, silk hangings tacked up on the mouldy walls and
scent sprinkled on them and the filthy floor in a vain
attempt to drown the smell of damp and dung. The
broken ladder to the loft was strengthened enough for

the victor of Lepanto to be carried up to his last earthly quarters.

He had loved splendour and pageant, had been " beautiful as Apollo, splendid as an Archangel " in his doublets of crimson and cloth of gold, sewn with pearls and belted with rubies, the white plumes of his hat and his white velvet cloak clasped with huge emeralds. He had been the hero of Christendom, the terror of the infidel. Now, poor, betrayed, a failure, he was dying in a ruined hut, his once gorgeous wardrobe a few shabby things, shrunk with wet, stained with yellow Flemish mud. " He died in a hovel, poor as a common soldier," wrote Fray Francisco to Philip : " In this he imitated the poverty of Christ."

The day before this last attack had begun the Prince had written hopelessly to Pedro de Mendoza at Genoa : " His Majesty is resolved on nothing. At least I am kept in ignorance of his intentions. Here life is doled out to us by moments. It is obvious that we are left here to pine to death. God guide us all as He thinks best, for in His hands are all things." And the same day to Doria : " They have cut off our hands. Nothing is left us but to stretch out our heads too." (Motley.)

He wrote one more letter to his brother between the paroxysms of fever and the terrible headaches which almost blinded him (September 20). It was a sketch of recent events, a warning against French influence and a last passionate appeal for orders for the direction of affairs, " desiring more than life some decision on your Majesty's part. . . . Our lives are at stake. All that we can hope for is to lose them with honour."

Early on Sunday, September 21, Don John told his confessor that, in spite of the doctors, he felt the end near. Not only was he enduring acute pain but the little strength left was fast draining away. It was a good thing to die poor, he said ; having nothing to leave he need not trouble to make a will, so could devote himself to making his soul. He then made his general confession, " with much humility and great grief," and received the Viaticum during the Mass celebrated by the Jesuit Father Fernandez in the " room." Later in the day as many officers as could crowd into the miserable place were summoned. Don John handed over all his authority, civil and military, to the Prince of Parma, naming him (in the event of his own death) Governor and Commander of the Netherlands till the King's pleasure was known. Alessandro accepted the responsibility, which, knowing the hopeless state of affairs, he would have certainly refused if he had consulted self-interest or ambition. When, kneeling beside the bed, he took the baton from the fever-wasted hand of his " most beloved uncle " he broke down completely, burying his head in his hands and sobbing bitterly, as most of the hardened veterans were doing.

His public duty done, the dying man could attend to his own few concerns. He told the Franciscan that he now gave up all he possessed—little as it was—to the King, only begging his Majesty to pension his faithful servants and to continue his care of Barbara Blomberg. The confessor and Ottavio Gonzaga (who had ridden with him from Madrid to Luxemburg) were to take charge of his body. If the King allowed, it should be buried beside that of their father, Charles V, in the Escorial. If not, in the monastery of our Lady of Montserrat, " for whom in life he had a special devotion." He ended the interview with a smiling question. " Is it not just and right, Father, that I who do not own a hand's breadth of earth should be made free of the wide realm of heaven ? "

The days crawled by. Alessandro, when not busy with military affairs, was continually at the bedside. Over it, on the rotting wall, hung the little charred Crucifix, when it was not in the hands of the dying man. The doctors martyred their patient with violent remedies and cruel draughts. In the attacks of delirium, which grew more and more frequent, Don John fought his battles again. He was in the valleys of the Alpujarras, under the crashing walls of Galera, standing in his tent with the red banner of Aben Aboo under his feet. " More I could not have desired, less would not have contented me." All his desires had crumbled into dust. He was emptied of all earthly things but pain. He was at Lepanto, the throbbing of his head the crash of meeting galleys, the blackness of his sight the drifting smoke of cannon. The strange sinking of everything under him was the rise and fall of the deck as the *Real* came to anchor off Carthage and he saw the flash of flamingoes, rose-flame like angels' wings against the sunset sky. Those watching by him heard him mutter continually : " Is this better for the King's service ? " Always the service of his brother, not his own.

There were lucid moments, when he talked with Alessandro, with his confessor, with Father Fernandez. It was to the Jesuit that he showed a little book which he pulled from under his pillow, with prayers written in his own hand, beginning with those he had learnt as a child with Doña Magdalena. He had never missed reading them for a single day in his life, he said. Now these blinding headaches made it impossible for him to see. The good Jesuit took the worn manuscript book and read the prayers as he had been asked to do. He told afterwards that the reading had taken an hour—an hour which Don John had somehow managed to snatch every day in dangers and actions of war on land or sea, from the burdens of organization and diplomacy, from the gaieties of siren cities. " In fact it was a complete index to his relations with God in all the crises of his life . . . which only the holy Father Juan Fernandez had the happiness to know." (Coloma.)

In another quiet interval he confided to Father Fernandez his resolution of months ago to withdraw to Montserrat, his wish to be buried there if not at the Escorial, though " it matters little where my body shall rest till the last day." He had already commended " his soul to God and his body to the country he loved most on earth." There is no word of her whose " love has never been nor ever will be equalled in this world." As at their last farewell at Abrojo, there was no need of words or messages.

Fray Francisco asked the Prince on September 30 if he would like Extreme Unction. The dying man could hardly manage to speak but just murmured : " Yes, Father, Jesus ! Quick ! "

The next day was the first of October, the month he had always called his luckiest, since the battle of Lepanto. Bodily agony was lessening. He was kneeling beside Doña

Magdalena at his First Communion in the chapel at Villa-garcia. Don Garcia and Fray Juan de Calahorra were smiling at him. He was back again in the present, dimly conscious of the weight of his body, pigeons preening themselves against the oblong of pale sky, the Franciscan's brown habit, the hardness of the wooden Crucifix under his cold fingers, the blackness of Alessandro's bent head, of the Jesuit's gown. Then they were all drowned in the rising tide of darkness.

Someone whispered in his ear. The Son of God, the Word Incarnate, had descended into this ruined, crowded room. Don John's hand went to his head, pulled off cap and compresses. His last movement was a salute to his divine Master. His lips continued to form the words: " Jesus, Mary." Then they were still.

There was no sound but the cooing of the pigeons and the prayers for the dying, those magnificent prayers in which the Catholic Church summons the whole Celestial Hierarchy and the Communion of Saints to assist one sinful soul in its passage from this world. The last faint breath ceased imperceptibly and the soul passed (in the Franciscan's words) " like a heavenly bird slipping through our hands without the least stir of life."

*   *   *   *   *

" *So he passed over and all the trumpets sounded for him on the other side.*"

(BUNYAN.)

NOTE

AUTHORITIES. Sir William Stirling Maxwell's *Don John of Austria*, in two large quarto volumes, packed with learning and profusely illustrated, is the only full and authoritative life of Don John in English, though a translation of Father Luis Coloma's *Jeromín* was published over twenty years ago. Both are now out of print. In Maxwell's monumental work the background of contemporary politics tends to dwarf and obscure the hero. The reverse is the case in the Jesuit's romantic sketch, parts of which are characterized by a sentimental piety alien to the English mentality.

Marmol and Mendoza, both of them contemporaries and eye-witnesses, are the chief authorities on the Morisco rebellion, Rosell and de la Gravière on the Lepanto campaign.

Professor Geyl's *Revolt in the Netherlands* is the last word on the troubles in the Low Countries and corrects Motley's strong prejudice and occasional inaccuracies.

The letters quoted in Parts I and II of the present sketch are from *Documentos Ineditos,* unless otherwise stated, those in Part III from Gachard's *Correspondance de Philippe II.*

PORTRAITS. A list of the few authentic portraits of Don John may be found in Maxwell. The bronze statue at Messina and the life-sized recumbent marble figure on his tomb in the Escorial give the best and most vital idea of him.

RELICS.   The silver shield and inlaid marble tables sent by Pius V after Lepanto are in the Armería and the Prado at Madrid.   Also in the Armería are a couple of red velvet banners from Lepanto, embroidered with Crucifix, Blessed Virgin and saints, Ali Pasha's long tunic with wide sleeves of cloth of gold and silver, Turkish arms, armour, standards and ships, lanterns taken at Lepanto.   " The Holy Christ of Don John's Galley," which hung on the mast of the *Real* at Lepanto, is venerated in Barcelona cathedral.   The remarkable sideways swing of the Figure is attributed by tradition to its having twisted during the battle to avoid a Turkish bullet.

The country round Villagarcia de Campos has changed little, if at all, since Don John spent his childhood there. The castle is a ruinous shell.   The foundations of its mighty yellow stone walls are fast crumbling away.   The church founded as a Jesuit college by Doña Magdalena is deserted, damp and desolate.   She and her husband are buried on either side of the high altar, with marble bas-relief portraits of each.   The alabaster carvings behind the high altar were sent by Don John from Flanders.   High in the dome hang the few tattered rags which are all that vandal " souvenir " hunters have left of the Turkish banners sent by Don John to his Tia after Lepanto.   The *Lignum Crucis* worn by him at the battle has been removed to a private house for safety.   The most precious relic of all is still in the reliquary chapel, " the Christ of his Battles."   The rudely carved Crucifix is mounted on a crystal sphere and wooden base. The Figure is about a foot high, the Face and left side of the Body so charred that the Features are almost indistinguishable. There is a small hole under the left Breast where the Turkish arrow pierced. This little Crucifix is interwoven with the whole of Don John's short, stormy, glorious, tragic life, from his childhood, when it hung over his bed in Villagarcia castle, to the day when he died in the ruined dovecote near Namur holding *El Cristo de sus Batallas*.

SOME BOOKS CONSULTED

Don John of Austria, by Sir William Stirling Maxwell.
Cloister Life of Charles V, by Sir William Stirling Maxwell.
Jeromín, by Luis Coloma, S.J.
Don Juan de Austria, by Vanderhammer y Leon.
Le Dernier des Paladins, by Des Ombreux (M).
Historia de Rebelion de los Moriscos, by Luis de Marmol.
El Combate Naval de Lepanto, by Rosell.
La Guerre de Chypre et la Bataille de Lepante, by Jurien de la Gravière.
Documentos Ineditos para la Historia de España.
Correspondance de Philippe II sur les Affaires des Pays Bas.
Rise of the Dutch Republic, by R. L. Motley.
Philippe II, une ténébreuse Affaire, by Louis Bertrand.
Philip II of Spain, by Martin Hume.
Philip II of Spain, by W. H. Prescott.
Master of the Armada, by J. H. Mariejol.
Queens of Old Spain, by Martin Hume.
Isabella of Spain, by T. Walsh.
Ferdinand and Isabella, by W. H. Prescott.
Reign of Charles V, by Prescott and Robertson.
Emperor Charles V, by E. Armstrong.
Emperor of the West, by Wyndham Lewis.
Moors in Spain, by S. Lane Poole
Turkey, by S. Lane Poole.
An Hour of Spain, by " Azorín."
Historia de España, by Ricardo Beltran y Rozpide.
Spain, edited by Allison Peers.
History of Spanish Literature, by F. Kelly.
Hand-book for Spain, by Richard Ford.
Annales d'Espagne et de Portugal, by Alvarez de Colmenar.
Portugal, by Morse Stephens.
The Spanish Inquisition, by J. Gordon.

The Spanish Inquisition, by H. L. Lea.

History of the Jews, by Dean Milman.

Decline and Fall of the Roman Empire, by Edward Gibbon.

History of Europe, by Bede Jarrett, O.P.

Celtic Peoples and Renaissance Europe, by David Mathew.

Universities of Europe in the Middle Ages, by H. Rashdall.

San Francisco de Borja, by an anonymous author.

St. Francis Borgia, by an anonymous author of the seventeenth century.

St. Francis Borgia, by A. M. Clarke.

The Jesuits, their Foundation and History, by " B. N."

Historia de la Compañia de Jesús en la Asistencia de España, by A Astrain, S.J.

Sea-wolves of the Mediterranean, by Hamilton Curry.

Story of Naples, by C. Headlam.

Queen Elizabeth, by J. E. Neale.

Queen Elizabeth, by E. S. Beasley.

Their Majesties of Scotland, by E. Thornton Cooke.

Love Affairs of Mary Queen of Scots, by Martin Hume.

History of the Popes, by Ludwig Pastor.

Encyclopedia Britannica.

Enciclopedia Italiana.

Enciclopedia Espasa Universal.

INDEX